Rebuilding Central Park
A Management and Restoration Plan

New York City
Department of Parks & Recreation
and
Central Park Conservancy

Elizabeth Barlow Rogers
Principal Author

Marianne Cramer, ASLA
Judith L. Heintz, ASLA
Bruce Kelly, ASLA
Philip N. Winslow, ASLA

John Berendt
Editor

The MIT Press
Cambridge, Massachusetts, and London, England

First MIT Press edition, 1987
© 1987 by the Central Park Conservancy

This book was set in Bembo by Trufont Typographes and printed and bound by Halliday Lithograph in the United States of America.

Library of Congress Cataloging-in-Publication Data

Rogers, Elizabeth Barlow, 1936–
    Rebuilding Central Park.

    Includes index.
    1. Central Park (New York, N.Y.) 2. New York (N.Y.)—Buildings, structures, etc. I. Berendt, John. II. New York (N.Y.) Dept. of Parks and Recreation. III. Central Park Conservancy (New York, N.Y.) IV. Title.
F128.65.C3R64 1987   974.7′1   86-27795
ISBN 0-262-18127-4

Table of Contents

List of Maps and Illustrations

Acknowledgements

A great long-term project such as the rebuilding of Central Park requires the creativity, collaboration and commitment of many people as well as the combination of many talents. Because the Park is a work of landscape art and a treasured New York City landmark, the primary authors of this plan are landscape professionals. But government officials, architects, engineers, urban sociologists, wildlife experts, and others have also played a large role in its development.

Mayor Edward I. Koch, by giving Park staff and consultants the widest latitude possible to entertain goals and objectives, has been a subtly potent force in its development. Parks Commissioner Henry J. Stern, actively involved in the day-to-day administration of the Park, has provided valuable counsel and leadership. Deputy Parks Commissioner Robert Russo and Manhattan Borough Commissioner Patrick J. Pomposello have lent managerial and operational expertise; Deputy Commissioner for Capital Projects Alan Moss has helped forge the strategy for the public-private funding of the restoration enterprise. Assistant Commissioner for Revenue Joanne Imohiosen has been especially helpful in attracting and supervising concessionaires that participate in the plan's objectives and uphold its standards.

Several consultants have contributed studies and reports which form the basis for many of the plan's conclusions and recommendations. William Kornblum and Terrance Williams of the Department of Urban Sociology at CUNY undertook a user analysis that provided much of the information to be found in "A Park for the People" (page 23). Lockwood, Kessler and Bartlett, Consulting Engineers, performed a hydrology study of Central Park and assisted the landscape team in developing some of the conclusions found in "Topography, Soils and Drainage" (page 45). Also contributing information to that chapter were the U.S. Department of Agriculture's Soil Conservation Service and the New York City Department of Environmental Protection, which respectively undertook surveys of the Park's soils and water quality. John Hecklau, a biologist, wrote a comprehensive wildlife report that gave important insight into the quantities and behavior of the Park's bird, mammal, reptile, amphibian, invertebrate and insect populations, and its conclusions are reflected in "Vegetation and Wildlife" (page 55). Pamela F. Tice, former Executive Director of the Central Park Conservancy, prepared a management study that was particularly useful in portraying current Park management practices as outlined in "Managing Central Park" (page 75).

The greatest help of all, however, has come from the men and women who work everyday in the Park and out of whose lives and careers the plan is taking substance. Ron Cianciulli, Chief of Operations for Central Park, is conceiving and supervising various strategies to upgrade maintenance and morale. Marianne Cramer, one of the authors of the plan, is currently the Assistant Administrator for Design and Planning, and, as such, she oversees the landscape architectural staff responsible for refining the plan and developing working drawings for the numerous projects that constitute its implementation. Timothy Marshall, Assistant Central Park Administrator for Construction and Preservation, has formed restoration crews capable of building rustic shelters, repairing stairs and walls and removing graffiti. In addition, he supervises projects built by outside contractors. Marie Ruby, Assistant Central Park Administrator for Visitor Services, continues to enrich and expand the programs offered at the Dairy, Belvedere, Bandshell and Conservatory Garden. She also supervises an active volunteer program. Frank Serpe, Director of Central Park Horticulture, is responsible to a significant degree for reestablishing groundskeeping (arboriculture, turf care, planting) in Central Park. Marie Sarchiapone is responsible for researching bronze and stone conservation techniques, and her crew deserves credit for keeping Central Park graffiti-free.

Staff photographer Sara Cedar Miller has taken most of the contemporary photographs in this document and has researched various photographic archives for historic views. Finally, we owe a special debt of gratitude to Heidi Humphrey, who has overseen the graphic production of this publication, and to Timothy Purcell, who has typed all of the drafts and revised drafts as well as the final manuscript.

The publication of this plan was funded through a grant from the National Park Service, U.S. Department of the Interior, under the provisions of the Urban Park and Recreation Recovery Act of 1978 (Title X, Public Law 95-625), the National Endowment for the Arts and the W. Alton Jones Foundation. Funding for the plan itself was generously provided by the American Telephone and Telegraph Company, The Vincent Astor Foundation, The Frederick W. Beinecke Fund, The Commonwealth Fund, The Dillon Fund, The Hearst Foundation, High Winds Fund, Hoffman-LaRoche, Inc., Ittleson Foundation, The J. M. Foundation, W. Alton Jones Foundation, Samuel Kress, Hale Matthews Foundation, McKinsey & Company, Henry and Lucy Moses Fund, National Endowment for the Arts, New York State Council on the Arts, New York Telephone Company, The Prospect Hill Foundation, Charles H. Revson Foundation, David Rockefeller, Richard Salomon, The Starr Foundation, Union Pacific Foundation and Lila Acheson Wallace.

In summary, the existence of this plan is product of the moral and financial commitment of the City of New York and its public servants as well as the faith of the trustees of the Central Park Conservancy and its many friends in the exhilarating enterprise of rebuilding the Park and operating it as a dynamic and cherished institution.

Elizabeth Barlow Rogers
Central Park,
August, 1986

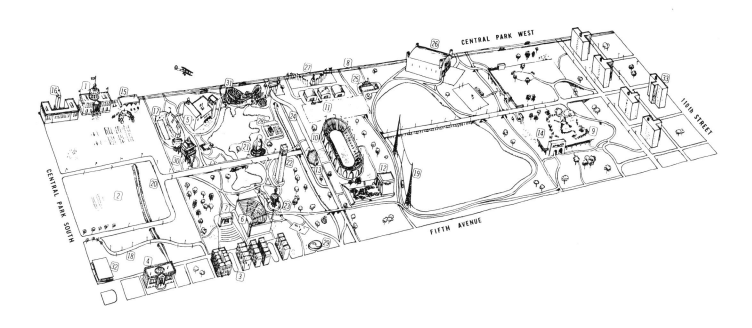

"Improvements" Suggested for Central Park since 1900

1. Exposition Building, 1903.
2. Drill ground, 1904.
3. Selling off lower park for building lots, 1904; proposed for west side of Fifth Avenue by Mayor La Guardia in 1930s.
4. Building for National Academy of Design, 1909.
5. Opera House, 1910.
6. Outdoor theater seating 50,000, 1911; opera amphitheater proposed 1933.
7. Marionette theater, 1912; proposed again, 1964 and 1965.
8. Relocation of Central Park West streetcar tracks, 1917.
9. Trenches in North Meadow as war display, 1918.
10. Large stadium, 1919.
11. Airplane field, 1919.
12. Sunken oriental garden, Memorial Hall for war trophies and sports amphitheater, 1920.
13. Music stand and road connecting drives to be called Mitchel Memorial, 1920.
14. Underground parking lot for 30,000 cars, 1921; proposed many times since.
15. Police garage, 1921.
16. Music and Art Center, 1922.

17. Swimming pool, circus and running track, 1923.
18. Filling in of Pond for new driveway, 1923.
19. Radio towers for city radio station, 1923.
20. Central roadway to relieve city's traffic congestion, 1923.
21. Statue of Buddha, 1925.
22. Carillon tower, 1925.
23. Fountain of the Seasons, 1929.
24. Promenade connecting Metropolitan and Natural History museums, 1930.
25. Recreation building and swimming pool, 1935.
26. Armory and stables, 1940.
27. Plaza of South America, 8 acres, 1941.
28. Recreation Center for the Elderly, 1955.
29. Garden for the Blind, 1955.
30. El Station as monument to Elevated Railroad, 1955.
31. Amusement Center, 1955.
32. Huntington Hartford Outdoor Café, 1960.
33. Housing Project, 106th to 110th Streets, 1964.

Sketch by Ken Fitzgerald, based on information supplied by Alan Becker

Central Park: A Paradigm for Socially Useful Landscapes

—James Marston Fitch, HAIA, FRIBA, D. Arts, D.H.L.

Central Park is by no means the first public park in the world. London's Hyde Park was opened to the public (on a fee-paying basis) in 1652, and the palace gardens of the Luxembourg and Versailles became public in the 1830s. The Boston Commons has been that since the seventeenth century—i.e., common lands set aside for use by the farmers for grazing their cattle. Both Georgian London and William Penn's Philadelphia had small, private and padlocked parks for use by the surrounding householders. But these were all spaces that entered the public domain by accident, so to say, long after they had been fully structured for other purposes. Central Park is the first grand open space specifically designed for public use, designed as a whole for that purpose and built in one campaign. It is significant, too, that it was sculpted out of raw farm and woodland where comparatively few man-made constructs had been before (the first Croton Reservoir, a fort from the War of 1812 and some farmhouses). In its present form, Central Park is thus a creation *de novo* of two remarkable men—Frederick Law Olmsted and his collaborator, Calvert Vaux.*

*The American Frederick Law Olmsted and the English-trained architect Calvert Vaux jointly won the 1858 competition for the design of the new park under the nom de plume "Greensward." This was to be the beginning of a long and fruitful collaboration, which was apparently satisfactory to both partners. At this late date, it is impossible to say precisely which man designed which specific parts of the actual fabric of the Park. But, assuming that Vaux's formal training as an architect qualified him as the active agent in architectural design (e.g., Belvedere Castle, the Dairy, the bridges), then it is equally logical to assume that Olmsted's experience in gardening and scientific agriculture would have made him the principal in landscape design. This, at any rate, has become the conventional approach to their collaborative work and the one that is followed here.

The basic armature of the Park was proven to be amazingly durable, physically as well as aesthetically, even when it is only now beginning to emerge from three quarters of a century of abuse and neglect. It is a tribute to the soundness of the original concept that, although it has lost almost all its original botanical material and is still defaced with the scar tissue of this neglect, it has never lost its sheer scenographic splendor. This splendor is a triumphant example of the nineteenth century "naturalistic" landscape, which is, in fact, an almost wholly man-made artifact, as carefully shaped, cut and polished as the geometric parterres of Versailles. Moving through the Park today, it is difficult to realize that

working with pick axes, shovels, horse-drawn carts and 20,800 barrels of gun powder, an army of laborers manipulated an estimated 4,825,000 cubic yards of earth and rock. This included about 700,000 cubic yards of imported topsoil, imported to supplement the Park's thin glacial till.

Yet the physiognomy of the completed landscape is by no means the single-handed "invention" of Olmsted. On the contrary, one cannot be unimpressed by the sagacity with which he took all the main features of the God-made landscape and used them to establish the parameters of his man-made transformations. This required, first of all, a truly scientific assessment of the basic landforms in which the Park was to be constructed. This the partners did with great precision. Topographically, they found that the tract on which the Park was to be constructed consisted of three basic types: meadow, parkland and woodland, laced with a filigree of brooks, ponds and little marshes. And a careful look at the Park today will reveal that it is composed of precisely these basic landforms: grassy meadows (the Sheep Meadow, Great Lawn, East Meadow and North Meadow); parklands with high shade and little understory growth (the more or less continuous

margins around the edge of the Park); thickets of native undergrowth (the Promontory and the Ramble—these last the hardest of all mini-landscapes to maintain since, left uncontrolled, such growth tends always toward full-scale woodland). Finally, the Park has a range of waters: the Pond in the Southeast Corner, the Lake at the center, the Meer in the Northeast Corner—all lovely little water bodies carved out of the original marshes of drowned streams. These are connected with a system of artfully landscaped brooks, many of them sadly silted up.

Although this terrain was already two and a half centuries distant from the primeval forests the Dutch had purchased in 1624, it had never been converted into tidy farmland, like Long Island across the East River. Its bony, glaciated topography of acid soils, thinly spread over schist and granite, did not encourage agriculture. The forests had long since been slaughtered, the second growth burned for charcoal. Contemporary photographs show that Olmsted began with a bare wasteland of squatters' shacks, tethered goats and garbage dumps at the south end, though there was a thin scattering of modest cottages and farmhouses in the north.

Central Park was actually designed in the dominant Romantic idiom of the mid-nineteenth century. The most powerful American advocates of this view of nature were the painters of the Hudson River School—artists who between the 1820s and 1880s had created a cult of natural beauty around such scenic spots as the Hudson Valley, the Catskills and Niagara Falls. Olmsted would have been thoroughly immersed in such images, as he would have been in the landscape theories of A.J. Downing, the autodidact nurseryman whose immensely successful books on landscape theory and garden design consistently extolled the "picturesque," naturalistic landscape. Olmsted would also have had the benefit of Calvert Vaux's British training as well as his own visits to such great English estates as those designed by Humphry Repton and Capability Brown. It is thus not surprising, when he came to build the Park in the midst of these inherently picturesque landforms, that he should choose the Romantic English rather than the formal French mode. But what the new Park was to look like was, in Olmsted's mind, intimately connected with how it was to be used. Here there is no possibility of misunderstanding his intentions: Form and function would be united in a popular, democratic environment; a haven of repose, relaxation and *recreation* (his emphasis) for the masses of ordinary people who were trapped in the hot, sterile geometry of Manhattan's streetscapes. Thus, the broad meadows, shady groves and cooling brooks and ponds were as much prophylactic as aesthetic amenities. This dialectic, which is central to all Olmsted's landscapes, here and elsewhere, is the basis of their astonishing durability.

Ever since its completion, the Park has had its own constituency, including both those who wanted "to keep it as it always was" and those who wanted to "improve it." Though, even today, the Park retains most of its original physiognomy, it has been the focus of various groups proposing changes in its condition. These groups have always described themselves as "progressive" and their proposals as "improvements." But, in retrospect, these proposed interventions can be seen as having seldom been wise, even when they were well intentioned. Had they all been implemented, the Park would have long ago been obliterated altogether. Fortunately, the Park has also had the other sort of friends who stubbornly resisted any change in the Olmsted-Vaux fabric. Though they were often in the past denounced as reactionaries, they would today be seen as preservationists. In any case, an awkward and sometimes faltering equilibrium between these two sets of forces has preserved the balance of the Park for the comprehensive program described in this book. Given the fact that this huge rectangle of 150 city blocks is placed in the center of a solid gridiron street pattern, traffic inside, around and across the Park has been handled with notable felicity—all while still conserving the visual integrity of the Park landscape. A circumferential drive, screened from the city by grading and planting, surrounds the Park. It picks up and discharges vehic-

ular traffic onto the surrounding streets at 17 evenly spaced points around the perimeter. But even more remarkable are the submerged transverse roads that carry crosstown traffic unobtrusively *across* the Park. This anticipation of crosstown traffic, at a time when the developed city lay almost wholly to the south of the Park, is but another example of the prescience of the designers.

This plan for the restoration, conservation and management of a great historic park will be of great interest to the friends and users of Central Park. But it has a far wider significance, since it is a prototypical study on the curatorship of a *landscape*—almost certainly the first of its kind in the breadth of its conceptual approach. It regards this landscape not only in the obvious sense that it is populated by millions of plants and animals and used daily by millions of people but also in understanding that its very face is slowly but continually being altered by natural forces—growth and death of vegetation, erosion, frost creep, topsoil accumulation—ineluctable processes that cannot be halted but can only be guided by wise policies. As was never possible before, it summarizes the best in current knowledge of natural forces embodied in the fields of archaeology, botany, ecology, zoology. In much the same fashion, the plan analyzes the social and cultural forces that play upon the Park, tracing the ways in which these forces have changed and/ or remained constant, and outlining what these changes imply for the future appearance of the Park.

No historic artifact as large and complex as New York's Central Park has ever been subjected to a more comprehensive program of research, analysis and design than that described in this volume. Now under way for over five years—long enough, in fact, for much of the conservation work it calls for to have been actually accomplished—this document is called a "restoration" plan. And so it is, but it must be understood in its broadest sense. For it deals with an old and very complex artifact (construction was started in 1857 and completed in 1876 on the 843 acres of land and water, every square foot of them man-modeled) that has undergone continuous change—some of it slow and natural (like forest creep and vegetative growth and decay), some of it sudden and arbitrary (like the construction of

new buildings and the paving of parking lots). Thus, the Park could not be literally restored, like a Renaissance painting or a classic sculpture, even if that were desired. What this document really envisions is an *extended life* for a noble old organism, a policy of curatorship that will preserve for another century, at least, the dialectic of stasis and change that has kept it Manhattan's greatest amenity.

In this plan, historic, archival and archaeological research has been employed to plot the morphological development of the Park across time. Parallel studies in the demography of the Park's users—who visited it, when and why—have been made, to establish the changing size and composition of attendance. Data such as these are already being used to establish benchmarks against which all proposals for future modification or retrofit of Park facilities can be measured. They offer the objective basis on which to evaluate such commonly heard charges as those that the Park is too "aristocratic" for today's users or "too old-fashioned" to meet today's recreational requirements. These surveys show that, to the contrary, the motivation of current users is very much the same as it was a century ago: simple rest and relaxation. "Eighty percent of the Park's visitors use it for passive activities," this report points out, "most notably enjoying the presence of one another and simply relaxing." And far from being exclusive or elitist, it shows that demographically, attendance almost exactly parallels the city's ethnic composition—55 percent white, 20 percent black, 19 percent Hispanic and 6 percent Asian—and that they come from all over the borough.

The Park counts some 13 million individual visits every year in search of widely varying recreational facilities. Many of these Olmsted anticipated from the beginning, as the report points out:

There was skating on the Lake the year it was filled with water (1858); horseback riding started in that year too. Concerts (1859), boating (1861), lawn tennis (1863), school ball games (1865), skating and curling on the Conservatory Water (1869).

But other recreation is newer (baseball, softball, volleyball and tennis), and mass spectacles such as the Metropolitan Opera concerts. These have tended to stress the Park's fragile landscapes and must somehow be programmed in the future. Central Park is also the habitat for an astonishing range of wildlife—especially indigenous and migratory birds—for which it provides both food and shelter. These last are not always as optimal as the Audubon Society would like to see, because in this Park there are aesthetic as well as environmental norms to be met. These are sometimes contradictory: The best cover for nesting thrushes may well be brambles, fallen limbs and "weed" plants (ailanthus, wild cherry). But the best site for a family picnic will be an immaculate lawn under high open shade.

In an effort to balance the conflicting demands of the Park's different types of users—birds and ball players, horseback riders and nature lovers, theatergoers and tennis buffs—the new plan analyzes them quantitatively and qualitatively, then tries to disperse them in time and space to minimize conflict. Thus some spectator sports may be transferred to other parks and playgrounds within the system, while events with large audiences—like the Metropolitan Opera summer performances—will be spaced across time to give the lawns time to recover. Then there is a general policy of making the north end of the Park both more attractive and more safe, thus lightening the wear and tear on the southern end of the landscape. The Park has had for several years a policy of requiring prepayment for cleanup costs after such massively successful events as the annual Puerto Rican Day celebration. By such a mix of plans and policies, the city administration hopes to serve the democratic constituency of the Park while preserving its historic and scenic integrity.

The plan itself is the product of the Office of the Central Park Administrator, a comparatively new type of agency in the New York City Parks Department. This office is, in turn, the outgrowth of a century's experience, during which the Park was managed by the department as just one of the 1,543 units in the metropolitan system. Such an arrangement, though it might have appeared sensible from the standpoint of municipal management, regarded the Park as just another 843 acres of the department's holdings. But the Park was never just an *ordinary* tract: Conceived as a unit and built in a single campaign, it was an unprece-

dented design that soon established a special identity around the world. Its very physical characteristics—its location in the heart of the greatest borough, its size and topographical variety, the international range of its visitors—all of these factors suggested that the Park required special housekeeping and maintenance. Yet this identity was increasingly compromised in recent decades as the Park was integrated into the system as a whole and compelled to share the steadily shrinking funds available to it. After decades of attrition, the decision was finally reached in 1980 to establish a special management unit for Central Park. Simultaneously, a private agency, the Central Park Conservancy, was established, whose task is to raise funds from private sources to amplify funding available through normal city budget channels.

Having recognized that the Park was indeed not "just another" unit in the municipal system but one with special cultural and physical characteristics, the new Administrator also recognized that it required special curatorial attention. Its management program frankly recognized this fact—a step not without its hazards, since it exposed the Administrator and Commissioner to charges of elitism—i.e., favoring one park with an undemocratically disproportionate share of the department's resources. To avoid such charges, Central Park operates under two separate but complementary budgets, with funds raised by the Conservancy being applied to those problems of construction and maintenance that are special to the Park. These problems derive mostly from the Park's age and historicity, as well as the intricacy and delicacy of much of its physical structure.

Some of the sections of the plan deal with the restoration of historic structures, like the 22 bridges that were a feature of the original Olmsted design. Others deal with the conservation of some very special miniature landscapes, such as the Ramble or the Promontory Bird Sanctuary. There are orthodox reconstructions of severely damaged structures, like the Dairy and Belvedere Castle. Both of these are projects of considerable magnitude which have already been completed and are now occupied by new activities—a Visitor Information Center and a Learning Center. Other equally important parts of the plan deal with

process—stonemasonry, rustic carpentry and conservation of bronze statuary; Dutch elm disease control; an ongoing graffiti-removal campaign; and rule enforcement by Park Rangers.

Many of the steps advocated in the plan have already been put into effect—remarkable in its own right, since so many published plans never get into effect at all. All of them are seen as part of an integrated process that, quite properly, regards preservation as the fourth dimension of restoration, i.e., capital investment in returning an historic landscape to its prime condition will be wasted unless it is matched by a simultaneous program of maintenance and repair.

Central Park at its prime (1898): a rich carpet of thick turf, well-tended shrubs and healthy trees reaching maturity. The scene is Pilgrim Hill, immediately south of the Conservatory Water.

Introduction

The contents of this book are drawn from the findings of a comprehensive, three-year study of Central Park. The purpose of the study was to analyze the Park's deteriorating condition and to produce a plan for the rehabilitation of its entire 843 acres. The planning team's intentions were to remain faithful to the spirit of Frederick Law Olmsted's original, naturalistic landscape while accommodating as varied a mix of contemporary activities as possible.

The Olmsted Tradition

Olmsted's Greensward Plan, submitted for the Central Park design competition in 1857, envisioned Central Park as a rural idyll in the midst of a noisy city. Central Park was to be a grand illusion, and it was one that worked remarkably well. It became a retreat where the city dweller could literally lose sight of the city itself. As to style, Olmsted had been inspired by the eighteenth-century English Romantic landscapes, in particular those designed by Humphrey Repton and Joseph Paxton. The look was an idealized version of a natural setting—clumps of trees, rolling lawns and tranquil lakes. Central Park became the first such landscape to be built in America, a style of landscape design later repeated in scores of city parks across the country. Because of the Park's prominence and its unique status, the effort to rehabilitate it warranted the extra care due an important historic landmark. Olmsted's copious writings, and the writings of those who influenced him, provide crucial insights into his approach to landscape design and the philosophy underlying what has come to be known as the Olmstedian landscape.

In 1856, the pre-Park site was a barren rectangle of rocks and swampland occupied by squatters, goats and a bone-boiling works.

We know that two books made deep impressions on Olmsted at an early age: Sir Uvedale Price's *On the Picturesque* and William Gilpin's *Forest Scenery*. Both offer fundamental clues to Olmsted's thinking. Price based his appreciation of nature on the study of painting; he cited the lyrical repose of Claude Lorrain's landscapes as an ideal. Gilpin evaluated various species of trees for their aesthetic qualities. "The oak," he said, "joins the ideas of strength to beauty; while the ash rather joins the ideas of beauty and elegance." Like Price, Olmsted was inspired by the artistically composed landscapes of Romantic artists. Like Gilpin, he came to look at trees not so much as a botanist or a gardener but rather as an artist considering choices on an arboreal palette.

The elements of Olmsted's landscapes were balanced compositions of placid lakes and gurgling brooks, broad green meadows, soft lawns and dappled woodlands. He arranged sequences of visual events to climax in stunning vistas. He integrated architecture into the landscape and separated different types of traffic. Olmsted's designs fell between the smoothed-out forms of the great English landscape improver Capability Brown and the more wild and rugged features of the "picturesque" school. Indeed, William Gilpin could have been describing Central Park when he recommended that parks contain "a varied surface—where the ground swells, and falls—where hanging lawns, screened with wood, are connected with valleys—and where one part is continually playing in contrast with another."

Though every inch of Central Park was shaped and molded by machines and men, the hand of man is never obvious. This is probably the least appreciated virtue of the Park—that it is a completely man-made landscape. Central Park is not simply a piece of real estate set off by a fence. It was sculpted out of a ragged northern fringe of New York City, a mostly barren rectangle of land inhabited by squatters and goats, littered with refuse, studded with jagged outcrops of Manhattan schist and miry with low-lying swamps.

A Brief History

The Democratic Experiment

The Park's creation was a monumental feat of engineering that cost $14 million—or $118 million, in 1984 dollars. Undertaken as a bold democratic experiment in which all social classes were invited to mingle in scenic surroundings of uplifting poetic beauty, the Park was artfully constructed in accordance with the Greensward Plan devised by Olmsted and his partner, Calvert Vaux.

Generally, the Park prospered throughout the nineteenth century and was a well-maintained, elegant pleasure ground successfully fulfilling its democratic mission. Although between 1870 and 1871 Boss Tweed and his Tammany Hall ring nearly undid the illusion of a natural paradise by cutting down great swaths of trees and shrubs, the Park's basic elements remained intact, and its designers' visions were realized as trees matured and grew to fine proportions.

Samuel Parsons, Olmsted and Vaux's successor, was a landscape architect and distinguished horticulturist who nourished and extended the original design concepts during a period of great botanical discovery. Parson's era saw the naturalization of many exotic species and hybrids in Central Park. Turn-of-the-century photographs and paintings show the Park at its prime, with thick turf and well-tended shrub beds and benches, ornamental fountains, arbors and boat landings in generally good repair.

The Rise of Recreation

By the end of the nineteenth century, the Park that Olmsted and Vaux created and Parsons perpetuated had been invaded by two alien ideologies: the City Beautiful Movement and the Reform Movement.

The City Beautiful Movement found its expression in the monumental neo-classical architecture of the Beaux Arts school, particularly after the trendsetting World's Columbian Exposition in Chicago in 1893. Olmsted vigorously fought the idea of grafting Beaux Arts

Central Park's major visual sequence: Visitors enter at Fifth Avenue and 59th Street; they move up the Drive to the Mall, continue on to Bethesda Terrace, to the Ramble's hilly woodland and finally to the Belvedere in the heart of the Park.

architecture onto Central Park, especially when a scheme was put forth to embellish the Park with a series of monumental gates designed by Richard Morris Hunt. Although Hunt's plan was defeated, the Park nonetheless gained certain monumentalizing touches, notably the Maine Monument erected in 1913 at the Columbus Circle entrance.

The reformers were less aesthetically inclined. For them, parks represented places where programmed recreation could be offered as a means to improve the lot of the underprivileged. The initial impact of this philosophy was, by and large, first felt outside Central Park, as playgrounds and public baths were built near the teeming tenements. But eventually the reform culture found expression within Central Park as well.

The 1902 Annual Report of the Department of Parks observes that Central Park provided "facilities for skating, lawn tennis, baseball, croquet, football, basketball and other games." Several slopes were opened that year for sledding. The demand for tennis was so great that in 1915 over 20,000 tennis permits were issued. Nets were set up on the Sheep Meadow, and clay courts were installed on the South Meadow, the site of the present courts.

In the 1920s, recreation in the Park became even more organized. There were canoe regattas and swimming meets on the Lake, miniature-airplane contests on the Sheep Meadow, roller-skating contests on the Mall, miniature-sailboat races and ice-skating derbies on the Conservatory Water, as well as tennis tournaments and marble-shooting contests elsewhere in the Park. Permanent facilities—playgrounds and courts for hardball, shuffleboard, bocci and basketball—had not yet been imposed on the Greensward Plan, but this situation would change with the long, influential tenure of Robert Moses as New York City Parks Commissioner.

The Moses Era

Robert Moses became New York's first citywide Parks Commissioner in 1934. He was a man with far-reaching authority and a powerful personality, and his tenure lasted 26 years. In that time Moses altered the Park's physical appearance considerably. Unlike Olmsted and Vaux, he did not see the Park as a series of naturalistic scenes nestled in

In the 1930s, recreational facilities were viewed as more important than Olmsted's naturalistic scenery; typical of this view is the Wollman Rink, which was built over part of the Pond and the Children's Zoo in 1960.

the heart of the busy city. He was a reformer and a builder. He built compactly scaled, soundly constructed and often whimsically ornamental recreational facilities. It was an ingratiating approach. Droves of delighted New Yorkers applauded his touches of fantasy and fun and the very real recreational opportunities he brought them.

Because ice-skating had been immensely popular since the Park's inception, Moses built the Wollman Rink over one arm of the 59th Street Pond and guaranteed hard ice every day of the season. It was deplored at the time by architectural historian Lewis Mumford and by later critics as a heavy-handed eyesore, but the Wollman Rink nonetheless became and remains one of the most popular recreational features in New York.

While most of the playgrounds and other facilities that Moses added have had enthusiastic constituencies, they were inserted into the Park with little consideration for the framework of the original plan. Not only did the new elements destroy some of the Park's most carefully conceived views; they created circulation problems as well.

Moses was not totally opposed to the idea of nature—his trained gardeners performed horticultural miracles, turning many parts of Central Park and other parks into showcase gardens—but he preferred nature somewhat tidied up and prettified rather than pastoral and semi-wild. A fairy-tale barnyard zoo was more to his taste than sheep grazing on the Sheep Meadow.

In the 1960s, following the retirement of Moses as Parks Commis-

sioner, the Park became more vulnerable than ever to encroachment. Plans were drawn up for burrowing a subway and a water tunnel under it; a café was proposed opposite the Plaza Hotel in the Southeast Corner. Never had its founders' ideal of a green oasis been more threatened. In a curious way, however, the social changes of the 1960s sowed the seeds of the Park's eventual salvation.

Decline and Reversal

During the 1960s, the Park's protectors were few but determined. They succeeded in defending its greensward from the imposition of the proposed Huntington Hartford Café, and soon after the city's Landmarks Commission was created in 1965, they campaigned for the then-novel notion of scenic historic landmarks and for the designation of Central Park as one of the first such landmarks. (Designation eventually occurred in 1974.) But the preservation of the Park and its current restoration might not have been possible if the Park had not become hugely popular once again. This popularity did more harm than good at first, as the landscape was trampled and abused, but it did reaffirm the Park's role as the life-enhancing heart of the city.

This was the era of Happenings, and under the brief, dramatic and well-publicized leadership of Mayor John Lindsay's first Parks Commissioner, Thomas Hoving, Central Park became a giant stage for the improvisational drama of urban life. The people of the city embraced their roles as actors in a

variety of spontaneous performances and planned spectacles: war-protest marches, gay-liberation rallies, a lunar-eclipse watch, New Year's Eve parties and the Schaeffer rock concerts. The Park wedding, with individually styled vows, became fashionable for a while. Barbra Streisand's concert on the Sheep Meadow in 1967 drew the largest gathering of people in the Park's 100-year history. Undoubtedly, the greatest contribution to the atmosphere of festivity during this period was the banning of automobiles from the Park on weekends.

Central Park was the locale of choice for many of the rallies, festivals and Happenings of the 1960s.

Pre-Park Site, 1857

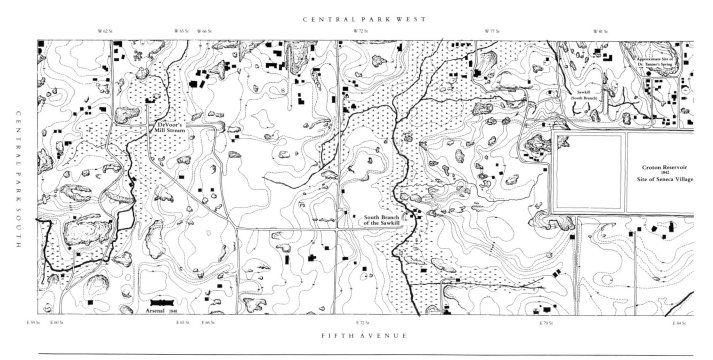

Park as built, 1873

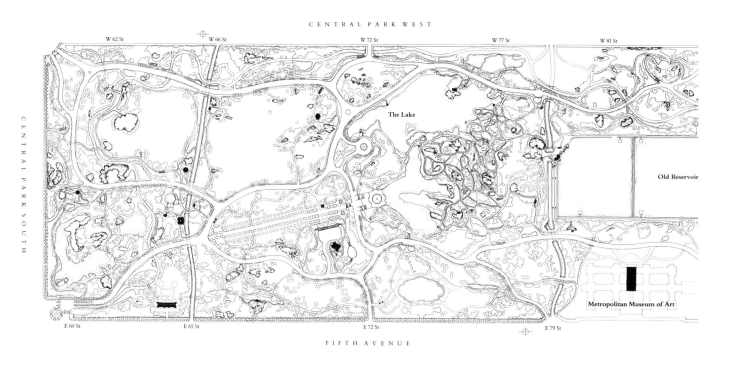

☒ Swamp   〼 Topographical contour lines

■ Building   〴 Streams

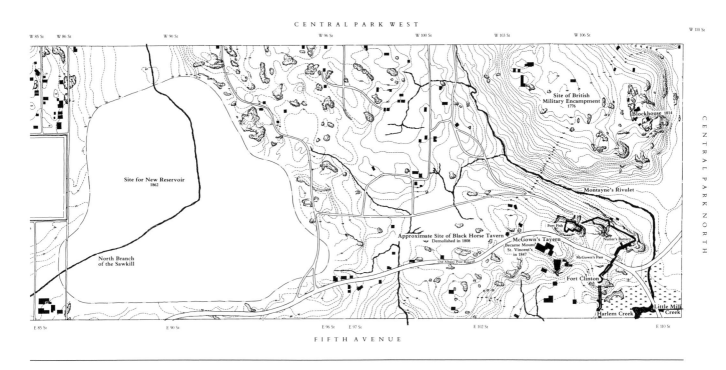

Olmsted and Vaux worked with existing landforms. Topographic low points were excavated to become water bodies, and high points were punctuated with rustic structures. Upland areas were modeled as rolling meadows. Pedestrian circulation was designed as a sequential experience.

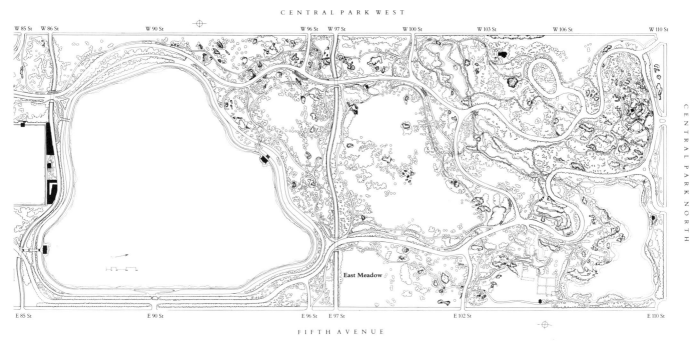

Concert at the Wollman Rink, 1970s.

From 1966 until 1972, the Parks Department was headed by August Heckscher, the grandson of the donor of the Heckscher Playground. Heckscher, who had previously served as John Kennedy's cultural affairs adviser, spoke eloquently about the importance of parks in urban life, but he was forced to accept the cuts imposed by City Hall, as Lindsay's budget officials searched for economies to help offset the city's rapidly growing debt.

During this period, only plumbing repairs of an emergency nature were performed, and comfort stations throughout the park system were closed one by one. Both drinking and ornamental fountains were allowed to go dry. By the mid-1970s, the Belvedere had become a vandalized ruin, its parapets broken and its rustic stonework laced with graffiti. Jacob Wrey Mould's elegant carved-stone Bethesda Terrace staircase, alive with the vitality of Victorian ornamentation, was similarly defaced. The Shakespeare Garden became a weed-choked ruin.

Heckscher's administration ended in 1972. His successor, Richard Clurman, sized up the situation and saw that the entire complex of recreational facilities that Moses had built could not be maintained. He reasoned that

planned—or worse, unplanned—shrinkage of the system was inevitable, and he consequently made what at the time sounded like a hard-nosed, but

An era of physical decline coincided with the city's 1970s budget crisis. Insufficient maintenance dollars and inadequate management systems caused severe Park deterioration.

later proved to be a merely practical, decision: "Let the communities take care of their parks, and where they are indifferent and allow them to become derelict, we'll close them down."

But Central Park was too popular and too significant ever to be closed down. Central Park was a major civic institution in its own right, important to residents and tourists alike. It had to be saved. As he walked through the Park, Clurman noticed how the dirt from the barren, unplanted slopes had washed into the 59th Street Pond, turning it into a mud flat filled with reeds and other vegetation. He noticed how the slab supporting the Wollman Rink had become warped and cracked. He assembled a team of Parks Department architects and outside consultants to develop a multimillion-dollar master plan for a staged rehabilitation of the Park, starting with the greatly abused Southeast Corner. This initial plan, while laying the groundwork for the current plan, could not become an agenda for action and therefore had to be abandoned: New York City was in a fiscal crisis; its budget was rescinded. The state-sponsored Emergency Financial Control Board took financial control.

During the administration of Mayor Abraham Beame, Clurman's successors—a series of four commissioners in as many years—could do little but preside over drastic budget cuts, which began with the layoff of 800 Parks Department employees in June 1975. Funds from the federal Department of Labor, through the CETA program, were used to keep a bare-bones work force alive, but capital projects for restoration were at a standstill.

Slowly, however, matters began to improve after the election of Edward I. Koch as Mayor in 1978 and his appointment of Gordon J. Davis as Parks Commissioner. Davis became an effective advocate of Parks Department needs at City Hall. As allocations were being made for the city's restructured and better-managed budget, Davis fought for and received sufficient appropriations to "buy back" most of the CETA employees when that program was terminated by the Reagan administration, thus reestablishing a career work force within the Parks Department. Additionally, he received funding for a program of Urban Park Rangers and for several restoration projects, some of which had been envisioned by the 1973 Central Park Master Plan.

In 1979, Mayor Koch created the position of Central Park Administrator, for the first time making a single individual responsible for supervising the ongoing restoration effort and coordinating the Park's day-to-day management and operations. Private funds were solicited to support the work of this new office within the Parks Department, and in 1980 the Central Park Conservancy was founded. The organization's primary mission is to find private financial backing for innovative programs and projects that cannot be done with city funds. Another of its functions is to provide firm guardianship to Central Park to help ensure that it never again becomes as abused, deteriorated and indifferently managed as it was in the 1970s.

At the time of the formation of the Administrator's Office and the Conservancy, the condition of Central Park was truly shocking. Once-green lawns were bare, dusty hardpan; slopes had been gullied by erosion; water bodies were silted and choked with weedy vegetation. Broken benches and clogged catch basins lined every path. Years of graffiti scrawlings covered almost every available stone, brick and wood surface. The traffic on streets and transverse roads was no longer screened, as a few species of hardy weeds and scraggly shrubs succeeded the once-dense growth of plants.

Restoration work began in the midst of this desolation. In 1979, the Sheep Meadow was completely resodded and the Southeast Corner of the Park was totally relandscaped. The Dairy was restored to its Victorian Gothic appearance, to be operated by the Conservancy as a visitor-information center and exhibition hall. Work was also started on the badly abused Belvedere Castle. More important perhaps than anything else, Conservancy-funded crews, composed primarily of young craftsmen and graduates of horticultural training programs, began to prune trees, plant shrubs, remove graffiti and rebuild the Park's lost rustic shelters.

As the city recovered from its fiscal crisis, more capital projects were begun with public funds. The Park soon began to resemble a patchwork of healthy landscapes amidst bare, eroded ground. The bright spots, of course,

The Dairy, 1979: a locked tool storage depot, deteriorating inside and out.

The Dairy, 1984: restored as a visitor services center with its colorful loggia entirely rebuilt.

made the decrepitude of the rest of the Park all the more apparent. They also gave the public tempting glimpses of how the Park as a whole might be saved. Soon it became clear that a project-by-project approach was not adequately addressing the problems of the Park, many of which are interrelated.

Central Park is not a free-form mélange of landscapes and recreational facilities. It was designed to be a single, unified park, and it still functions as one. The Park is an organic whole—a collection of integrated and interconnected systems of drainage, hydrology, traffic circulation, architecture and vegetation. Decay involving one area of the Park involves neighboring sections as well. In order to restore Central Park properly, it would be essential to regard it not piecemeal but whole.

In the past, expensive capital projects in Central Park and elsewhere had been followed by vandalism and deterioration. For a restoration plan to be effective, it would have to be coupled with a management plan. For such a plan to be realistic and workable, the people who actually run the Park on a day-to-day basis would have to be closely involved. The Central Park Administrator therefore personally took charge of the planning process, hiring staff and consultants to produce the plan and collaborate closely with other managers within the Parks Department. In 1981, a restoration planning team was formed: in-house managers and staff as well as outside consultants brought their backgrounds and expertise to the task at hand.

Girls' Gate at East 102nd Street before . . .

. . . and after restoration.

Ten studies, including wildlife and soil surveys, provide the information upon which the recommendations of the plan are based.

Methodology

Over the course of three years, the Central Park restoration planning team examined Central Park in minute detail from head to toe, as if it were a patient on an operating table. Its features were enumerated and catalogued (including a computerized inventory of its 24,000 trees), and the health of each of its vital systems was assessed. The studies performed by the planning team form a unique body of information. It is safe to say that no other landscape in the world has had its physical composition, its management and its uses so thoroughly scrutinized.

The most visible result of this effort is the management and restoration plan detailed in these pages and already being put into effect as this book goes to press. But of great importance, too, is the methodology the team devised for dealing logically and rationally with Central Park's complexities. It is a methodology that could well be followed in future scenic restoration projects anywhere else. In outline, it is as follows:

1. Formulation of policy
As a first step, basic parameters must be set. Questions relating to the purpose of the landscape should be raised and answered, such questions as: Is the landscape a historic one, and if so how faithful to the original should the restoration be? What uses will the landscape serve? What activities will be excluded? Who will use the landscape?

The members of the planning team were well aware that they were dealing with a historic landscape, and they were committed to restoring it *in the spirit* of the original, if not absolutely to the last detail. Central Park has evolved over time, and some of its modernizations would clearly have to stay—the automobile, for instance. However, the many unnecessary violations of Olmsted's design, such as the rimming of water bodies with concrete embankments, would not.

The question of what activities should be accommodated within Central Park has always been highly charged. The various user constituencies are strongly motivated and energetic in the defense of their turf. At the outset, therefore, the Central Park Conservancy commissioned a user study to find out exactly who was already using the Park. The study revealed that 80 percent of all visitors were "passive" users who strolled, sunbathed, ate food—and did not take part in active sports. This helped the planning team set up a framework of priorities, and the team ultimately decided that for the foreseeable future all present activities should be maintained at roughly the same capacity, but that no new facilities should be built and that ball fields and other existing sports facilities should be redesigned where possible to blend in better with the landscape.

2. Compilation of an inventory: historic view
Because a landscape is a living thing and always evolving, the landscape architect must look at it as a whole and study the history and evolution of all of its component parts: topography, geology, soils, hydrology, drainage, utilities, circulation, vegetation, wildlife, architecture, uses, management and security.

Ten such studies were undertaken for Central Park. What emerged from them was a picture of the Park in unprecedented detail and a narrative history of change and continuity over 125 years. With these studies in hand, the planning team was able to analyze the relationship between such things as pedestrian circulation and vegetation, vegetation and wildlife, and drainage and soil erosion. Patterns emerged and linkages became apparent. At this stage, the team sought to define parkwide problems.

3. Compilation of an inventory: present
A detailed inventory should be compiled of all the elements that make up each component considered in the second step. For instance, all trees, plants, buildings and park furniture (benches, water fountains, etc.) should be catalogued. All circulation routes, watersheds, drainage systems and catch basins should be mapped.

This was done for Central Park.

4. Dissection of the landscape
Unless a landscape is small enough to be restored all at once, it should be divided into manageable precincts. Factors to be considered in establishing these precincts are watersheds, visual continuity (viewsheds), user units, ecological units, physical elements (such as roads and buildings) or historic precedent.

Central Park was divided into 21 precincts, referred to as "scopes of work."

5. Maximization
Each precinct should be studied component by component (horticulture, drainage, circulation, etc.) just as each of the parkwide systems was studied in steps 2 and 3. And for every precinct, as an exercise and an important step in the planning process, the landscape architect should calculate what would have to be done to maximize each component. For example, what would have to be done, hypothetically, in a given precinct, to maximize wildlife, horticulture, drainage, security and usage. Clearly, many of these maximized conditions would be in conflict, which leads to an establishment of priorities for each precinct and for the landscape as a whole—step 6.

Studies were made of each precinct of Central Park. Depending on the complexity of the landscape and its uses, some were lengthy and extremely involved. The study for the 33-acre Ramble, for instance, ran to over 400 pages. The Ramble report included comparative plant lists from 1873, 1903 and 1978, a soils-analysis study, a detailed study of the ecological nitches of various species of birds, a visitor's survey and an inventory of all 6,000 trees (including the notation of their species and measurements and a rating of their horticultural quality and scenic value).

6. Establishment of priorities

For each precinct, priorities have to be determined. For instance, if scenic values are of primary importance in one place, then user activities or circulation might have to be somewhat curtailed there; if athletic use is the top priority, it might have to be achieved at the expense of scenery and horticultural interest. Priorities for each precinct therefore have to be considered once again in view of the situation in contiguous precincts and yet again in the context of the landscape as a whole.

7. Setting aesthetic goals

The landscape architect must approach each precinct with an eye to achieving a style consistent with that of the

landscape as a whole. This is the first step in which at least part of the solution will have to be subjective rather than objective; the landscape architect's imagination and taste come into play. If the style is to be formal and unchanging, the task is one of straightforward layout. On the other hand, if it is to be naturalistic—as is predominantly the case in Central Park—the landscape architect must anticipate a sequence of evolving scenes as the trees and plants grow to maturity over the years and the landscape undergoes shifts in scale, light, shadow, color and texture.

8. Devising solutions and making recommendations

Once the problems have been identified and the priorities agreed upon, two sets of solutions should be proposed: general parkwide recommendations and specific proposals for individual precincts.

The Ladies' Pavilion is cleaned prior to being painted.

9. Preparation of scopes and estimates

The landscape architect, having drawn up a rough schematic design, must then define the work to be done in each precinct and its cost. Calculations will necessarily involve a great deal of measurement and qualification. Previous surveys must be field-checked in order to correctly estimate linear feet of benches, square feet of paving and planting beds, numbers of drain inlets, size and condition of trees, quantity of topsoil needed and so forth.

10. Setting a project timetable

Each precinct should be evaluated according to a seven-point priority chart to determine in what order it should be done.

Although the criteria of this chart are all fairly objective, a realistic approach to Central Park has required that plans also be considered in light of political and financial considerations. How many capital and in-house construction projects could be financed in a given fiscal year? What were the expectations for public and private funding? What would a particular restored area require in the way of additional manpower and other resources? With all these factors in mind, a project implementation schuedule, or phasing chart, was then drawn up.

11. Fund-raising

At this stage, plans should be turned over to park managers to calculate how many people will be needed to maintain each precinct and the landscape as a whole. Their findings, combined with the cost estimates presented by the landscape architect, will constitute the total sum to be raised from public and private sources. In general, municipalities have proved more likely to approve money for building than for maintenance. What is not provided from public funds must be sought from foundations, corporations and individuals.

12. Public relations

Great care should be taken to involve the public in the restoration planning by means of conferences, booklets, news releases and newsletters. If the public's endorsement has been won early on, the formal approval process (through community boards and government agencies) is much easier.

13. The design process

The schematic design must now be put to the test of a preliminary working design in which it is determined whether or not the preliminary design is technically feasible. Adjustments should be made at this point and working drawings produced. Then the work can be let out for bidding on by contractors.

14. Construction
Once work begins on the restoration, the landscape architect should make frequent visits to the job site, because a certain amount of flexibility will be needed to achieve the effects he or she wants. Each plant has a unique form, and subtle changes in positioning will almost certainly be desirable. If workmen are left to follow the working drawings to the letter, the result is often a less pleasing landscape than one that embodies the landscape architect's eye and imagination throughout the construction process.

15. Maintenance
Day-to-day maintenance is all-important and never-ending, since it will prevent deterioration of the landscape and the need for another cycle of restoration. Plans should be drawn up for the continued maintenance of the project area with the same degree of care with which they were made for the restoration itself.

Carpenters building a rustic shelter out of unmilled cedar timbers.

In 1982, 57.7 percent of visitors surveyed listed "relaxation" as their primary activity in Central Park.

A Park for the People

Central Park was conceived as a democratic experiment, America's first public park—a people's park. The intention of its design was to provide the citizens of the growing city of New York with some relief from urban tension by means of tranquil, "rural" scenery, a place to stretch both legs and minds. Oddly enough, at the time the Park was proposed, many people doubted that this democratic vision for it would succeed. An 1867 *New York Herald* editorial protested:

It is folly to expect in this country to have parks like those in old aristocratic countries. When we open a public park, Sam will air himself in it. . . . He will knock down any better dressed man who remonstrates with him. He will talk and sing, and fill his share of the bench, and flirt with the nursery maids in his own coarse way. . . . Is it not obvious that . . . the great Central Park will be nothing but a great beer-garden for the lowest denizens of the city, of which we shall yet pray litanies to be delivered?

Once Central Park opened, however, it soon became clear that the democratic experiment was an overwhelming success. Olmsted himself noted with satisfaction that he saw the same people who had foretold doom for Central Park making more use of it "than they do the opera or the church."

Park Visitors

How Many Are There?
From the Park's inception until 1873, its managers kept a gate-by-gate count of visitors as they entered. The record of those years shows that even before its construction was completed, it was receiving ten million visitors a year.

Table 1

Annual Visits to Central Park, 1863–1873, and Percent Change from Preceding Year

Year	Annual Visits	% Change
1863	4,326,500	
1864	6,120,179	41.5
1865	7,593,139	24.0
1866	7,839,373	3.2
1867	7,227,855	−7.8
1868	7,089,798	−2.0
1869	7,350,957	−4.0
1870	8,628,826	17.4
1871	10,764,411	14.8
1872	10,873,839	1.0
1873	10,060,159	−7.5

Source: Adapted from Frederick Law Olmsted, Jr., and Theodora Kimball. *Forty Years of Landscape Architecture: Central Park* (Cambridge, Mass: The M.I.T. Press, 1973), pp. 534–536.

Method	Sample Size	Basic Purpose
Counting people passing through Park gates.	171,409	To estimate attendance.
Personal interviews with people entering Park.	734	To determine activities.
Personal interviews with people leaving Park.	618	To determine activities.
Personal interviews with people at specific locations in Park.	2,426	To obtain evaluations of specific locations.
Telephone interviews with residents of New York City.	650	To determine attitudes and characteristics of Park users and nonusers.

Source: E.S. Savas, Center for Government Studies, Columbia University, 1976.

Systematic counts of people entering the Park ceased in 1873 and were never resumed as a management practice. Two recent studies—one compiled in 1973, the other in 1982—represent the only meaningful subsequent attempts to determine a Park census. The 1973 study was conducted by Donald Sexton of Columbia University; the 1982 survey was performed by William Kornblum and Terry Williams of the City University of New York. In combination, the two studies examine the contemporary "human ecology" of Central Park and provide a complex portrait of the people who use it and how they use it. Much of this chapter is taken from the written reports based on those studies.

Professor Sexton employed the following variety of information-gathering methods in 1973,

The 1973 gate counts were made at preset time intervals (2,400 counts in all), and they remain today the most reliable sources of information for the number and demographics of Central Park's users. The counts were done on good-weather days when there were no major events planned for the Park: Tuesday, June 19; Saturday, June 23; and Sunday, June 24. Using these figures as typical of Park attendance for the month of June, Sexton calculated year-round figures by adjusting them according to the variation in concession revenues month by month.

From the gate counts, Sexton estimated that the average attendance on a fair-weather Sunday in June would be 120,000; Saturday, 70,000; and weekdays, 40,000. His extrapolations for the rest of the year can be seen in Table 2. Spot checks made during the 1982

Table 2
Annual Attendance Estimate
1976

Month	Normalized Concession Revenues	Estimated Attendance
January	.33	550,000
February	.28	470,000
March	.62	1,040,000
April	.93	1,570,000
May	.75	1,270,000
June	1.00	1,690,000
July	.85	1,430,000
August	.71	1,200,000
September	.73	1,240,000
October	.62	1,050,000
November	.44	750,000
December	.30	510,000
Total for Year		12,770,000

Source: E.S. Savas, Center for Government Studies, Columbia University, 1976.

study showed a 10 percent increase over 1973 in the number of people on major lawns such as the Great Lawn, Pilgrim Hill, the Mall and the Sheep Meadow. Otherwise the 1973 figures for Park attendance were found to be valid nine years later.

In the later (1982) study, Kornblum and Williams used a slightly different approach. Their intention was not only to obtain an overall census of Park users but also to ascertain their patterns of coming, going and roosting within the Park. To do this, they divided the Park into ten sectors, each of which was "swept" by teams of two trained observers during four distinct time periods: morning (8 to 9 A.M.), midday (11 A.M. to 1 P.M.), afternoon (2 to 4 P.M.) and evening (5 to 7 P.M.). On each sweep, people were counted and notes were made of their demographic character, their precise location and their activities. The information was broken down into a number of tables and summarized in graphic form in a "behavioral map" [see page 30]. As with the 1973 study, the 1982 study took place on typical days with no extraordinary events scheduled: Thursday, August 26, a clear, humid day with temperatures reaching the mid-80s; and Sunday, October 10, a crisp, clear fall day with temperatures in the 50s.

Who Are They?
On the basis of these two studies, we can estimate that today more than 3 million people use Central Park each year and that they they make upwards of 14 million person/visits annually. As to who these people are, the 1982 survey showed that although 68 percent are residents of Manhattan, at least 500,000 are out-of-towners, which makes Central Park one of New York's three leading tourist attractions, along with the Statue of Liberty and the United Nations.

Park users closely reflect the city's ethnic and racial demographics: 55 percent are white, 20 percent are black, 19 percent are Hispanic and 6 percent are Asian. Approximately 2 percent of the visitors are physically handicapped—a percentage that translates to

Table 3
Demographic Characteristics of Central Park Visitors, 1982
(in percent)

Sex	
male	66.5
female	33.5
Race/Ethnicity	
White	57.0
Black	20.0
Hispanic	20.4
Asian	3.2
Physical Handicap	2.0
Approximate Age	
Below 18	12.0
18–35	68.0
36–50	19.3
50+	12.6
Residence	
Manhattan	68.0
Other Boroughs	14.0
All Others	17.0

Source: City University of New York sample for Central Park Planners, 1982.

upwards of 1,000 handicapped people on an average Sunday. This number eloquently confirms the need for barrier-free facilities, like those recently installed in Central Park, in all parks.

The demographic similarity of the Park and the city as a whole in 1982 represents the most significant development in the 10-year period between studies. In 1973, blacks and Hispanics were underrepresented in the Park. The new racial parity indicates a basic change in the way the Park is being used, one that brings it closer to fulfilling Olmsted's democratic ideal.

The one remaining disparity between the Park's population and that of the surrounding city is the underrepresentation of women. From the Park's 1860s statistics we can see at least that this is nothing new. Women have historically accounted for around 40 percent of the Park's visitors. One reason is that there are more organized sports for men. Certainly men form the great majority of those who use the North Meadow, the Great Lawn and the Heckscher Ballfields. Women show up in greater numbers in such spots as the Zoo and the playgrounds, where they are supervising young children; in these places they are usually a majority. As it happens, this sexual imbalance is common in many urban public places. Women are more likely than men to remain at home during their leisure hours. In any case, other studies have shown that women have an average of 10 hours a week less free time than men (Vanek, 1974). Finally, women tend to feel more vulnerable in public places and are therefore less likely to use any park early and late in the day.

Activities in the Park
The standard dichotomy of "passive versus active" recreation hardly begins to describe the way people use Central Park. When visitors were asked what they did in the Park, their answers required more than 60 coding categories.

Table 4
Major Activity Categories, Central Park Visitors, Summer and Fall, 1982
(in percent)

Activity	Weekday	Weekend	Total
Relaxation	54.1	59.7	57.7
Sports	9.5	8.7	9.0
Water	2.7	2.3	2.4
Nature	4.2	3.3	3.7
Wheels	6.9	7.4	7.2
Music	4.8	5.7	5.3
Commute	6.5	2.2	3.8
Zoo	5.6	4.5	4.9
Playgrounds	2.8	3.7	3.4
Drugs/Deviance	2.8	2.4	2.6
Active	19.2	19.8	19.6
Passive	80.8	80.2	80.4

Source: City University of New York sample for Central Park Planners, 1982.

The striking fact is that virtually all of the most popular activities we observe in Central Park today were going on in it before the turn of the century. There was skating on the Lake as early as 1858, the year it was filled with water; horseback riding started in that year, too. Concerts began in 1859; boating, in 1861; lawn tennis, in 1863; school ball games, in 1865; skating and curling on the Conservatory Water, in 1869. In a very short time the Park had become the center for myriad activities.

The major difference today is that increasing portions of the Park have been dedicated to exclusive uses rather than left as flexible, unprogrammed space. The distinction between active, programmed use and unorganized, passive use of the Park is, of course, particularly relevant to the issues of Park restoration. The 80 percent of Central Park's visitors who use it for passive activities spend their time in a number of ways, most notably enjoying the presence of one another and simply relaxing. Because this large constituency of general Park users is unorganized and less vocal than other interest groups, their needs have been insufficiently taken into consideration in the past. Nor is the problem raised here unique to Central Park.

Table 5
Types of Relaxation by Central Park Visitors, In Rank Order and by Weekday and Weekend, 1982
(in percent)

Type of Relaxation	Weekday	Weekend	Total	Rank
People Watching	22.1	26.7	25.1	1
Relaxing	21.2	19.1	20.0	2
Thinking	20.2	13.2	15.6	3
Taking in the Park	9.4	11.3	10.7	4
Reading	11.0	10.1	10.1	5
Wandering	5.9	6.1	6.1	6
Sunbathing	1.3	6.0	4.5	7
Waiting	5.0	3.4	3.9	8
Picnic	4.0	3.0	3.3	9
Sleeping	0.8	0.7	0.8	10

Source: City University of New York sample for Central Park Planners, 1982.

The uses of Central Park have remained constant over the last 125 years.

Benches once had mudguards to protect ladies' skirts . . .

. . . otherwise not much has changed.

Winter in the Park, then . . .

. . . and now.

Biking, past . . .

. . . and present.

Table 6
Contrast between Weekday and Weekend Visitation in Central Park★
(in percent)

	Weekday	Weekend
Respondent was:		
Alone	63.8	46.7
With family	9.0	14.2
In a couple	20.0	30.1
With a group of friends	3.2	4.7
With a team	0.5	0.5
With a tour	0.5	0.2
Other	3.5	3.8

★Data on visitor use was collected in the summer and fall of 1982.

The setting aside of park space exclusively for active team sports is an issue that confronts most parks, and it is often an emotional one. Because encroachment upon green, open space by recreational interests is not viewed as critically as encroachment by highways or buildings, many parks have become little more than a collection of recreational facilities. Indeed, some modern parks—lacking the nineteenth-century scenic tradition — were never intended to be anything more. But, as will be seen in succeeding pages, it is a cardinal premise of the Central Park management and restoration plan that the Park continue to serve those who come there simply to find a bit of green grass or a tree-shaded bench to sit on. This does not, however, suggest indifference to the very real needs of an urban population for more vigorous forms of recreation. The issue is, in fact, one of city planning; and although the method of creating and precisely locating more athletic fields within the urban fabric of New York is beyond the scope of this plan, the need to do so underlies many of its recommendations. To grasp this important point one needs to observe the existing sports areas of Central Park today. The Park's playing fields are reserved to capacity during the most desirable post-workday and prime weekend hours. On any given weekend during warm weather, some 2,000 softball players occupy all the designated ball diamonds from the Heckscher fields to the North Meadow. At other times, these areas are only partly used. In winter, most of them receive only light use, and the Heckscher fields are totally empty. Thus, these popular sections of the Park are vibrant with activity some of the time but seem forlorn and vacant at other times because they are "off limits" to the general visitor, whose schedule of Park use is less precise but whose overall need is greater.

Regardless of whether a visitor's activity is active or passive, the 1982 study found a marked contrast in the social character of weekday and weekend visitation (Table 6). Weekday visitors tend to be solitary individuals; weekend visitors are more likely to be members of a family group or a couple. These findings highlight the fact that weekends in the Park are more often given over to social occasions, family outings and courtship.

The relative popularity of each of the Park's various features, both in the minds of those interviewed and by actual count of people, emerged from the 1982 study. Interestingly, the preferences of Manhattanites differ from those of people who live outside the borough. The ball fields of the North Meadow are, for instance, heavily favored by males living in nearby Manhattan neighborhoods. And although the Zoo is the clear favorite of the total Park-visiting public, residents of Manhattan, where the proportion of very young children is lower than elsewhere, have other preferences.

At the time Central Park was built, the population center of Manhattan was two miles away. The East Side was sparsely populated; the residential West Side had not yet even been built. In the early years, 70 percent of the Park's visitors entered from the south. Today the most consistently heavy traffic is through the main gates in the East and West Seventies, reflecting the fact that there is now a population of some 400,000 people living on blocks immediately adjacent to the Park—and a total of 726,000 people living within a 15-minute walk of it. Olmsted's prediction that Manhattan's population would eventually surround the Park has long since come true.

Table 7
Central Park Places Most Favored by All Respondents and Respondents from Manhattan 1982

Favorite Places	Overall Rank	Selected as Favorite by Manhattanites
Zoo	1	15.5%
Conservatory Water	2	11.0%
Reservoir	3	15.0%
Sheep Meadow	4	14.5%
Boathouse and Lake	5	12.0%
Great Lawn	6	6.0%
North Meadow	7	49.0%
Wollman Rink and Dairy	8	7.5%
Bethesda Fountain	9	24.0%
Heckscher Ballfields	10	6.5%

Source: City University of New York sample for Central Park Planners, 1982.

Table 8
Central Park Places Visited by All Respondents and Respondents from Manhattan 1982

Places Visited	Overall Rank	Visited by Adjacent Manhattanites
Zoo	1	4.0%
Conservatory Water	2	8.1%
W. 72nd Border	3	2.0%
W. 80/W. 94	4	8.3%
Reservoir	5	5.5%
Dairy	6	11.0%
E. 66–77	7	21.0%
Heckscher Ballfields	8	22.0%
North Ballfields	9	64.0%
Sheep Meadow	10	9.1%
Harlem Meer	11	50.0%

Source: City University of New York sample for Central Park Planners, 1982.

Daily Rhythms in Central Park

The data compiled by the user studies of Central Park provide an hour-by-hour view of the ebb and flow within its borders. It is a remarkable human ballet, as the following description paraphrased from the Kornblum and Williams report shows.

Sunday mornings in Central Park begin slowly. As the sun comes up, runners, bikers, dog walkers and bird watchers converge on the Park from all directions. By 8 A.M. on warm summer Sundays there are over a thousand people scattered around the Reservoir, the Great Lawn, the Conservatory Water and the Sheep Meadow. The areas around the Mall, Bethesda Fountain and the Ramble are still relatively quiet; a few scattered walkers and early-morning newspaper readers can be spotted here and there. Later in the day, this area from the Plaza gate to Bethesda Fountain will become the Park's population center, with people dispersing from it into the lower reaches of the Park. But in the early morning, these are quiet places.

By 9 A.M. most of the Park's summer inhabitants will have risen and begun their morning ablutions. There have been no firm counts of the number of homeless people who actually live in the Park during the warmer months, but observers counted seven vagrants awakening in the rock formations below the Dairy, from five to 15 vagrants who had slept in the West 59th Street area above the Heckscher Ballfields and at least 20 more indigent Park dwellers or overnight visitors who had strayed into the Park after a Saturday-night binge. In all, there are usually between 50 and 100 people who awake in the Park after having slept there.

Early morning is prime time for the Park's birders and nature lovers. Bird watchers have better luck in the transition hours from dawn to day, and they also have the pleasure of peace and quiet. Unlike the joggers, who puff along on the edges of lawns, or the early-morning dog walkers whose pets habitually demand hurried visits to spots at the Park's edge, the nature students and bird watchers browse throughout the Park and come to know all its inhabitants. The Ramble is their favorite haunt, but the entire Park offers possibilities for observation. They are the eyes and vocal chords for

Bird watchers, on the lookout for the Park's 269 species of birds, are among the earliest visitors to the Park each day.

the Park's plant and animal life. They penetrate less trodden areas and regularly report on their condition.

On Sundays, the rush into the Park has begun by midmorning (10 A.M.). Fortunately for those who seek the relative repose of the Park morning, the full onslaught will not get underway until midday or early afternoon. But by midmorning all the athletic facilities in the Park are being used to capacity. The tennis courts and softball fields are completely occupied by 10 A.M., unless the day is so hot or it is so late in the season that Jones Beach, Fire Island and other more distant spots will have drawn away the largest crowds. But from the first weeks of spring bloom to the onset of summer's

dog days, the Park will be used to capacity during most daylight hours.

The behavioral map (on page 28) shows a good deal of passive recreation directly adjacent to the most actively used sports facilities (the Great Lawn, the Heckscher Ballfields and the North Meadow fields). The rings of passive use surrounding active zones is visual proof that one group's exercise is another's entertainment. In addition to groups of spouses and children who take part in spectator picnics around ball games, elderly men frequent the bleachers at the Heckscher fields and come to know the various teams well enough to place friendly bets on the outcome of games. This same group of retired, predominantly white Park reg-

Nineteen playgrounds are sited near the perimeter of Central Park.

The Pace of Activity in Central Park

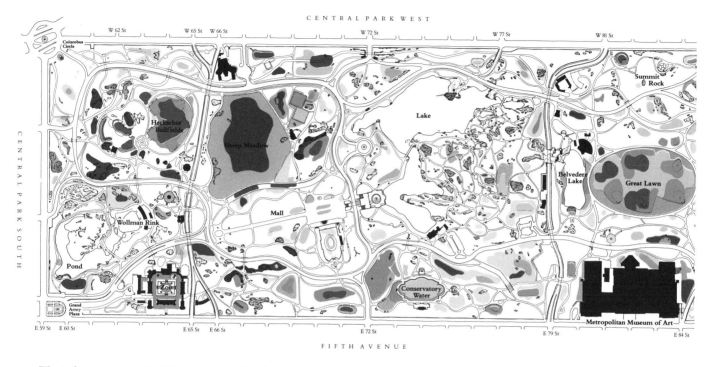

The information used for this map was gathered on two days in 1982, in August and October. Each was a typical good-weather day when no large events were planned. For purposes of observation, the Park was divided into 10 sections, each of which was "swept" four times during the day by a two-person team.

Active Uses: *The designation includes ball games, rowing, jogging, horseback riding, ice-skating, roller-skating and biking. The darkest patches—the areas most heavily used for active recreation—are invariably on flat open ground: the Heckscher Ballfields, the Great Lawn, the North Meadow, the East Meadow, the tennis courts and numerous lawns and playgrounds.*

ulars often remains until dusk for a spirited dice game, one of many in the Park almost any day of the week.

Between 2 and 4 P.M., the Park reaches its period of peak use. Families, couples and friendship groups stream through the big gates—those at the Park's southern corners, the East and West 72nd Street entrances, and the northern entrance at Adam Clayton Powell Boulevard and 110th Street. The Mall and the internal approaches to the Zoo become a huge impromptu "no-ring" circus with clowns, jugglers, mimes, musicians, acrobatic disco skaters, volleyball players, Frisbee art-

ists and kibitzers. Lines form by the vendors' carts. Eager children pull their parents toward the Zoo. The benches along the Mall become crowded, but there always seems to be a spot from which to view the activities.

The newly restored Sheep Meadow is the Park's center for relaxation, just as the Mall, the Zoo, the Lake and the Drives are its prime strolling thoroughfares. At any given moment in the late spring or early summer, there will be from 300 to 900 people reposing on the meadow. No area of the Park, however, is ever entirely peopled by sedentary users. At its most crowded, the Sheep Meadow may host a number of Frisbee games, a football catch game or two and assorted kite artists. It is, in fact, this mixture of activity that accounts for much of the

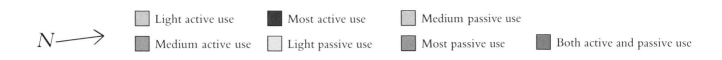

| Light active use | Most active use | Medium passive use |
| Medium active use | Light passive use | Most passive use | Both active and passive use |

Passive Uses: *Sunbathing, resting, sleeping, picnicking, people-watching and strolling. Sloping lawns are favorite places for passive activities, as are the perimeters of active-use areas, where spectators sit to watch the action. Places with pleasant views, such as Bethesda Terrace and Cherry Hill, are especially popular passive-use locations.*

Park's popularity: People come, as we have seen, for many reasons, not the least important of which is the enjoyment of observing the skills and pleasures of one another.

Toward 5 P.M., the Park begins to empty rapidly. At dusk the human rhythms are once again dominated by the flow of runners, bikers and dog walkers. Yet there will be hundreds of strolling couples and solitary walkers in most lawn areas. On especially hot evenings, family and neighborhood gatherings above 96th Street may linger far into the night, as people seek to escape the heat of their apartments. In

the south end, especially below the Dairy and on the slopes above the Heckscher Ballfields, the vagrants and homeless indigent bed down for the night.

Weekday Park rhythms contrast markedly with those of Saturday and Sunday, even if there are also some important similarities. Morning use of the Park begins earlier. Runners and dog walkers must be finished in time to get ready for work. Then, from around 7:30 to 9 A.M., a few thousand pedestrian commuters cross the Park on their way to Midtown from the West Side.

Weekday peak hours are at midday, when thousands of lunch-hour visitors stream into the Park's lower corners and fan out along the Mall, the Lake and the Zoo. Peak times on the Park's

29

Table 9
Hourly Flow of Visitors to Central Park
1982

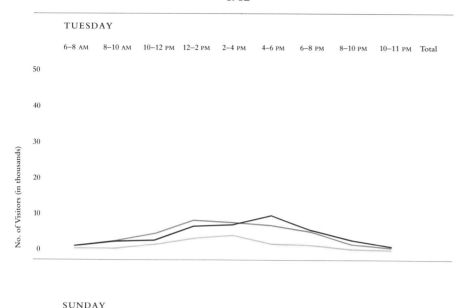

TUESDAY

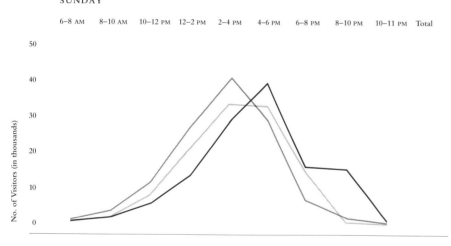

SUNDAY

Entering ——— Leaving ——— In Park ———

Source: City University of New York sample

sports fields are between 4 and 7 P.M., when organized adult sports leagues from Manhattan fill every available space. But before the regular league games begin, the Park's playing fields are heavily used by children from the more than 30 private schools within easy walking distance. Pickup games of soccer and Frisbee crowd the outfields and lawns adjacent to the formal ball fields.

Comparisons between weekday and weekend use can be easily overstated, however. Park attendance on warm summer weekdays bears a strong resemblance to weekend days, because so many New Yorkers and their families

will be on vacation—from their jobs or from school. The major differences are the times of peak use, as noted, and in the volume of weekday visitors who come to the Park alone (see Table 6). And, of course, specially scheduled evening music and theater performances bring added thousands of late-hour visitors into the Park on certain summer weekdays.

As can be seen by comparing the 1863-1873 figures and the contemporary census counts of the Park, the population trends of New York City as a whole have not been mirrored by the number of people visiting the Park. Central Park received maximum use

early in its history, but attendance leveled off despite huge population increases from 1870 to 1950. Similarly, the Park's use remained stable despite the 10.4 percent drop in population that New York experienced in the decade between 1970 and 1980.

One factor accounting for the present stability of Park use is the fact that so many nearby apartment dwellers consider Central Park to be quite literally their backyard. Manhattanites now account for 68 percent of Park users. Though this should not be surprising, it does represent an increase over 1973. Several factors account for this, chief among them the sustained physical fitness movement and the continuing popularity of special events. Officials of the Central Park Police Precinct estimate that approximately 5,000 joggers use Central Park every day. Joggers alone account for over 1.5 million person/visits a year. Special events, like the New York Marathon and the outdoor concerts, account for at least another million.

Another factor is the perception that the Park is safer now than it used to be. In 1973, 13 percent of those interviewed said they thought the Park was "safer than two years ago"; in 1982, 30 percent thought so. Greater presence of rangers and policemen as well as cleanup and repair programs are largely responsible. So is the almost constant presence of joggers, who, in using the Park from early morning to late at night, extend the period of heavy use and create an atmosphere of safety.

Crime in Central Park

Because park crime is random and opportunistic, it therefore gets greater, more sensational media coverage than crime committed elsewhere. Central Park especially enjoys a notoriety in this regard that is far in excess of what actual statistics warrant. Its stature as the country's premier urban park means that even its smallest problems receive national attention. This unwonted emphasis distorts the public's view of the Park. After one has discounted the fact that the Park is more notorious than it ought to be, one must nevertheless acknowledge that actions to further increase its security need to be taken. Some of these are already underway, and others being planned are discussed on page 81.

Goals, Priorities and Recommendations

User Studies as a Routine Practice
More important than any single recommendation derived from the recent user studies of Central Park is the recognition that user studies themselves are an invaluable tool for planning. They should once again become a routine management function in Central Park. This is the best way to assess the needs, desires and attitudes of the Park's constituency on a continuing basis.

Improving the Least-Visited Areas
The most pressing problems in Central Park generally have to do with overuse. But just as Central Park's visitors have favorite places, 20 percent admit that there are parts of the Park they avoid. Six of the seven Park areas that people said they stayed away from most were in the north end. And, indeed, the north end suffers from underuse (see Table 10). Only part of the reason for this can be attributed to the fact that the north end is adjacent to Harlem, where many whites are reluctant to go. The hilly and heavily wooded character of the Park in this quadrant is just as much a factor; blacks find it hostile too.

The James Taylor Concert on the Great Lawn, 1979.

Table 10
Places Central Park Visitors Said They Most Avoid, 1982
(in percent)

Park Area	Rank	Percent
Above 96th	1	5
Conservatory Garden	2	3
North Meadow	—	3
Harlem Meer	—	3
The Loch	—	3
Great Hill	3	2
The Ramble	4	1

Source: City University of New York sample

Some Park activists have pointed out that of the 86 events that took place in Central Park in 1982, only six were located above 96th Street. Events are programmed in the middle and south sections because that is where sponsors want them, regardless of their ethnic or cultural nature. This imbalance is being corrected somewhat with the recent restoration of the Conservatory Garden and the Great Hill. When the 110th Street Boathouse is rehabilitated, the north end will have yet another attractive venue for large gatherings.

Recommendations for making the overgrown and somewhat forbidding landscape of other parts of the north end more inviting will be found in the section of this book that deals with individual project areas.

Sports Fields Versus Meadows
The question of whether to dedicate the Park's meadows to programmed athletics has been touched on above. Given the fact that the preponderance of visitors are passive users of the landscape, the management and restoration plan recommends improving and maintaining those fields already in existence and not building any more— a policy consistent with wishes expressed in interviews conducted as part of the 1982 user study. Not one respondent asked for more ball fields, just better ones.

Policies Regulating Management and Use Throughout the Park
The Park, like any other structure, will need periodic capital reconstruction. As this current plan makes clear, Central Park has been constructed not once, but several times over its 130-year history. But because of excessive unregulated use and management neglect, at various times its appearance has become derelict and its agenda of capital investment has been greater and more frequent than it should have been. It will always be necessary to rebuild parts of the Park as long as it remains a popular and actively enjoyed place. This process can be greatly decelerated, however, by the enforcement of sensible policies and simple rules.

Policies for the management and use of the Park's three primary landscape types (meadow, woodland and parkland) necessarily differ, and within each category different parts of the Park support different uses and have different management needs. The successful management of the Sheep Meadow (used for passive recreation) and the Heckscher Playground (used for athletics) over the past six years proves that carefully thought out and consistently enforced use policies coupled with good maintenance can prevent the deterioration that is an inevitable consequence of heavy unregulated use. The extension of the same kind of careful and specific management techniques that account for the continuing health and beauty of these restored areas is being applied elsewhere throughout the Park. Special attention should be given to management and use policies in those delicately balanced environments within the Park that support wildlife populations.

Regulation of Park Noise
If the Park is to function successfully as the peaceful refuge it is meant to be, the current experiment of designating certain sections "quiet zones" where the use of loud radios is prohibited should be continued and extended.

72nd Street Cross Drive on a busy Sunday.

Circulation: Drives, Paths and Bridle Trail

The traffic circulation system in Central Park, quite unlike the street plan of the surrounding city, was designed as a recreational and scenic work of art. It leads visitors along a carefully arranged trail of visual experiences, through sunny meadows and shaded woodlands, from the water's edge to high rock outcroppings, from rugged landscapes to areas of intense architectural sophistication.

The inspiration for this approach to landscape design came from landscape paintings of the seventeenth century, particularly those of Claude Lorrain, and from the landscaped parks of. the eighteenth-century English aristocracy. In both the paintings and the living landscapes, the eye was attracted from one view to another. In Central Park, as in the English estate parks, vistas were meant to appear and disappear as the observer moved onward, beckoned by such landscape ornaments as Bethesda Terrace, Bow Bridge, the Belvedere and the bold rock outcrops crowned by rustic shelters.

Central Park's Four Types of Circulation

The four circulation systems of Central Park are the transverse roads, the Drives, the pedestrian paths and the Bridle Trail. Each is grade-separated from the others. As Olmsted described:

Observations of [traffic difficulties] both in our streets and in European parks, led to the planning of a system of independent ways; first for carriages, second for horsemen wishing to gallop, third for footmen, and fourth for common street traffic requiring to cross the Park. By this means it was made possible, even for the most timid and nervous, to go on foot to any district of the Park . . . without crossing a line of wheels on the same level, and consequently, without occasion for anxiety or hesitation. [Olmsted and Kimball, 1973, p. 47]

The ingenuity of Olmsted and Vaux's Central Park circulation plan is legendary. Given a long, narrow, rectangular site to work with, they succeeded in creating an illusion of randomness and rural freedom by their artful placement of curving drives, paths and a bridle trail. Each type of path or roadway was separated from the others, passing over or under them by means of arches and bridges. No two of the 36 arches and bridges used to carry out this scheme are alike; the designers used the opportunity to create an exuberant mélange of architectural motifs in a variety of materials—cast iron, rubble stone, cut stone, brick, granite, brownstone and wood.

The Park's circulation systems were not intended to be design elements themselves but rather to be inconspicuous routes by which the carefully orchestrated sequence of landscapes could be experienced. Their widths were scaled according to the volume of use they were to bear, and the landscapes connected by them differed according to the mode and speed of travel going through. Those adjacent to the Drives were broad and sweeping; beside the paths they were more intimate in scale and detailed in design; along the Bridle Trail they became rugged and picturesque. Views were composed, as in landscape paint-

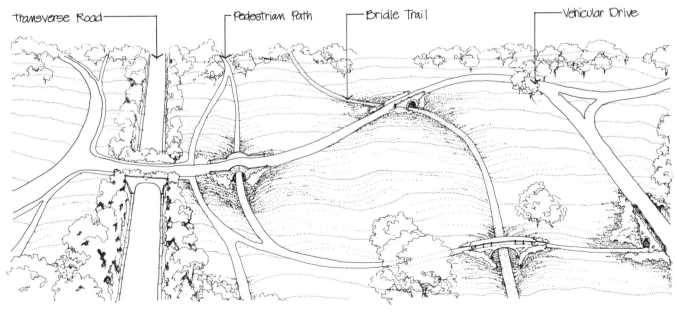

The various elements of Central Park's circulation system—pedestrian paths, Bridle Trail, transverse roads and vehicular drives—are grade-separated, thus preventing the interruption of the flow of one traffic mode by another.

33

Cast-iron bridges carry pedestrians over the Bridle Trail.

ings, with attention to foreground, middle ground and background. The materials of the artists' palette were water, trees, shrubs, lawn, rocks and the topography itself. Individual objects, even the most charming works of architecture or the noblest or most exotic trees, meant nothing by themselves; composition was everything.

The Transverse Roads
It was a brilliant foresight to build the four sunken, east-west transverse roads so that crosstown city traffic could tunnel swiftly and unobtrusively under and through the Park. The truly remarkable thing was that there was no

need for the transverse roads when Olmsted and Vaux designed them. The city lay almost entirely to the south of the Park; the land to the east and west was still undeveloped. And yet Olmsted had the prescience to write:

The time will come when New York will be built up, when all the grading and filling will be done, and when the picturesquely varied, rocky formations of the Island will have been converted into formations for rows of monotonous straight streets, and piles of erect buildings. There will be no suggestion left of its present varied surface, with the single exception of the few acres contained in the Park.

In hindsight, Olmsted's prediction sounds obvious enough, and yet at the time it was written, some of the wisest minds in New York thought it foolhardy. August Belmont and Robert J. Dillon argued that the transverse roads should be omitted from the plan, claiming that "there will be little or no such business relations of one side with the other as to require vehicles of traffic to cross the Park."

In time, however, the city did envelope the Park on all sides, and today the transverses (at 65th Street, 79th Street, 85th Street and 97th Street) are vital, heavily used thoroughfares. They permit commercial traffic to flow smoothly across town, virtually out of sight, without interrupting the scenic impressions or the recreational pleasures inside the Park.

The Paths
Most people come to Central Park as tourists, to wander without a specific destination and to be uplifted by the moods induced by scenery. But many also head for specific recreational facilities by the shortest possible route—not always on the established paths. In addition, more people are now playing sports or engaging in other activities that cause them to leave the circulation system and distribute themselves onto the landscape. Although Olmsted and Vaux had brilliantly anticipated the need for crosstown vehicular traffic through the Park, they did not foresee that a strong east-west pedestrian impulse would develop as well. Therefore, new pedestrian entrances had to be cut into the Park wall at 61st, 66th,

Passages under the Drive are handsome stone arches, each different in design.

The below-grade transverse roads permit crosstown vehicular traffic to cut through the Park without interrupting people at play.

When established paths do not give ready access to major destinations, visitors create desire lines.

79th, 90th, 93rd, 103rd and 106th streets on the west side and at 60th, 67th, 69th, 76th, 85th, 97th, 99th and 102nd streets on the east side.

One consequence of additional Park facilities, additional entrances and new pedestrian habits has been the creation of a well-defined second circulation system, one that has a greater east-west orientation than the original. Although some of the new paths have been designed, most are *ad hoc* additions, or "desire lines"—dirt foot trails that cut across the landscape and cause soil erosion. Since many of these foot trails have been "legitimized" with pavement, the Park landscape has become more and more chopped up and webbed with asphalt. In some places, particularly at the south end, lights, signs and benches are more in evidence than grass and trees.

Originally the paths, as well as the Drives described below, were made of cinder and gravel, with granite block gutters. They served not only as circulation routes but also as a part of the surface and subsurface drainage system. Water seeped through the gravel to underground drainage pipes. In later years, when these routes were paved and curbed, water could no longer seep into the ground and had to be carried off by a series of catch basins and drainpipes. The catch basins and pipes of the new system are generally too small and, lacking proper maintenance in recent years, apt to become clogged with debris. Consequently, after every rain, there are large pools of standing water along the pathways and Drives.

The Drives
The East Drive and West Drive combine to form a six-mile scenic loop of Central Park, linking the entire 843 acres. Originally, these Drives provided a recreational tour for carriages. Going for a drive in the Park was by itself a major form of recreation. Some of the Park's loveliest scenery was designed to be seen from the Drives, and there were carriage drop-offs and parking areas along the way to promote further pedestrian exploration. In turn, people on the pedestrian paths enjoyed watching the passing carriages, or as Olmsted put it, viewing "the equipages and their inmates." [Olmsted and Kimball, p. 232]

The advent of the automobile naturally had a substantial impact on the Park. At first, these "pleasure vehicles" joined the carriages along the Drives as part of the great, leisurely vehicular parade. But as cars multiplied and carriages disappeared, the Drives became an extension of the city streets. Automobile and taxi drivers sped through the Park on their way from one part of the city to another. For them, the Park became not a destination but a shortcut. The use of the Park Drives as important traffic arteries was further encouraged by the addition of new vehicular entrances at Sixth and Seventh avenues on Central Park South and at 67th, 77th, 90th and 106th streets on Central Park West.

When one-way traffic was introduced in the city in 1934, the Park Drives—by now an integral part of the city street system—were also converted to one-way use. At the same time, the carriage Drives were re-engineered and straightened to accommodate faster traffic. Among the alterations to their original looping course were the smoothing out of the curve where the East Drive met the Center Drive at the south end of the Mall, the closing of the Center Drive itself, and the burial of the Marble Arch at 65th Street.

The first tentative steps to reverse this trend of domination by the automobile were taken in 1966, when, over major opposition from the taxi industry, management began closing the Drives to cars in daylight hours on weekends and holidays from Memorial Day to Labor Day. Gradually these closings were extended so that today the Park Drives are closed on weekends all year and on weekdays from May to October, from 10 A.M. to 4 P.M. Although this policy has its dissenters, the re-dedication of the Drives for recreational use during non-rush hours, the warm weather season and on weekends helps strike a balance between the Drives' function within the Park's internal circulation system and their role as city traffic arteries.

The Bridle Trail
For years, one of the Park's finest recreational features was the Bridle Trail, which hugs the perimeter. But it has a soft surface that requires constant maintenance, and large segments of the trail have become gullied, rocky and very dangerous. Unlike the paths and Drives, which have proliferated over

the years, there is less of the Bridle Trail now than there used to be, particularly in the southern sector, where the Zoo, the Wollman Rink and the Heckscher Ballfields have pre-empted it. Today, this truncated part of the trail simply dissolves into a mud puddle near Seventh Avenue and Central Park South. The northern loop, skirting the Reservoir and extending beyond it into the rugged scenery of the north end, is more heavily used by horseback riders. Though not as badly deteriorated as the southern segment, it too is in need of major repair.

Elements Associated with Central Park's Circulation Systems

The architectural elements of the Park, particularly its arches and bridges and other amenities such as lights and benches, should be considered in relation to its circulation system. Rustic shelters, like the beckoning Belvedere, served as punctuation marks in the landscape. Park visitors were thus subtly guided through the landscape by a series of visual experiences constructed of water, vegetation, topography, architecture and sculpture.

A closer look at these circulation-related elements reveals problems as well as opportunities for park preservationists.

Bridges
As has been mentioned, no two of the 36 bridges and arches in the Park are the same. Unfortunately, many of the pedestrian bridges no longer serve the purpose for which they were designed. Some became isolated relics as new pathways skirted around them. Others are dark and dank and are simply avoided.

Stairs
Some stairs are connected with bridges; others are picturesquely built into rock cliffs and rock faces or set into steep hillsides. Today, many of them have been heaved by frost and dislodged by erosion.

Architecture
Bridges, arches, stairs and vine-clad arbors were, of course, integral to the Park's circulation system, and nearby rustic shelters accented the landscape and promoted its exploration. However, such large-scale architecture as the Dairy, Bethesda Terrace, the Boathouse, the Metropolitan Museum and the Casino were tucked out of the way so that they would not interrupt the overall *rus en urbe* impression and would simply be "discovered" by the casual stroller. Subsequent architectural additions such as the Lasker Rink, the Wollman Rink and the Tennis House have, unfortunately, not been as sensitively sited.

Circulation amenities
Benches
Fences
Signage
Drinking fountains
Trash baskets
Lighting
Comfort stations

The most important path amenities —the rock outcrops—were in the Park long before the arrival of the designers, and they, in fact, determined the positioning of the circulation system itself. These magnificent, glacially polished protrusions of Manhattan mica schist served as an armature for the design of the landscape.

A Circulation Field Study

In 1983, a survey of the four-part circulation system of Central Park was compiled for the Central Park Conservancy by landscape architect Philip Winslow. Every path segment of the system was described in detail, and the following maps were produced:

Historic comparisons
The original circulation system of Central Park—transverse roads, paths, Drives and Bridle Trail—was depicted, along with additions and subtractions occurring throughout the history of the Park.

Steps cut into the Park's Manhattan schist bedrock at the Kinderberg.

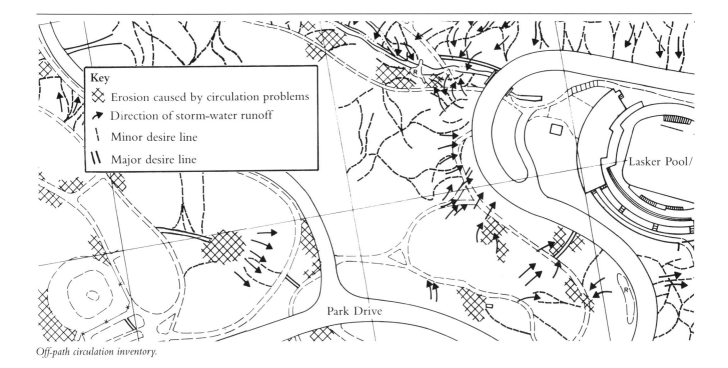

Key

⊠ Erosion caused by circulation problems

➚ Direction of storm-water runoff

\ Minor desire line

\\ Major desire line

Lasker Pool/

Park Drive

Off-path circulation inventory.

The desire-line circulation system
Paths created by the users of Central Park were mapped, together with the direction of erosion caused by desire lines. All present path intersections were numbered, and the conditions around them were recorded—specifically, notes regarding bare spots worn by short-cutting.

Significant pedestrian routes
Whether they follow constructed pedestrian paths, desire lines, the Bridle Trail, the Drives or the transverse roads, all major routes of foot travel through the Park were mapped.

Amenities along pedestrian paths
All amenities such as benches, lamps, garbage cans, water fountains and fences bordering the paths were charted.

Vehicular use of pedestrian paths
The major circulation routes of maintenance, security and sanitation vehicles were mapped to assess the efficiency of the operations they serve and the extent and effect of their intrusion on the pedestrian circulation system.

Problem Solving

The proposals in this chapter attempt to reintroduce the "experiential" quality of Central Park's circulation system by restoring the relationship between scenery and circulation wherever possible. At the same time, this plan takes into account the fact that there are two kinds of pedestrians who enter Central Park: those who are content to meander and those who are headed for a specific destination. A fundamental objective, therefore, is to design the circulation so that both types of visitors keep to the paths and do not trample lawns and shrub beds to get where they want to go. By considering paths in the context of the entire landscape and by using all facets of the landscape to direct the stroller, this objective can be accomplished.

Poor pathway drainage encourages desire line traffic.

Circulation: The Growth of Concrete

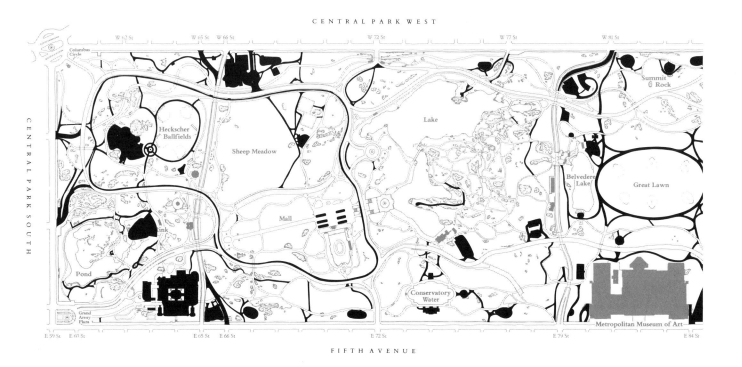

Problem: How to Prevent Desire Lines

Solutions:
1. Mounding
2. Mounding plus vegetation
3. Fences
4. Benches as fences
5. The elongated intersection

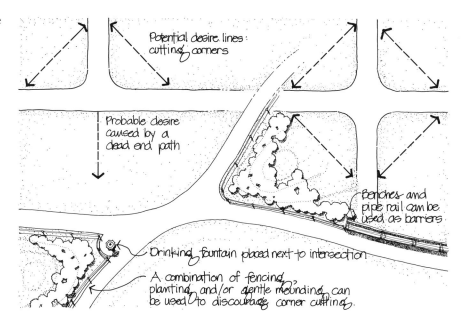

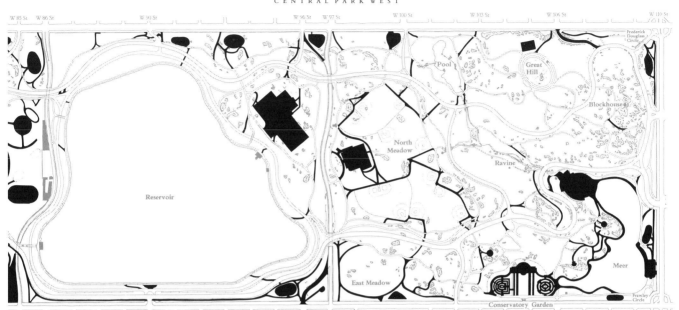

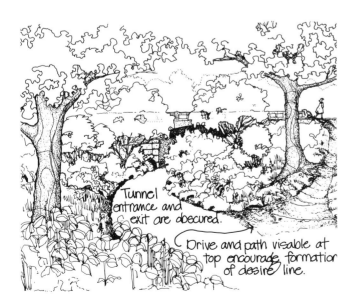

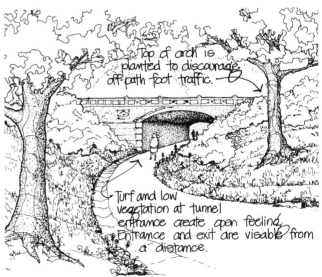

Problem: How to Orient the Pedestrian

Solution: Visual Cues

Typical Central Park
Furniture and Amenities

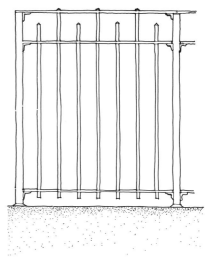

RUSTIC FENCE
Used in picturesque landscapes, such as the Ramble

STEEL PICKET FENCE
Four or seven foot height

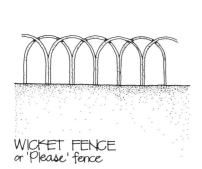

WICKET FENCE
or 'Please' fence

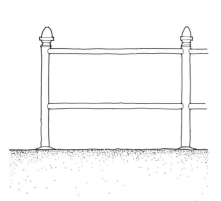

WOOD GUARD RAIL
Used on Park Drives

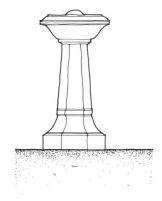

TWO-RAIL, PIPE-RAIL FENCE

DRINKING FOUNTAIN

TRASH RECEPTACLE
Wire Mesh

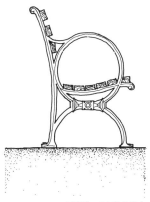

WORLDS FAIR BENCH
Cast iron and wood

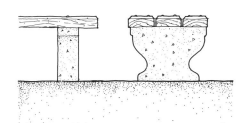

BACKLESS BENCH · Wood & Concrete
Used on the Park perimeter

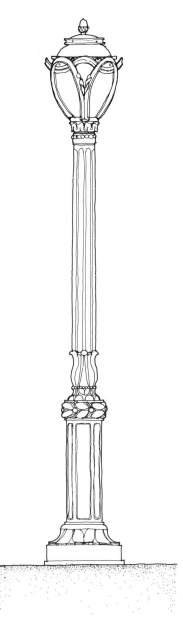

CENTRAL PARK LUMINAIRE
on 'B' POLE

RUSTIC BENCH
Used in picturesque landscapes

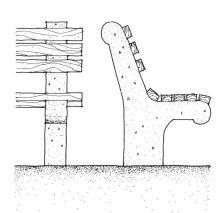

WOOD and CONCRETE BENCH
Function well as barriers and at entries

Problem: How to Make a Curving Path Seem to Be the Shortest Distance Between Two Points

Solution

Illustration: A gently curving path describing a very slender "S" overlaid by an arrow to show that, even though the path bends, it does not take the pedestrian the least bit out of his way.

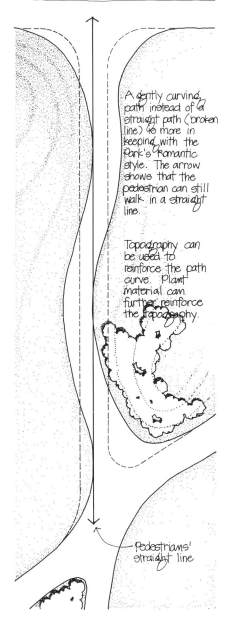

DRIVE

A gently curving path instead of a straight path (broken line) is more in keeping with the Park's Romantic style. The arrow shows that the pedestrian can still walk in a straight line.

Topography can be used to reinforce the path curve. Plant material can further reinforce the topography.

Pedestrians' straight line

One of the few grade crossings in Central Park, an unpleasant interruption of the Park experience during hours when Drives are open to traffic.

Recommendations

Pedestrian Paths

A functioning hierarchy of paths should be established with widths and paving materials determined by use and destination.

Pedestrian traffic should be channeled and controlled, especially at the Park entrances, to avoid further trampling of the landscape. Off-path movement should be discouraged by a variety of design strategies: the use of grading, shrub planting, benches and pipe-rail fencing. Desire lines should be eradicated and replanted. In some places, the circulation system should be partially or completely redesigned to eliminate confusing or redundant path systems.

The path systems serving non-original attractions, such as the Great Lawn, the tennis courts and the two skating rinks, should be redesigned to meld more gracefully into the landscape.

In areas rich in historic design, special attention should be paid to building with negotiable curves and with sub-surface and surface engineering appropriate to the loads they must bear.

Lighting should be concentrated along major pedestrian routes. Major cross-park paths should be well lit, as should evening- and nighttime-event spaces. However, the Park's woodlands and other secluded sections should not be

lit at night in order to discourage nighttime visitation and to preserve their appearance as natural areas. The Mall and the entrance to the Park at Grand Army Plaza should receive distinctive lighting to distinguish and dignify them as major formal spaces. Special features, such as Bethesda Fountain and the Belvedere, should be illuminated for aesthetic and security reasons.

Stone arches should be restored so that once again they serve their aesthetic and functional purposes. Drainage must be corrected, vegetation obscuring their entrances should be pruned or removed, and the arches should be invitingly lit.

There should be at least one route to all major destinations that is accessible to handicapped people. Where steep slopes make this impossible, other arrangements should be made to accommodate the handicapped.

Drives

In general, the Drives should be downplayed as thruways to Midtown and the suburbs. Their use as a touring road for viewing the Park should be encouraged by lowering the speed limit to 20 miles per hour. Traffic lights should be timed accordingly.

Special graphics should be designed for use in all the city parks to reduce the visual disruption created by highway-

Redesigned path, Strawberry Fields.

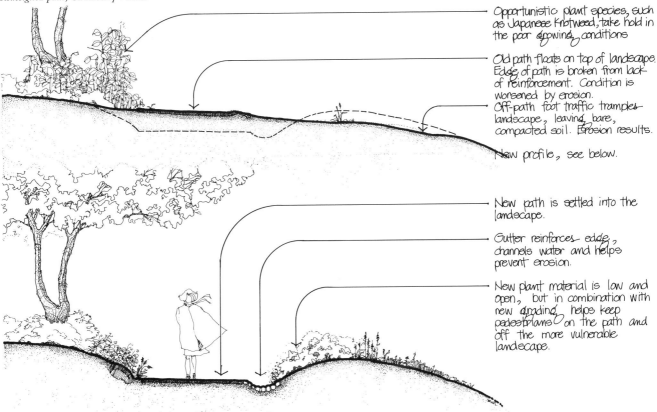

Opportunistic plant species, such as Japanese Knotweed, take hold in the poor growing conditions

Old path floats on top of landscape. Edge of path is broken from lack of reinforcement. Condition is worsened by erosion.

Off-path foot traffic tramples landscape, leaving bare, compacted soil. Erosion results.

New profile, see below.

New path is settled into the landscape.

Gutter reinforces edge, channels water and helps prevent erosion.

New plant material is low and open, but in combination with new grading, helps keep pedestrians on the path and off the more vulnerable landscape.

Cross section of Strawberry Fields path before and after restoration.

style signs. Furthermore, such park-specific signs will deliver an unwritten message that these are not city streets and therefore the rules are different.

Parking within the Park, including employee parking, should be reduced as much as possible. Essential parking should be made inconspicuous.

In order to reestablish the integrity of the Park landscape along its southern edge, the feasibility of closing the entrance Drives at Sixth and Seventh avenues should be studied.

Bridle Trail

Since the southern portion of the Bridle Trail has already been severely truncated and the more scenic, extensive, flatter northern portion is adequate to serve horseback riders, the part below 86th Street on the west side should be converted to a badly needed major north-south pedestrian path.

Above 86th Street, the Bridle Trail should be completely rebuilt with adequate underdrainage, relandscaped to control slope erosion, and given a new soft surfacing and proper maintenance to prevent future deterioration.

The Transverse Roads

Since the transverse roads are sunk below grade, they are low points in watersheds and frequently become impassable after rainstorms. Their drainage should be repaired by decreasing storm water flow from above, by increasing the capacity of the underground drainage system and by routine removal of debris.

In addition, the walls of the transverses should be repointed, and the tunnels—some of which have no functioning lights at all—should be lit 24 hours a day.

43

Sheep Meadow, 1979, during restoration. A network of drainage tiles beneath the Park's surface carries off storm water.

Topography, Soils and Drainage

The Bare Bones

The site that was destined to become Central Park was both frustrating and fortuitous for its designers. It was frustrating because of its long, narrow, rigidly rectilinear shape; its broken, agitated topography; and its lack of significant natural scenery. There were no venerable stands of trees, fine meadows or placid lakes but rather two large swamps, a portion of salt marsh, an upland bog and uneven, thin-soiled, boulder-strewn tableland dotted with squatters' shacks, bone-boiling works and piles of refuse from the burgeoning city that lay to the south. It was an altogether un-prepossessing landscape. But there was potential for landscape art nonetheless. Outcrops of Manhattan mica-schist—so troublesome to the city's builders, who were busily blasting them away elsewhere in order to make street grades as level as possible—offered striking forms and topographic accents for the park-to-be.

These ancient outcrops form a fascinating chapter of geological history and are in many ways the most beautiful features of Central Park. They are composed of very hard, erosion-resistant metamorphic rock baked in the earth's interior 450 million years ago as part of the mountain-building event that produced the Appalachian chain. Ribboned with granite intrusions from a second epoch of geological unrest 100 million years after their initial formation, they protrude from the surface of the ground throughout the Park, polished stumps of once lofty peaks, looming gray presences flecked with silver flakes of mica and also containing the minerals quartz, feldspar and hornblende. They, more than any other aspect, give Central Park its essential and distinctive landscape character.

In addition to the rock outcrops, there were other major features already in place on the site of the future park. The northern end contained a steep, wooded stream valley and a brook flowing through a break in a series of low bluffs, which had served as for-

Umpire Rock, with grooves marking the passage of the Wisconsin glacier from northwest to southeast.

tified lookout points during the Revolutionary War and the War of 1812.

The original site also contained two reservoirs: the present irregular one, called the receiving reservoir, built while the Park was in construction, and the rectilinear Croton Reservoir, built in 1842 on the site now occupied by the Great Lawn. These two bodies of water, 143 acres in extent, effectively separated Central Park into two parts, an Upper Park and a Lower Park, and presented a considerable challenge to the designers in their efforts to achieve an integrated plan for all 843 acres.

Meeting the Challenge

It took an army of laborers to build Central Park, most of them newly arrived immigrants. Working with pickaxes, shovels, horse-drawn carts and 20,800 barrels of gunpowder, they manipulated an estimated 4,825,000 cubic yards of earth and rock. This included about 700,000 cubic yards of topsoil imported to supplement the Park's thin glacial till soil. The terrain was modeled into long wide swales, small knolls, and hummock and saddle formations; these gave the Park its

gently rolling character reminiscent of pastoral countryside. Construction teams dredged the swamps and incorporated the organic matter from them into the newly configured upland areas, at the same time installing complex piping systems that would turn these basins into artificial lakes and ponds. Some 476,000 cubic yards of rock were excavated, removed and reset. Much of this was bedrock that had to be blasted away in order to create the Park's four sunken transverse roads.

Olmsted's design for Central Park was one of considerable brilliance. It took advantage of existing natural landforms, particularly the spectacular rock outcrops. The most impressive outcrops received names such as Summit Rock (the highest natural elevation in the Park), Spur Rock and Drip Rock. Others, like the Kinderberg and seven rocky elevations in the Ramble, were crowned with rustic shelters to emphasize their presence in the landscape. Thus they became focal points as well as viewing platforms. Vista Rock, which plunged a sheer 20.3 feet to the old Reservoir and also contained the tunnel of the 79th Street transverse

The Meer's natural shoreline was replaced with a continuous rock edge, above, which in turn was replaced with a concrete wall in the 1940s.

The 79th Street transverse is the only one that burrows through solid rock.

road, received the most dramatic treatment: a Victorian Gothic castle built largely out of the parent bedrock and called the Belvedere because of its three viewing terraces. This ornament, which today houses a U.S. weather station and the Central Park Learning Center, was placed on an axis with the Mall and Bethesda Terrace.

Workmen used much of the excavated rock debris to define and control the embankments of lakes, ponds and streams. They built two streams. One, the Gill in the Ramble, is wholly artificial. The other, in the northern end of the Park, was made from Montayne's Rivulet, its streambed was excavated, and boulders were placed artfully along its course to form the Pool, the Loch and a series of five waterfalls (two of which have now disappeared) emptying into the Harlem Meer. The designers also created two other seemingly natural bodies of water: the large 20-acre Lake (including a man-made island) embracing the Ramble and, in the Southeast Corner, the Pond. In addition to the rocky material that helped impound their water and hold their shores in place, some of the water bodies had gravel paths along the edges with stone curbing set two and a half feet below the summer water level. When the water was lowered in winter, skaters could sit on the stone curb and walk on the gravel. This and other measures helped forestall shoreline erosion and damage to the vegetation from human traffic.

Olmsted and Vaux used boulders as naturalistic side walls for stairs set into

hillsides, as barriers to control erosion or simply as elements of visual interest. They used them in constructing the Park's grade-separated circulation system. Twenty-three underpasses appear to grow gracefully and naturally out of the landscape; the steep embankments of many were formed and held in place by boulder construction.

Thus Central Park was sculpted into more or less the form we know today. In this process, the designers were mindful of another imperative besides those of landscape beauty and convenience of circulation: the achievement of good drainage throughout the Park.

Drainage

Before construction, the Park consisted of five major drainage watersheds. Originally these basins were part of a natural drainage system that flowed both into and out of the Park to the East River. But when uniform city street grades were established on all four sides of the Park and the ground surface was raised or lowered in many places, the natural drainage corridors were destroyed. Isolated and rimmed by a perimeter wall, as it is today, Central Park has had to depend on an artificial drainage system to carry off storm water. Two systems, in fact, were constructed: one for the general landscape and another for the circulation system.

Soil compaction caused drainage problems from the outset. Olmsted complained that in the recently excavated areas the ground held water like

putty when wet and that the soil was "suitable only to the growth of swamp plants." During periods of drought it became rock-hard, creating "a hydrollic floor between the thirsty roots in the surface soil and the moisture which would otherwise be afforded them from the cool earth below." Olmsted had made a considerable study of underground drainage, and working with a drainage engineer, Colonel George E. Waring, Jr., he planned a field drainage system for most of the Park landscape, notably the bog in the Ramble, the swamp in the Southwest Corner and the streambeds, which had been filled in during the Park's construction. This system consisted of clay tiles, one and one-quarter to six inches in diameter, laid approximately 40 feet apart. Elsewhere, tiles were laid where water collected along the underground surface of the bedrock, where it could not percolate through impermeable subsoil or where the water table was naturally high. These drainage tiles slowly funneled the water into basins attached to an underground collector system that fed the Park's streams and ponds.

A second drainage system was constructed parallel to the Park's circulation system. Drives, a Bridle Trail and transverse roads were crowned in the middle and had open gutters, lined with granite block or other stones, on both sides. These gutters emptied water into a series of catch basins, which in turn were connected by pipes to the storm-water collection system that emptied into the Park water

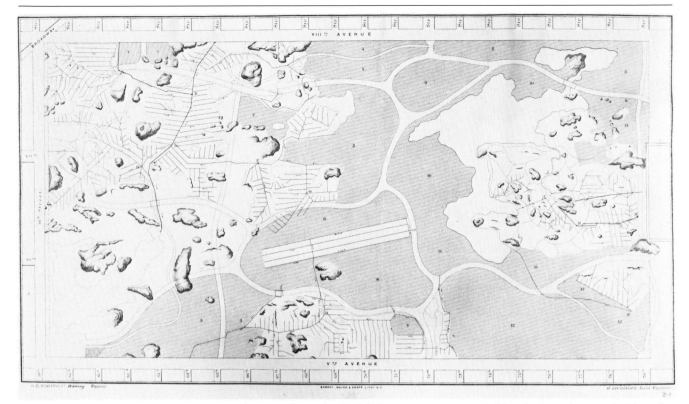

This 1859 map by G. E. Waring, Drainage Engineer, shows part of Central Park's field drainage system, constructed of clay tiles. It was known as the "thorough drainage system," then a new technology imported from Europe.

bodies or, in the case of the sunken transverse roads, directly into the city sewer system. Beneath most of the paths were laid more drainage tiles like those in the open landscape. The path system was mostly unpaved at first, and water could drain down through the porous surface materials. Where the topography made it necessary, catch basins were positioned to prevent storm-water runoff from washing out paths and creating gullies on the Bridle Trail and the Drives. Catch basins were also needed where the artificial topography of the grade-separated circulation system interfered with the Park's natural drainage, subdividing its five drainage basins and creating new low points.

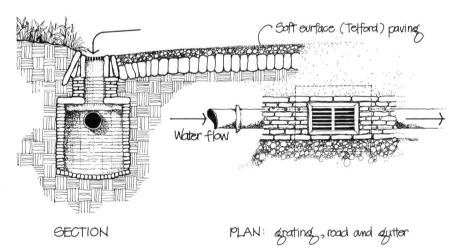

Section of the Carriage Drive showing layers of gravel and drainage system according to 1865 design.

Hydrological Problems and Changes

The Park's ponds and streams were lined with clay to ensure that they retained a proper volume of water, but in times of drought not enough water flowed into them to maintain constant circulation. Early annual reports frequently describe the water bodies as green, stagnant and generally offensive. Because of a widespread fear of malaria, there was at least one proposal to fill the Park's water bodies with earth. The dumping of raw sewage from Park comfort stations into them posed a more serious health hazard, however. Not until 1905, when sewer pipes connected the interior of the Park to city sewer lines, was the problem corrected. With the completion of the Catskill Aqueduct in 1915, more water was available to flush the lakes and maintain an adequate water level.

Also at that time, gravel and cement were applied to lake and pond edges; beaches were widened, smoothed and cemented. Dams were constructed in the Gill. The Meer was edged with a new dry-rock rubble edge, and in 1929

47

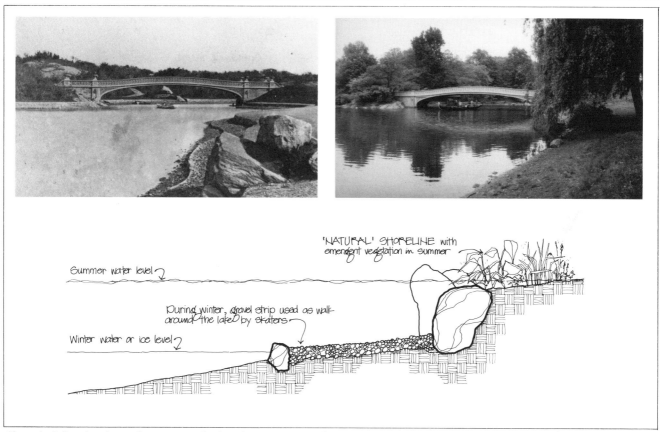

Above, the Lake at its winter and summer water levels. Below, a cross section of its carefully constructed "naturalistic" shoreline.

a new rock edge was constructed around the Lake. The configuration of pond and lake shorelines, however, remained essentially the same as they had been originally. But this was not true for long. After 1934, Robert Moses adopted a landscape approach that emphasized engineering more than design. Errant circulation and erosion at the water's edge were remedied with asphalt paths and rock walls partially rimming the Pond and entirely surrounding the Meer. In building these hard, regularized edges, coves and peninsulas were modified and water-surface area was reduced. Water surface in the Park was further diminished by the imposition of Wollman Rink on an arm of the Pond, the Loeb Boathouse on the northeast inlet of the Lake and Lasker Rink at the mouth of the Loch. Because of all these changes, plus the effects of siltation, 21 percent of the original water-body surface area has been lost.

Islands, too, have disappeared. Erosion claimed the island in the Lake, the Pool island was washed away after a water-main break in the early 1960s, and the Meer island disappeared be-

neath Lasker Rink. With all this melting away of islands and the tremendous sedimentary load washed down from the surrounding watersheds, the depth of the Park's water bodies was greatly reduced. Today, the Park contains an accumulation of 30,000 cubic yards of dredge material—a figure that does not include sediment found in its two streams. Analysis of this fine sediment reveals it to be high in iron and organic content, providing food for the explosive growth of algae and other water plants. This accounts for the highly eutrophic condition and murky green color of all the Park's water bodies in summer.

As the water bodies continue to silt up, the same kind of plant succession observable in old bogs has begun to occur. Aquatic plants and wetland vegetation have taken hold on the edges. When they die in winter, the resulting mat of debris furthers the filling-in process. Unless routine dredging is performed, siltation of the Park's water bodies will continue until they revert to swamps and finally to dry land ribboned by smaller streams and marshes similar to those depicted

on the map of the pre-Park site. (See page 14.)

Thus Central Park's designed landscape continues to shift. Uninformed public opinion believes that somehow the Park's delicate balance of land and water manages to take care of itself. Nothing could be further from the truth, as a brief examination of its drainage and soil problems will show.

Drainage Additions and Problems

Central Park's carefully conceived system of drainage pipes was adequately maintained and functioned well for about 50 years. But after the turn of the century, the field drainage system began to break down. During 1907 and 1908, 4,025 linear feet of new drain tiles were laid in order to correct standing water problems in several low-lying areas. Shortly thereafter, asphalt, then a new road material, was used to pave the Drives; curbs were installed in place of the gutters to contain storm-water runoff and guide it into catch basins. The paving of the Drives and later the paths increased the

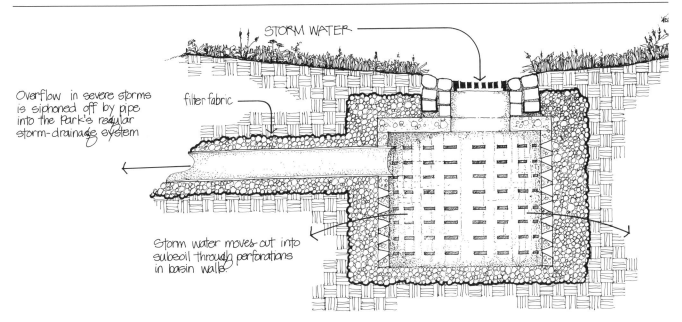

STORM WATER

Overflow in severe storms is siphoned off by pipe into the Park's regular storm-drainage system

filter fabric

Storm water moves out into subsoil through perforations in basin walls.

Cross section of a recently installed seepage basin. It is designed to keep as much storm water as possible in the underground water table.

volume of water emptying into the underground drainage system. Even more critical was the proliferation of new paths and pavement for parking lots and playgrounds. Between the turn of the century and 1960, there was a 57 percent increase in the amount of hard surfaces within the Park. All of this greatly reduced the amount of water percolating into the ground water table and increased the burden on the existing drainage system. The siphoning off of rainwater from the Park has, of course, affected its ecol-ogy, with particular consequences for its vegetation.

After 1960, the entire system experienced accelerating deterioration as the Parks Department became under-funded and regular cleaning of 700 catch basins, miles of drainage pipes

A transverse road, showing the effects of clogged catch basins after a rain. Since 1985, this problem has been practically eliminated by routine maintenance procedures.

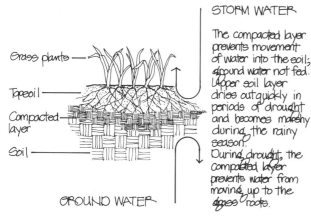

STORM WATER

The compacted layer prevents movement of water into the soil; ground water not fed. Upper soil layer dries out quickly in periods of drought and becomes marshy during the rainy season.
During drought, the compacted layer prevents water from moving up to the grass roots.

Grass plants

Topsoil

Compacted layer

Soil

GROUND WATER

Grass Roots and Subsurface Compaction

STORM WATER

Water should circulate up and down freely, as shown. Grass roots grow deeper, and during a drought can depend on ground water.

Soil should be 50% soil solids and 50% pore space for equal amounts of air and water.

Grass plants

Soil

Healthy grass root system

GROUND WATER

Grass Roots in Uncompacted Soil

and numerous water bodies came to a halt. To make matters worse, the updating of maps to show the location of all underground piping, catch basins, gate valves and outflow structures was abandoned. As employees who possessed an understanding of Central Park's infrastructure retired, valuable information was lost. Increasingly, unpleasant emergency situations arose because of drains so clogged with debris that after every rain, storm-water lakes would inundate walkways or stall traffic on the drives and transverse roads. Today's Park managers and planners find themselves in the unenviable position of trying to remedy this complicated and difficult situation with inadequate maps and charts.

Soil Conditions

As we have seen, Central Park was not abundantly endowed with rich native soil. Tons of imported topsoil were used in its construction, and many amendments have been necessary because the imported soil was also acidic and poor in organic matter. Three aspects of the Park's soil are of concern to us here: its erosion, its compaction and its fertility.

Today, erosion of the topsoil in Central Park is severe. In 1982, almost 25 percent of the Park's soil had no vegetation to hold it in place or keep it from being washed into low-lying areas. Erosion is minimized when soil

is covered by turf, protected by shrub lateral branching, ground cover, litter layer or mulch, or when it supports plants with dense fibrous root systems. The same lack of sound management and work force attrition that permitted the drainage system to deteriorate has taken its toll on the landscape. Because no new planting of the ground plane has been done for so long during a period when the Park was becoming increasingly popular and subject to heavy use, erosion has increased and has been accompanied by severe compaction of the soil.

On bare soil, even a drop of rain becomes a compaction force, pushing

A clogged catch basin.

fine soil particles into spaces that should hold air or water. A surface "crust" forms, restricting seed germination and the infiltration of water. As the ground becomes progressively harder and storm gullies form, what plants remain are further deprived of needed moisture.

Soil compaction has yet another unfortunate consequence. We have seen above how over the years increased paving of the Park's circulation system has added to the burden of its underground drainage system while robbing its water table of the ability to recharge itself quickly. Hardpan, which acts like pavement, has the same effect. Water that should be kept on site to benefit the vegetation is diverted instead to an already overloaded drainage system. Moreover, the amount of impervious surface in the Park today causes rainwater to course in raging currents, scouring adjacent topsoil and debris, and thereby further clogging up the catch basins and drainage pipes. As catch basins overflow everywhere in the Park, storm-water lakes are formed, rendering paths and landscape unusable for several days after a rain and ultimately leaving a layer of muddy sedimentation on top of the ground.

Soil Quality

A soil survey conducted in Central Park in 1982 showed that the soils are of low fertility. Subsequent chemical

A catch basin along a pedestrian pathway is cleared of debris.

A crew cleans out a catch basin in a transverse road.

analysis of more than 250 samples has revealed that the soil throughout the Park is predominantly acidic, with one-third of the samples having a pH value of 5 or below. Because grass thrives best where the pH is between 6 and 7, it is necessary to use a great deal of lime on the lawns to keep them green. On the other hand, trees and many shrubs like rhododendrons, azaleas and other ericaceous plants are well-suited to grow in Central Park's soil if other conditions are right. Heavy foot traffic and leaf raking in high-use areas have denied the accumulation of organic materials in the soil, so it is usually necessary to add organic matter wherever new landscaping projects occur. There is also a general paucity of available phosphorus and calcium.

Since 1982, the Central Park Conservancy has supported a soil laboratory as well as a composting operation. The soil lab provides horticultural personnel with immediate information about new planting sites and assists them in prescribing soil improvements and appropriate plant species. A soil scientist monitors moisture levels in the soil in order to adjust watering schedules and save valuable manpower while maximizing the benefit to the vegetation.

The composting operation has initiated the production of good new humus within Central Park and achieved a savings in labor costs formerly allocated to transport leaves and other organic debris to dump sites

outside the Park. To be truly effective and efficient, however, the operation should be reconstructed, streamlined and more highly mechanized.

Goals

A primary goal of this plan is to achieve a well-drained Park with retention of as much water as possible in the ground below the surface. A second goal, supporting the first, is a maintenance program to ensure that catch basins do not silt up, pipes can flow freely, and lakes, ponds and streams are routinely cleaned and dredged. A third goal is the production of an up-to-date survey of the Park's underground drainage structures.

The control of erosion in the future and maintenance of a stable landscape and healthy soil are goals concomitant with those of drainage improvement. They can be achieved by continuing and expanding the work of the soil lab to include hydrological measurements and by upgrading the Park's composting operation.

Recommendations

Storm-water runoff should be decreased by stabilization of the Park's landscape. To do this enormous task sensibly and successfully, restoration must start at the highest elevations in a given watershed and proceed downward. Before this is begun, the extent, severity and causes of erosion at each site must be surveyed. Compacted soil

should be broken up, enriched and possibly added to. Boulders may be needed to hold soil in place on steep slopes, and, most important, slopes must be covered with vegetation.

The specifications for fill soil and the preparation of landscape restoration sites should be rewritten to ensure that in the future the Park has the highest quality topsoil and that it drains properly. Of special importance is the amendment of topsoil with coarse sand, composted leaf mold and humus, instead of the customarily specified peat moss, which acidifies the soil. These specifications should be individually tailored to the needs of specific project sites after testing by the soil lab.

For each project site, soil scientists from the lab should assess and advise on soil conditions, including levels of compaction, both before construction specifications are written and following restoration. They should engage in pilot projects that expand the Conservancy's leadership role in urban-soils research. The lab should be responsible for a computerized soil data base, and it should also oversee composting.

The present composting operation should be restudied. It should possibly be relocated or, at least, reorganized to take up less space. If it is to provide a reliable supply of good compost, it should have one full-time person in charge and the necessary machinery to make it efficient.

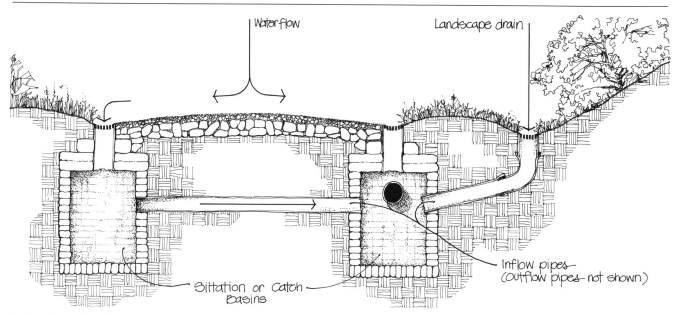

Waterflow

Landscape drain

Siltation or Catch Basins

Inflow pipes (outflow pipes not shown)

Section of soft-surface footpath and drainage according to 1865 design.

Park soil should continue to be enriched and pH levels adjusted on a site-specific basis prescribed by soil lab technicians. Its humus content should be increased selectively, especially on planted slopes. Its porosity should be increased on flatter, heavily used areas by the addition of coarse sand in order to promote good drainage. Specifications for soil, drainage and irrigation should be closely linked with the intended use of a given area.

Much of the Park's drainage system may have to be reconstructed and enlarged from 4- or 6-inch pipes to 10- and 12-inch pipes, depending on the capacity of the downslope trunk lines. In order to determine the amount of work necessary to repair or reconstruct the system, there must first be a survey of the amount of collapsed pipe and the number and location of catch basins that have been invaded by tree roots. A computerized mapping of the Park's drainage system that can be progressively updated should then be prepared and maintained.

The impermeable surfaces of the Park should be reduced wherever possible in order to make the ground plane more porous and the water table more capable of being recharged. Some path widths should be reduced, and wherever hardpan has formed it should be

Rough-hewn paving blocks set into sand make an attractive gutter for path drainage.

broken up, tilled to a sufficient depth to ensure proper drainage and replanted. Seepage basins, dry wells or other such means of keeping water in the landscape rather than allowing it to drain away should be studied. Also toward this end, the Park's two drainage systems—the one that is integral to the circulation system and must carry

off water immediately and the other that merely prevents water from standing in the landscape—should be made as separate and distinct as possible.

The maintenance crew that was recently assembled to perform routine drainage repairs and systematic cleaning of catch basins in order to control the flooding of Drives and paths should continue its work throughout the Park. Systematic catch-basin maintenance will prevent the reversion of newly restored meadows and lawns to muddy bogs. The work of this crew is also essential to performing the drainage survey recommended above.

The Park's water bodies should be thoroughly dredged after their surrounding watersheds have been restored and stabilized. In conjunction with dredging, water-body edges should be softened with vegetation and returned, where possible, to their original historic configuration. All outlet structures to the city's combined sewer system should be rehabilitated. And with the addition of more skilled personnel and the cooperation and advice of the New York State Department of Environmental Protection limnologists, the soil lab should be enabled to monitor the condition of all water bodies on a regular basis and to recommend remedies when needed.

Water Needs in Central Park

Early drinking fountains like this one in the Mall used a common cup.

This newly restored system will provide adequate water to do the following:

Supply water to the Park's 67 drinking fountains and to service buildings.

Supply water to the existing display fountains and two proposed display water features.

Flush the lakes and keep them at acceptable levels.

Increase the number of irrigation systems in the Park.

Irrigation Needs

To protect the extensive capital investment in turf and plant material throughout the Park, water must be available for periodic irrigation and watering. When a drought emergency exists, Park managers, like private citizens, are forbidden to use city water for this purpose. For this reason, the Parks Department plans to drill wells in certain major parks, including Central Park.

Three complementary watering strategies are necessary to ensure green lawns during hot, dry weather.

Fully Automated Irrigation. This system is now in place at the Sheep Meadow, Bowling Green, the East Green and the Tennis Courts.

Semi-automated Irrigation. This system, which consists of underground piping with quick-couplers and above-ground hose connections, serves the Heckscher Ballfields, Strawberry Fields and various smaller landscapes throughout the Park. While requiring less capital investment and technical maintenance than fully automated irrigation, this type of irrigation is more time-consuming to operate.

Water trucks. Trucks filled from fire hydrants or well heads provide a good means for watering new plantings. Although this practice is labor-intensive, watering schedules can be relaxed once plant material is established.

Potable Water

Early in the Park's history, the two reservoirs supplied all the fresh water needed for drinking fountains, irrigation and running water for the buildings. This system was dependent on the water available solely from the two reservoirs, but over the years the system has eventually tapped into the City's overall distribution system.

The Parks Department is currently rehabilitating all water mains and control valves. Using surveys from 1910 and metal detectors, the contractors are locating the water pipes, grinding out mineral deposits accumulated over the past century and relining them with concrete. They are also replacing broken pipes, eliminating outmoded lines, standardizing control valves and, most important, mapping the system for future use by Park plumbers.

Gear-driven rotary sprinkler system with automatic timer on the East Green.

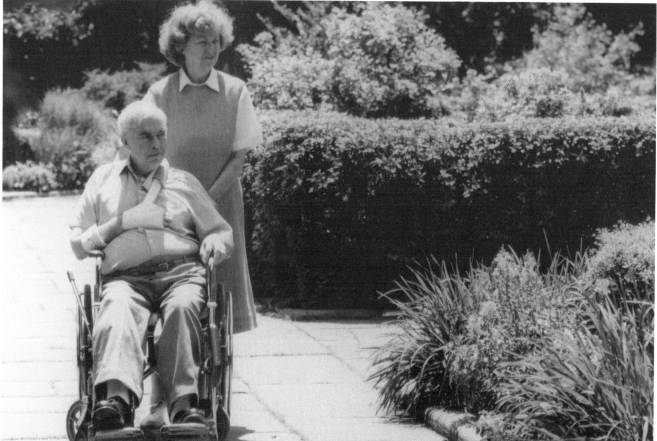

Cedar Hill in winter and the Conservatory Garden in summer.

Vegetation and Wildlife

Central Park's vegetation, more than any other of its features, defines its character and identifies its function. Because the Park is old, we assume its vegetation is constant and fairly immutable. But, in fact, Central Park has been host to a succession of overlapping, constantly changing vegetative communities.

The primeval forest of oaks and beeches that once covered Manhattan Island was gone by the time Central Park was laid out. New Yorkers had been forced to cut down the trees for fuel during the Revolutionary War when the city was an isolated British outpost. As a result, the pre-Park site was largely denuded, though not entirely bare.

We know from the writings of Clarence Cook and Frederick Law Olmsted that there was some noteworthy vegetation growing on the Central Park site. There were firs on the Promontory; willow trees grew near what became Willowdell Arch; large oak trees were growing east of the Mall site; and a stand of hydrophyllic, or water-loving, plants was thriving on the rocky upland swamps that became the Ramble. Among this pre-Ramble vegetation, for example, were sweet gum, spicebush, tulip trees, sassafras, red maple, black oak and native American azaleas and andromedas. Olmsted described the northern end of the Park site as bold and sweeping and containing a second growth of native American trees which, he thought, could be turned to good advantage in the design of the Park. The southern end, by contrast, was rocky, swampy and nearly barren.

In 1857, while he was superintendent of the pre-Park site and solely in charge of clearing the land, Olmsted began to develop a planting philosophy—before he had ever thought of becoming a landscape architect. (Olmsted's predecessors called themselves "landscape improvers"; he and Vaux actually christened their profession "landscape architecture" in 1863.)

Bank Rock Bridge and the Ramble in the 1870s: A multitude of evergreens once grew in the Park; now they are relatively scarce.

Olmsted Formulates a Plan for Central Park

In his preliminary study, Olmsted divided the Park into four quadrants. In rugged areas, comprising three quarters of the first quadrant (from 59th Street to 71st Street), he envisioned "the stiffer forms of evergreen trees to accord with and set off the picturesque rocks which are a marked feature of the landscape." For areas with thin soil and in clefts of rocks, he saw European larch, Scotch fir and American arborvitae. The more sheltered low areas, especially those near water, seemed to call for deciduous cypress, white cedar, swamp arborvitae, and red and black American larch. For this first quadrant of the Park, Olmsted asked for the following plants to be purchased as soon as possible:
3,000 Norway spruce
3,000 hemlock
500 black spruce
500 larch
500 arborvitae
150 Scotch fir
150 deciduous cypress
150 white cedar

For the second quadrant, best described as tableland (approximately 71st Street to 83rd Street), Olmsted preferred the softer evergreens and called for the purchase of:
300 white pines
150 Corsican pines
150 Scotch pines
150 pinaster pines
150 cembra pines

Nearly one third of the second and third quadrants (71st Street to 95th Street) already had groves of young deciduous trees. Olmsted proposed that in the eastern part of these sections an "artificial style" might be adopted. In the western part of this sector, he called for the same evergreens he had selected for the first quadrant.

In the fourth quadrant (95th Street to 106th Street, 106th Street being at that time the northern boundary of the proposed Park), Olmsted found "much fine young wood of the native deciduous species admirably grouped by nature." He called for "the largest and finest trees of our climate"—hickories, oaks, elms, beeches, chestnuts, ashes and especially maples. They would be used in groups and singly on lawns. He called for 1,000 of each of these trees, specifying that they be uniformly healthy, simple in outline, and dense and retentive of foliage. These large deciduous and coniferous trees would be the backbone of the Park's vegetation, and smaller trees and shrubs would be added for interest and variety in scale.

For the smaller trees and shrubs, he recommended that several thousand of the following be purchased:

honeysuckle
Kalmia lalifolia
dogwood
privet
hawthorn
buckthorn
Osage orange
Magnolia glauca
Magnolia obvata
Magnolia conspicus
dwarf horse chestnut
Missouri currant
Virginia fringe
spirea
syringa and *Hydrangea quercifolia*

And as a base in a park nursery:
viburnum
althea
acacia
indigo bush
Deutzia seabra
And every smooth-leaved evergreen that would endure (Rhododendrons, azaleas, andromedas, etc.)
Weigela risea
papan quince
Daphne mexerium
burning bush
laburnum

Olmsted and Vaux submitted their Greensward Plan in 1857, as number 33 in the design competition organized by the Board of Commissioners. It was judged the winner, and work on the Park began at once. Since there is no surviving planting plan, it can never be known for certain how closely the rough scheme quoted above was followed. The first methodical counting of trees, by Robert Demcker in 1873, includes not only all of the species mentioned in Olmsted's original report but also many more, suggesting that Olmsted broadened the range of plants as work progressed. Plants were seen by the designers as the Park's most important building element. Their intentions were first to screen out incongruous objects beyond the Park's borders; second, to assign as much flatland as possible to tranquil, open,

pastoral lawns and meadows; and third, to fill the rest—the rocky, uneven terrain—with picturesque detail.

By 1865, the Park's vegetation was already beginning to fill out. That year, the Report of the Park Commissioners observed: "The foliage, becoming dense with the lapse of time, constantly presents new and more striking effects." The next few years were largely spent building the architecture. The Belvedere, the Kinderberg, the Dairy and other structures were added as embellishments to the landscape. In 1870, the corrupt Tweed administration took power and reorganized the Park's board to make plush political appointments and to hand out patronage to cronies. Olmsted and Vaux resigned, and the Park fell under the control of people who were unsympathetic to the original design.

Tweed's Acting Chief Landscape Gardener, Frank A. Pollard, declared that Central Park's trees were too thickly planted, and he thinned them. His efforts were strong, direct and self-assured but wholly at odds with Olmsted's romantic planting concept. Pollard removed plants from clumps and spaced them out, often in rows along the edges of walks and drives— something Olmsted detested. In general, Pollard presided over a horticultural regimentation and "neatening up."

The Tweed era in Central Park ended abruptly in 1871, and a new Park board was formed that included the former president of the old board, Henry Stebbins, and landscape artist Frederick Church. They reappointed Olmsted and Vaux.

The designers immediately set about correcting some of the mistakes of the Tweed administration, compiling a long list of horticultural instructions to be followed at once and some philosophical precepts to be observed, as far as they were concerned, in perpetuity. "Avoid pretty temporary effects at the expense of the advantage for the future," they cautioned. "The less anything appears done by human hands the better. . . . The main features of the park are already outlined. What remains is to cure some defects, foster the right growth of what is art, and add beauty and interest of detail."

Throughout the last quarter of the nineteenth century, the Park had its ups and downs, depending largely on the political environment. Olmsted was, for the most part, not closely involved.

In general, the Park's condition deteriorated from 1875 to 1885, after which it improved, largely as a result of the efforts of Samuel Parsons, Jr. Parsons served as Superintendent of Parks (1885-1897), Central Park Landscape Architect (1898-1911) and Commissioner of Parks (1905-1907). The son of a nurseryman, Parsons's tenure is often looked upon as a golden age of Central Park, a time when much of the vegetation had reached a well-cared-for maturity. Parsons was a brilliant horticulturalist; he added numerous native American species to the Park (he thought the Park was deficient in this one respect), and he remained loyal to the basic concept of the original design. The 1903 text *Trees and Shrubs of Central Park*, by Louis Harriman Peet, while not a comprehensive list, probably names most of the species then growing in Central Park. The Peet list, when compared to a comprehensive list of the plants in Central Park in the 1873 Report of the Board of Commissioners of the Department of Public Parks, makes clear the ways in which Parsons expanded the range of American plants in Central Park. Parsons described his own philosophy in two books: *Landscape Gardening* (1881) and *The Art of Landscape Architecture* (1885).

After the turn of the century, a management more responsive to demands for programmed recreation than to horticulture allowed the Park's vegetation to deteriorate and its botanical variety to dwindle. A study conducted by landscape architect Herman Merkel in 1927 found an "appalling" number of dead and dying trees, a dearth of ground covers and a profusion of volunteer growth. Of the 50 types of conifers originally planted in the Park, all but three or four species had disappeared because of city soot, pests and trampling by users.

As a result of the Merkel report, 3,000 new trees and 70,000 new shrubs were planted. This was done as Robert Moses was beginning his 26-year tenure (1934-1960) as Parks Commissioner, and the style of planting differed markedly from the original. Trees were not planted in "composed" groups of several varieties, as Olmsted and Parsons had done. Instead, they were planted in homogeneous rows, boulevard-fashion, lining paths.

Nevertheless, horticultural care was revived during the Depression, when gardeners who had formerly been employed on great estates joined the Parks

Lack of maintenance permits a vacant-lot ecology: erosion, spread of weeds and spindly, self-seeding trees.

Department under Moses and worked on a number of federally funded "spruce-up" projects. Gone, unfortunately, were the romantic pastoral scenery and picturesque detail of the old Park; but gone, too, were the vegetative eyesores—dead trees, bare and weed-choked lawns, and scruffy shrub beds.

By the 1970s, the Moses-era layer of vegetation had mostly disappeared, at least on the ground plane, as much of Central Park was given over to concerts, rallies, festivals, Happenings and other mass events. The old, European-trained gardeners had also disappeared through attrition and retirement. Little was planted during this period, but a great deal of spontaneous vegetation—self-seeding cherries, sycamore maples and ailanthus, among others—sprouted up, obliterating views and giving the Park a generally wild, untended appearance.

The state of vegetation in Central Park in the years following the Moses administration was therefore one of

steady deterioration as abuse, overuse and lack of management took their toll. Extensive vegetative analysis and the reintroduction of horticultural practices were imperative if the Park's landscape architecture was to survive.

Existing Conditions: Taking Horticultural Stock

As an essential preliminary step in preparing this management and restoration plan, an inventory of plants and trees was undertaken in 1982. The inventory was divided into two sections: trees six inches and over in diameter at breast height (DBH) and all other types of vegetation under six inches DBH—saplings, understory trees, shrubs, herbaceous material, grasses and various ground-plane plants.

The Tree Survey

For purposes of collecting data, the Park was divided into grid cells 50 feet

square. (The information was also coded by lawn area number, since that is the traditional Central Park maintenance unit.) Trees were mapped by grid cell, given a number and identified by species, caliper, height and crown spread. In addition, they were evaluated on 17 variables such as percent of dead wood, pests, cavities and root conditions. The fieldwork was carried out by forestry students and supervised by horticulturalists and professional foresters.

The tree survey identified a total of 24,600 trees with a six-inch or greater DBH. Detailed information about them was tabulated in a computerized inventory. Among the findings was the fact that while 143 species of trees exist in Central Park, 10 species comprise 62 percent of the tree population. Of these, five are self-propagating—the elm, cherry, locust, Norway maple and sycamore maple—and therefore account, in addition, for much of the sapling growth in the Park, trees with less than a six-inch DBH.

Tree Canopy, 1873

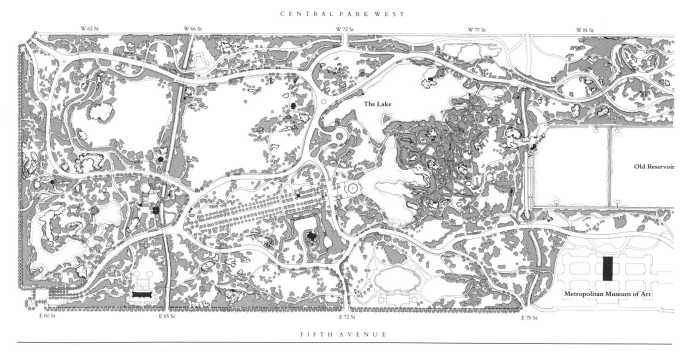

Tree Canopy, Present

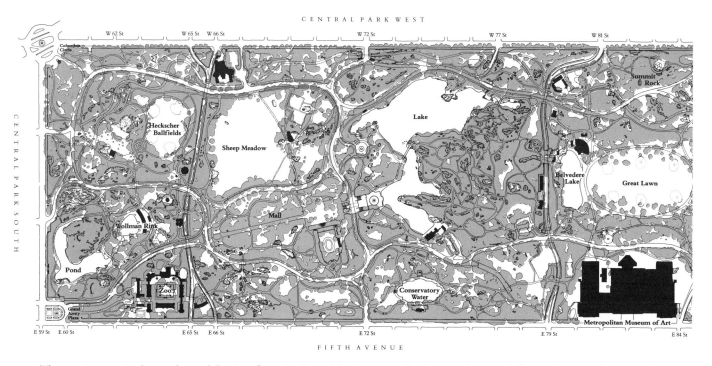

The vast increase in the number and density of trees in Central Park accounts for the most dramatic difference between the Park today and the Park as it was in 1873. Hundreds of trees have been planted by a succession of Park managers, sometimes wisely, sometimes not; even more trees took root by self-propagation.

It was Olmsted's intention that a solid tree canopy occur in only a few places (parts of the Ramble and north end and along the transverse roads and the edges of the Park). Today, however, a continuous canopy nearly blankets the Park. Over time, the spreading

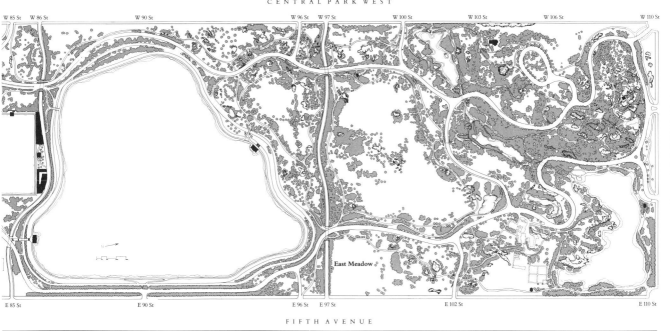

canopy has engulfed many small meadows and encroached upon the large open spaces.

The original Greensward Plan called for a loose configuration of trees at the edges of meadows in order to give the impression of receding lawns rather than ones that terminate abruptly. The latter effect, unfortunately, now prevails. The individual specimens and loose clumps of trees that once gave the meadows an illusion of indefinite space have been cut back to make room for ball fields and tennis courts. Meanwhile, the trees behind them have filled in, creating solid walls of green.

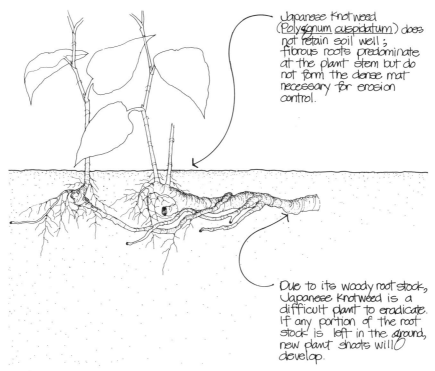

Japanese knotweed (*Polygonum cuspidatum*) does not retain soil well; fibrous roots predominate at the plant stem but do not form the dense mat necessary for erosion control.

Due to its woody rootstock, Japanese knotweed is a difficult plant to eradicate. If any portion of the rootstock is left in the ground, new plant shoots will develop.

Growth habit of Japanese knotweed.

Table 1
Dominant Tree Species in Central Park

Species	Number over 6 inches in diameter
1. Black cherry (*Prunus serotina*)	4,260
2. American elm (*Ulmus americana*)	1,835
3. Pin oak (*Quercus palustris*)	1,730
4. Black locust (*Robinia pseudoacacia*)	1,632
5. London plane (*Platanus acerifolia*)	1,320
6. Norway maple (*Acer platanoides*)	1,314
7. Plantree maple (*Acer pseudoplantanus*)	935
8. White ash (*Fraxinus americana*)	837
9. Red oak (*Quercus rubra*)	766
10. Ginkgo (*Ginkgo biloba*)	549

This trend, if allowed to continue, represents a liability for the Park's future beauty and health. North America has experienced several serious tree devastations. Dutch elm disease has killed dozens of Central Park's elms and threatens the rest; diplodia has attacked the Austrian pines; the chestnut blight of 1904 wiped out the Park's stands of chestnuts. Unforeseen disasters like these can eliminate an entire species in a relatively short time. Therefore, it is shortsighted to allow a small number of species to gain dominance in a park. The demise of a particular species can leave great holes in the Park's structure—visually, horticulturally and ecologically.

The 1982 inventory revealed a significant depletion of conifers; there were only 961 pines with a DBH of six inches—4 percent of the tree population. Olmsted had planted thousands, prizing them for their interesting forms and for their winter color. Table 2 lists 10 unusually fine trees that were represented only sparsely in 1982.

Not only has there been a loss of botanical variety in Central Park, but a comparison of today's Park with that of Olmsted and Vaux reveals that there is a much denser tree canopy today. Of course, when the Park was young and newly planted, its trees were much

Table 2
10 Uncommon Native Trees in Central Park

Species	Number over 6 inches in diameter
1. *Nyssa sylvatica* (tupelo)	27
2. *Quercus coccinea* (scarlet oak)	21
3. *Aesculus glabra* (Ohio buckeye)	21
4. *Tsuga canadensis* (Canadian hemlock)	19
5. *Taxodium distichum* (common bald cypress)	15
6. *Quercus macrocarpa* (bur oak)	15
7. *Fagus grandifolia* (American beech)	14
8. *Quercus prinus* (chestnut oak)	8
9. *Carya ovata* (shagbark hickory)	5
10. *Ilex opaca* (American holly)	2

smaller. But there was also, by design, more space devoted to lawns and meadows. For its authors, the highest desideratum of Park scenery was rolling meadowland. Because of Central Park's narrow width and somewhat agitated topography, this was not always easy to achieve. In the Sheep Meadow and the North Meadow, they were able to realize this scenic ideal. Elsewhere, they managed to lay out small lawns and sunny glades, many of which have severely shrunk or disappeared altogether.

Rampant Cherries
The most aggressively self-seeding tree species in Central Park is the black cherry (*Prunus serotina*). According to the 1982 tree inventory, more than 19 percent of the trees with a six-inch DBH are black cherries. But when one adds the black cherry saplings to this number, the predominance of this one species is even greater. Fifty-nine percent of all lawn areas are populated with cherry saplings under six inches

DBH. In the Ramble, the percentage is around 80. If no new planting were to occur and the Park were left in an unmanaged state, its vegetation would be increasingly composed of these short-lived trees with an estimated span of 70 years, as opposed to oaks and other long-lived species.

The volunteer cherry population has not only crowded out less aggressive species; it has encroached upon open meadow spaces. This encroachment was abetted in the 1970s during the city's fiscal crisis, when the Parks Department, in order to curtail manpower, began using heavy, oversize mowing machines that can cut a wide swath but are unable to cut close enough to rock outcrops to prevent cherries and other opportunistic plants from sprouting up around them. The cherries grew and multiplied, and each year the mowers had to mow a little farther away. Today, groves of cherries surround and obscure many of the Park's handsome rock outcrops. Fortunately, the use of specialized mowing

equipment appropriate to parks rather than highway medians and shoulders has been reinstated in Central Park.

The Ground Plane
The mapping of the Park's vegetation that has a less than six-inch DBH was more generalized than the mapping of its mature trees. This plant material was in many cases identified in masses rather than by individual specimens. The "ground-plane" vegetation survey identified 339 plant species—50 species of saplings, 47 species of understory, 130 ground-cover or herbaceous species and five water-edge plant species.

While this total number is impressive, it should be noted that most species exist in very small numbers, and a relatively few dominate. Those that dominate are generally old and not particularly healthy and lush. Notable in this group are privet (*Ligustrum spp.*), which was once planted heavily throughout the Park, and black haw (*Viburnum prunifolium*). While the wintergreen barberry (*Berberis julianae*),

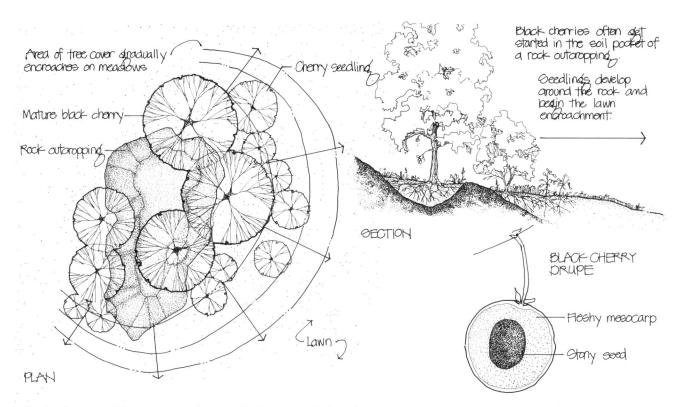

Black cherries (*Prunus serotina*) tend to become established in places around which it is difficult to mow, such as rock outcroppings. Seedlings develop outside the drip line of established cherries, where sunlight is greatest, gradually encroaching on meadows and lawns, diminishing Park open space.

The black cherry has a durable, stony endocarp, or seed, less easily damaged than the seeds of more desirable tree species, such as oaks or beeches.

Propagation of the black cherry, a prolific self-seeder.

The Ground Plane

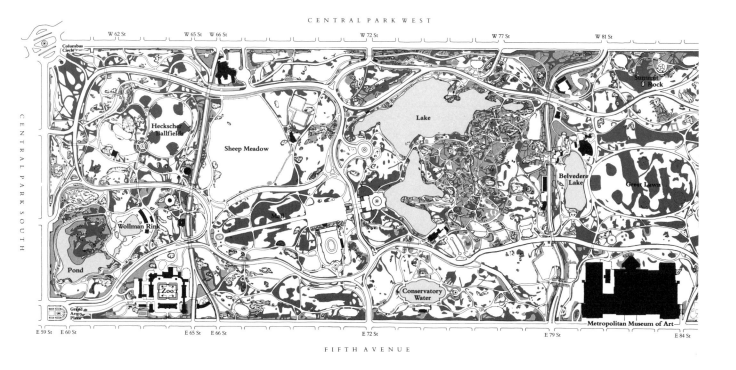

Japanese barberry (*B. thunbergi*), Japanese holly (*Ilex crenata*) and various types of hawthorn, viburnum, euonymus and forsythia are hardy and dependable, none appears to be self-propagating. If this structural layer is to remain diverse, these plants must be planted, maintained and replaced on a regular basis. But they will not by themselves adequately fill out the generally sparse understory in the Park's woodlands and meadow edges, where flowering trees and ericaceous shrubs are also desirable, especially those that produce food and cover for wildlife.

The understory survey, like the tree inventory, produced several interesting and rare finds, including papaw, wild rice, crape myrtle, partridgeberry, bamboo, southern magnolia and cucumber magnolia.

Well known as a problem plant in Central Park, Japanese knotweed (*Polygonum cuspidatum*) was mapped separately by the survey teams so that planners could begin to grasp the extent of this invasive, aggressive plant. Since it thrives even in poor soil, its presence can indicate that the soil in a particular area is disturbed. Its tuberous root system does little to deter erosion, unlike the more fibrous root systems and low-leafing branches of shrubs and other ground covers. Eradication of knotweed is difficult, because its tuberous roots store food and allow the plant to resprout after it has been seemingly destroyed by thorough grubbing.

The Three Types of Park Landscapes: Meadows, Parkland and Woodland

Olmsted and Vaux designed three major types of landscapes in Central Park: meadows, parkland and woodland. The features of the pre-Park site determined what the ultimate forms would be: flat tableland became pastoral meadows; rolling terrain became parkland, composed of turf, specimen trees and tree groves; craggy uplands were turned into woodland. Each landscape acquired and imparted value from its contrast with the others. The Ramble—wooded, rugged and lush—contrasted with the sweeping, smooth lawns and specimen trees of Cherry

☐ Water ☐ Grass, roads ▨ Herbaceous vegetation, including understory trees

■ Bare areas ■ Buildings

CENTRAL PARK WEST

Reservoir

Pool

Great Hill

Blockhouse

North Meadow

Ravine

Meer

East Meadow

Conservatory Garden

Fowler

FIFTH AVENUE

CENTRAL PARK NORTH

Hill. By design, the emotional atmosphere changed with the scenery—from pastoral and calmly soothing to picturesque and pleasantly agitated—expressing the same Romantic nineteenth-century imagination as painting and literature.

The three landscapes differ visually, structurally and compositionally, and lend themselves to quite different uses and management techniques.

Meadows

Meadows are open grassy or turf areas of any size or configuration. Central Park's original meadows had soft, indefinite borders of loosely spaced trees beyond which the greensward, dappled with shadows, seemed to go on forever. The Sheep Meadow and the

North Meadow were the two spaces that best approximated the designers' ideal park scenery, but the East Meadow and the South Meadow (now the tennis courts) also provided good examples of rolling meadowland. The Great Hill, the west side perimeter from 97th Street to 102nd Street, and the East Green, at 72nd Street and Fifth Avenue, are examples of smaller meadow landscapes within the Park. Two athletic fields were once greensward—the Heckscher Ballfields and the Great Lawn, built in 1934 by Robert Moses.

Sports Fields

Athletic uses present the primary management issue with respect to meadows. Intense use compacts the soil and renders it unsuitable for reseeding or

sodding without extensive soil reconstruction. This has been a concern since the Park's inception. Olmsted wrote in 1865:

Nothing is more certain than that the Park's lawns would soon be rendered disagreeable if games were to be constantly played upon them. If the play of one club is allowed, others will demand the same privilege; and these clubs are so numerous that if space were provided for the ordinary practice of games, it would tend to depreciate the attractions of the Park to the far greater number who visit it for the refined pleasures that its landscape affords to those who are sensitive to natural beauties.

In the intervening 120 years, not much has changed except that the demand for sports fields has increased. At least 75 public and private schools

63

Meadowland: wide-open areas with, ideally, a loosely defined border of trees.

Parkland: trees growing singly or in clumps, with little understory and grass used as the primary ground cover.

Woodland: tree canopy, a lush understory and varied ground cover.

use Central Park for their gymnasium and outdoor sports facility. Many, in fact, advertise their proximity to the Park in their brochures.

During the spring and fall of the school year, the open lawns are used from nine in the morning until four or five in the afternoon. There is no time during the day for the lawns to recover, and most of them are used regardless of their condition, even if they are wet from a rain and therefore vulnerable to compaction and other types of damage. In addition to this school use, there is the regular baseball season from mid-April to mid-September. On a weekday, there are approximately 45 games parkwide for which permits are issued; on a weekend day, 130.

While active sports are an important use of parkland, they do preempt valuable lawn space, pushing out other less-organized forms of recreation. Although the Sheep Meadow is now managed for passive use exclusively and is especially popular as a kind of giant "backyard" for thousands of sunbathers, kite-fliers, Frisbee-throwers and so forth, the North Meadow and the Great Lawn rarely see any activity other than intensive active sports, which take a great deal of space for relatively few people. For example, at its period of peak use, the Great Lawn serves only an average of 144 people on its 14 acres, about 10 people per acre. The 22-acre Sheep Meadow, on the other hand, serves more than twice that number. It is reasonable to assume that whenever there is flat, open land in a park as densely populated as Central Park, organized sports will continue to supersede passive recreation unless policies reserving certain meadows and lawns either exclusively or partially for such use are enforced as they now are on the Sheep Meadow.

Grasses
The type of grass used in a public park has significant management implications which should be understood before lawn restoration is undertaken. The Sheep Meadow has been an instructive case in this regard. It was resodded in 1978 with a bluegrass-fescue mixture commonly used for estate lawns in the Northeast. Its maintenance requirements are costly in terms of manpower.

The use of wild grasses in certain park situations is therefore a desirable alternative to the use everywhere of a standardized high-quality turf with its heavy requirements for irrigation, mowing and fertilization. Wild grasses, which require infrequent mowing and no irrigation, would be inappropriate for lawns and athletic fields, but they are suitable for some of the Park's smaller open spaces where cropped grass is essential, such as the woodland glades in the north end, where in fact they already thrive.

Trees
As discussed above, the tree canopy over Central Park is much denser now than it was in the late nineteenth century, when the Park's original design outlines were achieved (see page 58). The incursion of trees into open spaces has happened in all sectors of the Park, both by self-seeding species and as a result of planting without reference to a comprehensive landscape design. One result has been a loss of the indefinite border by which Olmsted and Vaux created an illusion of infinite pastoral openness. Instead, most of the meadows are now surrounded by solid "walls" of trees. This plan seeks to re-create some of the illusion of unrestricted openness that was such a happy psychological result of the original Greensward Plan. The removal of unhealthy trees and a policy against new or replacement planting that would further tighten and constrict the tree "walls" ringing meadows are therefore recommended below. Regarding the politically sensitive issue of tree removal: While the existence of any form of spontaneous nature within the urban setting is something to be celebrated, landscape architecture—which is the art of *arranging nature* and enriching it horticulturally—cannot be practiced without judicious, selective tree removal.

Parkland

Parkland is a combination of trees and turf. It is the most common landscape type in Central Park, best represented by the Dene and the landscape around the Conservatory Water. The deer parks surrounding the great country houses of England were Olmsted's model—forests with no understory, only leaf mold, low brush and grass or ferns. In these private parks, hunters on horseback could follow their hounds with ease; there was no underbrush to impede them. French parks with their formal parterres were designed with fine, well-graded sands and gravels in place of grass. However, in Central Park, where people obviously enjoy sitting or lying on the ground, grass is the only acceptable choice for ground cover.

The ideal composition of parkland is a small number of specimen-quality trees, standing singly or in small groves, on green lawns, their canopies sufficiently open and well spaced so that a dappled rather than a dense shade prevails. Unfortunately, the parkland landscapes in Central Park, like the borders of its meadows, have become too thickly populated with trees for this design concept to work successfully. The turf beneath the closely spaced trees can neither withstand their dense shade nor compete with their root systems for moisture and nutrients, and the trees themselves are, for the most part, weak and their crowns too crowded to develop full canopies.

If one accepts as generally appropriate for Central Park the English deer park model with its turf/tree combination rather than some other combination (gravel/tree, sand/tree, bare ground/tree, ivy/tree, pachysandra/tree), then one must also accept a policy of judicious, selective tree removal. A policy that seeks to avoid this difficult and unpopular task invites further erosion of the bare ground and further weakening of the trees.

Woodland

The woodlands of Central Park are, for the most part, imitations of a natural forest environment. They exhibit many of the characteristics of New York's original climax forest, which was temperate and deciduous and dominated by oak and chestnut. But they are more than pastiches of the native ecology: Central Park's woodlands are stylized Victorian versions of woodlands. Landscape essays in the style of the picturesque, they include, in addition to native species, a number of exotic and oriental plants, which were newly imported to America at the time the Park was being built. Typically, Central Park's woodlands have multilayered vegetation, from vines and ground covers to underbrush to mid- and understory plants to overhead canopy. Woodland trees are designed in masses; they are not meant to develop to their optimal proportions like specimen trees growing in a parkland setting.

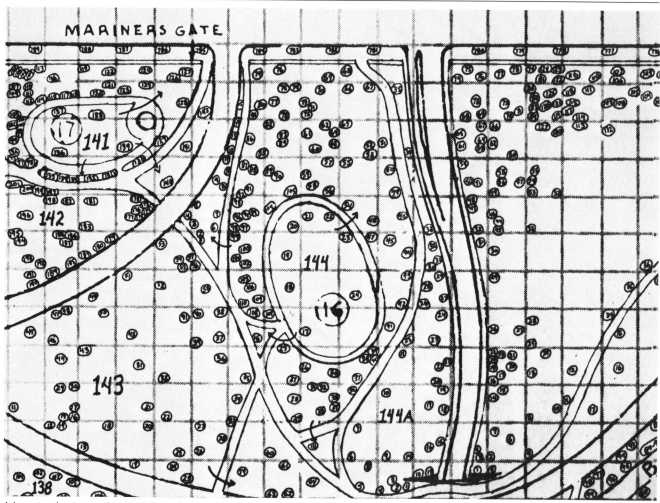

A base map showing numbered Park lawns and trees located within grid cells. Information completed from this 1982 survey of Park trees over six inches in diameter was subsequently programmed into a computer and can be regularly updated.

The three major woodland areas in Central Park are the Ramble, the Northwest Corner and the Promontory, or Bird Sanctuary.

The Ramble
The Ramble is Central Park's most visited and varied woodland. It is traversed by winding paths that carry one through a sequence of scenic "events." Here plant material is used as a shaper of spaces, as a concealer of other paths and people; it is used to tantalize and intrigue. The path system controls the way in which the landscape is experienced; it leads the stroller in turn through densely planted forest and small glades, crossing and recrossing the Gill, an artificial stream punctuated with rustic bridges and miniature waterfalls, with here and there a glimpse of the Lake beyond

and, like a beacon at its northern extremity, the Belvedere. Because of this complicated scheme, the Ramble seems more extensive than its actual 30 acres. It was meant to be seen from afar as well as from inside, a wild contrast to the more "civilized" formal areas such as Bethesda Terrace and Cherry Hill.

The Northwest Corner
The Northwest Corner differs in several respects from the Ramble. For one thing, at the time of the Park's creation, the Northwest Corner had a developed natural forest ecosystem. Olmsted and Vaux needed to modify very little to achieve the scenery they wanted here. Succeeding Park managers also left it alone; maintenance and design initiatives were undertaken elsewhere in the Park. Nor has the

Northwest Corner ever had as many visitors as the parts of the Park lying farther south.

Generally, the Northwest Corner exhibits many more of the characteristics typical of a New York area forest than the Ramble does. The landscape is cooler, drier, better drained and rocky, while the Ramble is essentially an upland bog. The north end has a variety of microclimates: stream bottom wetlands (with willows and sweet gums), steep slopes (with American beeches) and upland meadows (with grasses and black locusts). The north end is a more ecologically stable landscape than the Ramble, and its design is not as complex and intricate. However, it suffers from invasion by Japanese knotweed even more than the Ramble.

Park edge: bare, eroded ground—a bleak gap between city and Park.   *A lush and varied edge—a buffer zone between the Park and street.*

The Promontory

The Promontory, jutting into the 59th Street Pond, was never meant for visitation. It was intended to serve as a scenic backdrop for people strolling around the Pond. It never had any walks or paths. The overhead tree canopy was originally scattered, with openings being left to lie as grassy glades. Evidence shows that conifers were once numerous, planted to accent the huge rock outcrops that cover much of the site. It was fenced off as a bird sanctuary in 1934.

The Promontory offers a good illustration of what happens when there is an almost complete absence of human intervention in a Central Park woodland ecosystem. Most of the results are positive, and viewed from the shores of the Pond, the wild lush vegetation is quite beautiful. Closer inspection, however, reveals how the proliferation of self-seeded black cherry trees has closed in the canopy, creating dense shade, which in turn has killed off grass and other understory vegetation and made the area vulnerable to erosion.

The individual problems faced by each of these woodland areas, and the recommendations proposed for dealing with them, are discussed later in this book. The point to be reiterated here is that while they are designed to look natural, they are not. They are artificial ecosystems that require continuing care and maintenance. All have been invaded by Japanese knotweed, wild cherry and other self-propagating

trees, and thereby suffer a loss of horticultural variety. Ground-plane erosion is evident in all of these areas to a greater or lesser degree. As their canopies have thickened, the small openings that were part of the original design have disappeared.

Park Edges

In addition to the three major landscape units discussed above, there are strips or edges of the Park that deserve careful attention: the perimeter just inside the Park wall, the shorelines of water bodies and the borders of the Park Drives.

The Perimeter

Olmsted envisioned a dense perimeter planting of trees as a green screen to shut out the sights and sounds of the growing city. Commenting on his design in later years, he explained how he foresaw that the Park was to be:

. . . surrounded by an artificial wall, twice as high as the Great Wall of China, composed of urban buildings. Wherever this should appear across a meadow-view, the imagination would be checked abruptly at short range. Natural objects were thus required to be interposed, which, while excluding the buildings as much as possible from view, would leave an uncertainty as to the occupation of the space beyond, and establish a horizon line, composed, as much as possible, of verdure.

While perimeter planting cannot hide the twentieth-century towers that surround the Park today, it does pro-

vide an effective buffer between street and Park, enhancing each. These edges ideally should have the same configuration and layering of vegetation as the edges of natural woodlands, where along the sunny outer fringe one finds thick ground covers and herbaceous material banked by shrubs, understory trees and forest saplings overarched by a mature tree canopy.

Perimeter plantings in parks, like such natural woodland edges, are plantings without emphasis on individual trees or shrubs. Here and there a single tree or shrub may stand apart from the mass, but the overall composition of an undulating wall of green is what counts. The perimeter is one of the most stressed zones in Central Park because of the heavy foot traffic it receives, much of it the trampling, off-path variety. It is the part of the Park most frequented by dog owners and their pets. Ten percent of the visits to Central Park in 1982 (approximately 1.3 million) were made by people who brought a dog. The high ammonia content of dog urine burns the plant foliage, which receives further stress from the dirt, heat, fumes, reflected glare and building shadows of the adjacent city streets. Plants on the Park's edge also receive the full brunt of sharp winds, which gather force as they are channeled through the streets. The cumulative effects of all these punishing factors has led in many places to a bare, eroded perimeter, loss of topsoil, a lack of understory material and generally unhealthy trees.

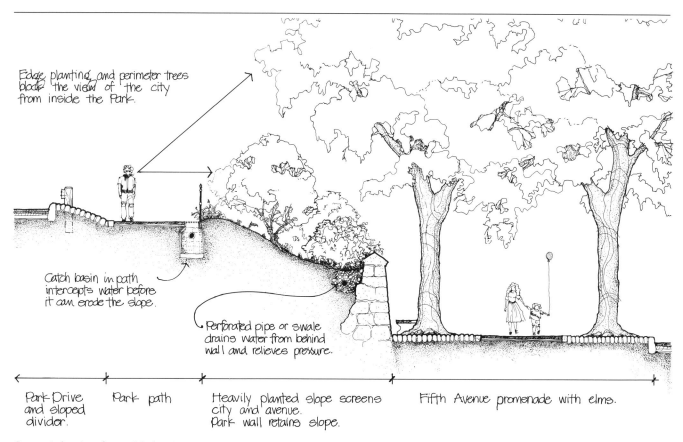

Edge planting and perimeter trees block the view of the city from inside the Park.

Catch basin in path intercepts water before it can erode the slope.

Perforated pipe or swale drains water from behind wall and relieves pressure.

Park Drive and sloped divider.

Park path

Heavily planted slope screens city and avenue. Park wall retains slope.

Fifth Avenue promenade with elms.

Prototypical section of restored Park perimeter.

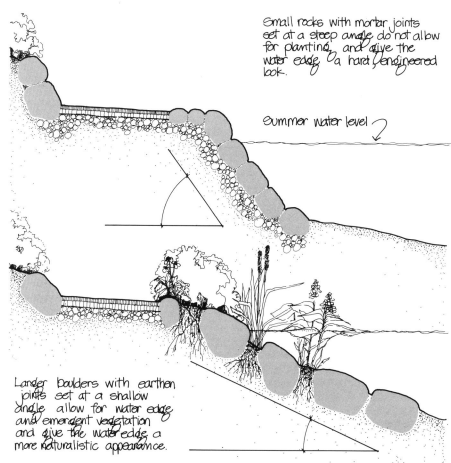

Small rocks with mortar joints set at a steep angle do not allow for planting, and give the water edge a hard, engineered look.

Summer water level

Larger boulders with earthen joints set at a shallow angle allow for water edge and emergent vegetation and give the water edge a more naturalistic appearance.

Prototypical sections of "hard" and "soft" water edges.

Since the appearance of the perimeter creates the first impression of the Park as a whole and to the casual observer reflects its overall level of maintenance and care, the renovation and maintenance of this important edge is a priority for managers.

Water Edges
Originally, all Central Park water bodies had "soft" naturalistic edges. Rows of boulders and stabilized earth formed the shoreline foundation. Unless they were intended to be picturesque, the boulders were low enough to disappear under the summer water level. This partially invisible barrier served as a deterrent to rowboat landings while holding the soil embankment in place.

Since water is a great attraction for people, and since Central Park has always accommodated a large public, these soft water edges eventually became trampled and eroded. One by one, they were replaced by low-maintenance riprap or concrete edges. Although hard embankments stabilize the water edges, they are alien to Olmsted's pastoral ideal and provide no shelter for birds or aquatic animals.

The Pond, in the Southeast Corner of the Park, is a good example of the visual harshness of an engineered edge. The concreted stone riprap completely covers the south and east shores, leaving no pockets of soil for shoreline plantings. In direct contrast to these hard edges is the soft edge of the Promontory on the opposite shore. Its original foundations of stone and concrete, set in place to hold back soil and plantings, are still intact. Though artificial, the edge of the Promontory is natural in appearance.

Drive Edges
There is no pattern to the design of vegetation adjacent to the Park Drives; it changes from sector to sector as the Park itself changes. One point worth making, however, is that the use of salt as a de-icing agent in winter is extremely harmful to Drive-edge horticulture. The saltwater that is not spattered directly onto foliage along the Drives seeps down into root systems and finally drains into the lakes and streams. In this way, foliage along the Drives is scorched, roots are burned and water bodies become polluted with salt. Roadway salt should be used sparingly!

The sunken transverse roads are screened from view by thick vegetation.

Erosion is one of Central Park's most serious problems.

The sunken transverse roads are a special case. Their molded embankments are densely planted with trees and shrubs to screen out the sight, sound and fumes of cross-Park traffic. These plantings withstand especially tortuous punishment, particularly from exhaust pollution. They require continuing care and replacement.

Soil Erosion, the Number One Problem

Today, almost 25 percent of the ground plane of Central Park, excluding paved areas and water bodies, is completely devoid of vegetation. It is bare, compacted earth, eroding away with every rain. As soil erodes, it clogs catch basins and drainage pipes until they no longer function. It also washes into the lakes as sediment, decreasing the water volume and the surface area and adding an excess of nutrients, which causes summer algae blooms.

The reasons for the Park's heavy erosion are: first, the profusion of "desire lines"—impromptu dirt paths cut across the greensward, through shrubbery and parallel to the Drives; second, unregulated use of lawn areas by athletic teams; and third, the combination of dense shade and root competition among trees not spaced sufficiently apart to permit the growth of a healthy understory.

The Wildlife Habitat

Despite its location in the center of the biggest metropolis in America, Central Park plays host to an extremely varied wildlife population, both resident and transient. Gone, of course, are the white-tailed deer, gray wolves, black bears, bobcats, beavers, wild turkeys and ruffed grouse that roamed the area when New York was being settled in the mid-seventeenth century. But there are still rabbits, woodchucks, bats, raccoons, squirrels, frogs, turtles, fish and scores of bird species.

In the Park's early days, animals were placed in it as decorative components of the landscape, much like shrubs and trees. Such living ornaments included swans, pea fowl, guinea fowl, English sparrows, rabbits, and even herds of deer and sheep. Today, Central Park's wildlife is confined mostly to its waters and woodlands, where it survives with remarkable persistence. A wildlife inventory survey by biologist John Hecklau was published in 1984. Its findings are summarized below.

Inside the Urban Barrier
By the turn of the century, Central Park had become an island habitat, surrounded by an urban barrier zone capable of being crossed only by birds, insects and urban species such as rats. After 1900, most species lost to the

Park could be reestablished only through release by visitors.

Birds
Because Central Park is located in the middle of the Atlantic flyway, it acts as a green oasis in the midst of an urban desert, attracting species of unusual interest. Between 1873 and 1984, some 269 species were sighted in the Park, 42 of which were resident. Some of the rarer species seen in the Park have been: loons, grebes, cormorants, herons, ibises, snow geese, mute swans, black vultures, bald eagles, plovers, sandpipers, barn owls, great horned owls, snowy owls and mountain shrikes.

Mammals
With the exception of bats, mammals are less able than birds to cross the urban barrier. Thus, as the city grew and mammalian species were driven from the Park, they did not return unless reintroduced by man. Still, raccoons, muskrats and woodchucks were among the mammals sighted in the Park in 1982-83:

Raccoons living in the Park.

that a total of at least nine species of reptiles and amphibians reside in the Park today.

Various exotic reptiles and amphibians have also been reported in the Park. These individuals, all of which

were introduced by Park users, include pine snake, boa constrictor, western garter snake and a variety of southern turtles, such as terrapin, red-eared slider and red-bellied turtle. With the exception of the red-eared slider, most of the exotics are unlikely to survive in the Park.

Fish
A sizable population of fish exists in the Park's water bodies today.

Table 5
Fish Recorded in Central Park During 1982-83.[1]

Species	Water body in which found[2]
Pumpkinseed	ACDEFG
Bluegill	AD
Golden shiner	F
Yellow perch	F
Banded killifish	ADG
Largemouth bass	ABCDG
Brown bullhead	G
Goldfish	EFG
Guppy	E

[1]Determined by seining Park water bodies (except the Reservoir) with scientists from the American Museum of Natural History (L. Smith and L. Stillman), and through personal observation.

[2]Locations: A = the Harlem Meer
B = the Loch
C = the Pool
D = the Lake
E = the Pond
F = the Belvedere Lake
G = the Conservatory Water

Table 3
Mammals Recorded in Central Park During 1982-83.[1]

Species	Resident
Dog (ferral)	✔
Cat (ferral)	✔
Big brown bat	
Little brown bat	
Red bat	
Hoary bat	
Silver-haired bat	
Woodchuck	✔
Gray squirrel	✔
House mouse	✔
Norway rat	✔
Eastern cottontail	✔
Raccoon	✔
Muskrat	✔

[1]Presence determined through personal observation and interviews with Urban Park Rangers and with scientists at the American Museum of Natural History (including J. Farrand, S. Anderson, M. Klemens, C. Koopman, R. VanGelder and K. Chambers).

Reptiles and Amphibians
Reports from scientists at the American Museum of Natural History and from the Urban Park Rangers indicate

Table 4
Reptiles and Amphibians Recorded in Central Park During 1982-83.[1]

Species	Presence Confirmed[2]	Evidence of successful reproduction
Bull frog	✔	✔
Green frog		
American toad		
Eastern painted turtle	✔	
Snapping turtle	✔	✔
Red-eared slider	✔	
Musk turtle	✔	
Garter snake		
DeKay's snake		

[1]Determined through interviews with Urban Park Rangers and with scientists at the American Museum of Natural History.

[2]Confirmed through trapping and personal observation.

Invertebrates
While not formally surveyed by Hecklau, some of the more interesting invertebrate species were recorded—butterflies, moths, crayfish and freshwater jellyfish. The crayfish undoubtedly constitute a prey base for bass and large sunfish, raccoons, herons and kingfishers.

Within the three wooded zones described above, where most of the Park's wildlife is concentrated, many factors create an assortment of ecological niches that favor species variety: variations in foliage height, leaf and branch structure, amount of deadwood, number of food-producing plants, presence of evergreens for winter cover, and the existence of running water and wetland areas—individually and in combination.

The quality of the Park's wildlife habitats is related to the health and diversity of the Park's vegetative community. Many of the problems cited for the other parts of the Park are problems for the Park's wildlife areas as well. In addition, vegetative elements that enhance the wildlife population, such as small herbaceous openings, deadwood, thick brushy areas, running water, wetlands and winter evergreen cover, are often missing or exist in less than optimal quantities.

Goals

The overriding goal for the Park's vegetation is to make it a healthy and diverse community. This includes ensuring the survival of the Park's fine old trees and providing for a successor generation. It also entails replanting the now-missing middle layer of vegetation—the shrub and understory trees that once provided both an effective buffer between Park and city and a congenial habitat for wildlife—and re-establishing a completely covered ground plane. Other goals include the continued reinstatement of irrigation, standards of turf management and Park rules that will enable visitors to enjoy soft green lawns, good athletic turf and meadows spangled with flowers. Similarly, the major goal for wildlife in the Park is to maintain a wide variety of species through habitat improvement, sound ecological management and protection from human interference.

General Recommendations

The following recommendations apply throughout the Park:

Plant diversity should be increased throughout to provide greater botanical interest and ecological richness. A variety of turfs should be maintained, ranging from wild meadow mixtures to manicured lawns and bowling greens.

While tree density should be decreased, *overall plant density*, including the density of understory trees, shrubs, grasses, vines and herbaceous material, should be increased to control erosion and screen traffic along the Park's borders and transverse roads.

Japanese knotweed should be controlled.

Open spaces should be enhanced and increased where possible. There should be no further shrinking of existing open glades, lawns and meadows. Throughout the Park new trees should be planted according to only the following criteria: (a) augmentation of an important or underrepresented species; (b) introduction of new species; (c) replacement of an appropriately placed dead or dying tree; (d) restoration of a historic effect.

Leash laws should be enforced.

Salt should be applied in minimum quantities as a de-icer.

Evergreens should be reintroduced throughout the Park, particularly in woodlands, wildlife areas, along the Winter Drive and at picturesque rock outcrops.

Meadows

Even though the Park is surrounded by buildings, it is still possible to re-establish the illusion of unlimited space in parts of the Park. The meadows offer this opportunity. To re-create a sense of free, unbounded openness, it is necessary to apply the same artistry in landscape composition as was used during the Park's first 50 years.

Meadow edges should be made irregular and indefinite. Where now a virtual wall of trees exists, ever tightening and shrinking the meadows' boundaries, there should be indentation and spatial extension of the tree line. This in-and-out effect will cause the eye to perceive a flowing, apparently limitless greensward rather than a tightly defined open space. In order to achieve this, it will be necessary to remove some trees and to plant others. However, specimen trees should be retained even if they are inappropriately sited, but not replaced when they die.

Turf management should combine the use of an improved "tough turf" grass mixture and new drainage systems.

Double-grade drainage systems are especially effective for meadows used for sports. Recently developed, this system consists of an interaction betweeen two layers of soil: surface and subsurface. The surface soil has a high coarse sand content; it is very porous and quick-draining. The subsurface layer underneath is somewhat compacted; it catches the moisture as it filters down and passes it off through a network of

Competition for sunlight causes stunted and lopsided tree crowns, while excessive shade and root competition prevents grass from growing.

Removal of one tree to eliminate crowding allows crowns to fill out. Filtered sunlight reaches the ground plane, allowing grass to grow.

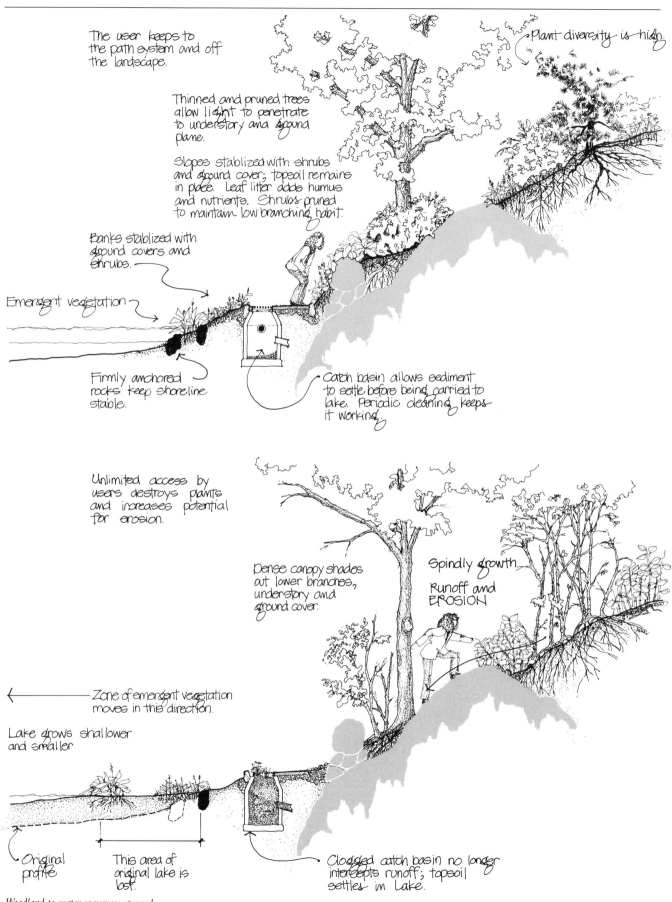

The user keeps to the path system and off the landscape.

Thinned and pruned trees allow light to penetrate to understory and ground plane.

Slopes stablized with shrubs and ground cover; topsoil remains in place. Leaf litter adds humus and nutrients. Shrubs pruned to maintain low branching habit.

Plant diversity is high.

Banks stablized with ground covers and shrubs.

Emergent vegetation

Firmly anchored rocks keep shoreline stable.

Catch basin allows sediment to settle before being carried to lake. Periodic cleaning keeps it working.

Unlimited access by users destroys plants and increases potential for erosion.

Dense canopy shades out lower branches, understory and ground cover.

Spindly growth

Runoff and EROSION

Zone of emergent vegetation moves in this direction.

Lake grows shallower and smaller

Original profile

This area of original lake is lost.

Clogged catch basin no longer intercepts runoff; topsoil settles in lake.

Woodland-to-water sequence: stressed.

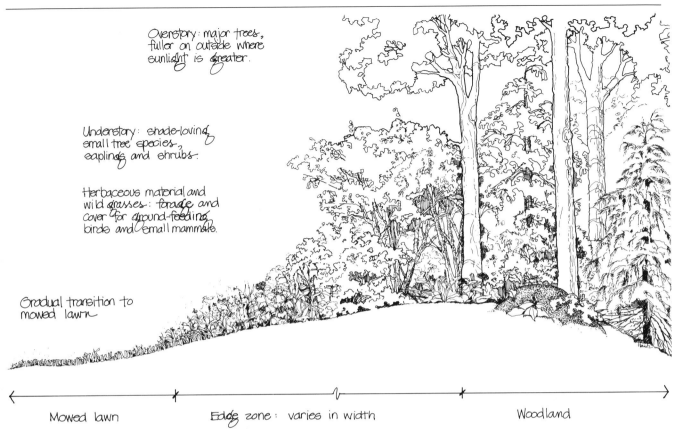

Overstory: major trees, fuller on outside where sunlight is greater.

Understory: shade-loving small tree species, saplings and shrubs.

Herbaceous material and wild grasses: forage and cover for ground-feeding birds and small mammals.

Gradual transition to mowed lawn

Mowed lawn | Edge zone: varies in width | Woodland

Prototypical woodland-to-meadow sequence.

perforated pipes. What makes this system unusual, and versatile, is that in dry weather the subsurface drainage pipes can be closed off so that the water is held by the compacted layer of soil like a subsurface reservoir, preventing the surface layer from drying out. This particular soil structure encourages deep roots, which enable the grass to stand up better under hard use. It also promotes healthier grass that is less prone to disease and infestation by pests.

Parkland

This is the general and predominant Park landscape, grounds that are neither meadow nor woodland but open lawns with scattered trees.

Turf management should be continually practiced to ensure a continuous greensward. This includes soil reconstitution and lawn reconstruction; proper drainage and irrigation; application of different seed mixtures to correspond with environmental conditions (sun, shade, slope) and intensity of use; and periodic liming, fertilization, aeration and overseeding.

Tree thinning and pruning should be practiced where necessary to prevent unhealthy competition and shading out of lawns. Fertilizing, cabling and other types of tree care should be applied as necessary.

Woodland

Although the three wooded sections of the Park—the Promontory, the Ramble and the Northwest Corner—differ in character and have different needs, the following general recommendations apply to all of them.

Overstory tree replanting should be based on priority for native food-producing species.

Understory trees and shrubs should be increased in number and variety. Rebuilding this middle layer of the Park's woodlands with shade-tolerant evergreens such as American holly and Eastern hemlock will greatly enhance their beauty and multiply the opportunities for wildlife. It will be necessary to remove a certain amount of volunteer growth and improve the condition of the soil in order to do this.

Small openings such as glades and lawns, some with only limited mowing to keep down woody growth, should be reestablished. Their edges, which are ecologically significant

zones, should be developed or allowed to develop as brushy and densely planted zones where irregularity and structural complexity are the desired effects.

Picturesque details—intimately scaled vines, mosses, bulbs and ferns, where possible—should be reintroduced to surprise and delight the eye.

Dead trees typical of "old growth" forests should to some extent be left in place because they are part of the woodland ecology hospitable to wildlife. Some fallen deadwood must remain as well. Leaf litter must also remain, because it enriches the soil, reduces erosion and provides essential foraging for ground-feeding birds.

A staff ecologist should be hired to participate in management and restoration decisions in the woodlands. Such a perspective would increase the health of the ecosystems within the Park, thereby benefiting its wildlife and enhancing its landscape beauty. As an example, monitoring the natural regeneration of particular plant populations such as those in the Ramble will lead to management decisions that encourage and promote a more diverse forest community in the Park's woodlands.

Managing events accounts for one-third of the time spent by Park maintenance workers during warm weather months.

Managing Central Park

Introduction

A man may buy and fit up a costly house, but if, after he has done so, he finds coal and ashes scattered over his carpets, if decorated ceilings are stained and marred, if pictures are defaced, windows and doors kept open during storms, beds used as tables and tables as beds, and so on, all that he has obtained for his expenditure will be of little value to him . . . through inefficiency of housekeeping. In the same way a park, as in the case of Central Park, will depend on the prevention of mis-use, which again is a question of the efficiency of park-keeping.

—Frederick Law Olmsted

The "efficiency of park-keeping" in Central Park has, unfortunately, never been commensurate with its maintenance needs. Today's planners and managers, with the aid of early photographs, can conjure up a vision of thick carpets of turf, beautiful shrub borders, flourishing trees and structures always in a state of good repair. Such scenes did and still do exist here and there, but in reality, routine maintenance in Central Park has never been adequate to preserve Olmsted and Vaux's landscape masterpiece. Instead, Central Park has had to undergo periodic major capital reconstruction to shore it up and reverse the process of deterioration.

The purpose of this chapter is to show how, through sufficient maintenance, the large capital reinvestment recommended in this plan can be protected.

A Brief History of Central Park's Management

In the winter of 1858, Olmsted boasted in a letter to his father to "have got the Park into a capital discipline, a perfect system, working like a machine, 1,000 men now at work." Later that year there were as many as 2,500 under his direction. This army of laborers was employed mainly on the construction of the Park, a welcome public-relief project following the financial panic of 1857. There are records of both construction and maintenance expenditures for these early years, and they reveal, not surprisingly, increased maintenance needs as more parts of the Park were finished. Early Park budgets show an emphasis on landscape management, maintenance of the unpaved Drives, and security and rule enforcement.

In 1873, approximately 550 of the Parks Department work force of 882 men were assigned to Central Park. Although the building of the Park was nearing completion, more than half the work force was still engaged in construction work. Throughout the remaining years of the nineteenth century, foresighted planners laid out a comprehensive park system, with parkways linking large parks in each of the five boroughs of New York City. Central Park became just one of many New York parks, albeit the most popular and famous. In 1914, four commissioners were appointed to administer these parks, one for each borough, with Manhattan and Richmond (Staten Island) operationally linked under a single commissioner.

The full-time work force in the period before World War I looked something like this: 1 arboriculturist, 19 mechanics, 7 climbers and pruners, 4 foremen, 10 gardeners, 14 drivers and hostlers (horses performed much of the work done today by motorized vehicles) and 100 laborers. There were also perhaps a dozen permanent recreational employees working in the Park, supplemented by another 15 seasonal recreational employees.

After World War I, the Park's landscape was allowed to deteriorate severely. This decline was detailed in a 1927 report by Herman W. Merkel, the Parks Department Landscape Architect. His recommendations included, among other things, the assignment of an individual supervisor to Central Park and the subdivision of the Park into seven or eight sections, with a foreman and gardening crew assigned to each. (It is approximately this system that survives today, although the recently formed horticultural crews are organized along functional lines—tree care, planting, turf management—and they perform their duties on a park-wide basis.)

During the Depression, federally funded work programs and the bold leadership of Robert Moses transformed Central Park's landscape and its administration. Moses employed hundreds of architects at the Parks Department's headquarters in the Arsenal to design projects that relief workers could undertake. The Central Park projects were announced in rapid succession as work progressed. In 1934, Moses's first year, a prodigious amount of work was reported in the *New York Times*:

February 28, 1934: The conversion of the Sheepfold to a picturesque popular restaurant.

April 6, 1934: Plans for the 32-acre site of the old reservoir to become the Great Lawn.

May 1934: An increase in Park play facilities such as handball courts, roller-skating areas and sandboxes; the conversion of the stable north of 97th Street into a field house and the completion of 13 ball diamonds.

November 11, 1934: The razing of the Conservatory at 104th Street and Fifth Avenue.

November 21, 1934: A new entrance completed at 61st Street and Fifth Avenue.

December 1934: The new Central Park Zoo opened.

A camel from the Menagerie helped mow the grass in 1860.

A modern tractor-mower on the Sheep Meadow.

In addition to the reconstruction of specific sites, Moses's workers also planted trees and shrubs, weeded and reseeded lawns, and repaired walks. A *Times* article of October 24, 1935, notes that 2,100 laborers and 500 mechanics worked on the Park's $2 million rehabilitation, approximately the same number that worked on the Park's construction in 1858-59. Because of the Depression, and with federal funds at its disposal, the Parks Department was able to recruit exceptionally

able employees who could not find work in the private sector. Moses enlarged the department's staff of architects and engineers to 1,800 and hired hundreds of former estate gardeners.

Moses also abolished the positions of the relatively autonomous Borough Park Commissioners, centralizing all authority under himself—an act that makes an accurate assessment of Central Park's budget allocations after 1934 difficult. But it is fascinating to look at

the entire parks system during the subsequent 30 years as it underwent a fivefold expansion.

The 2,600 laborers and mechanics who performed the stem-to-stern renovation of Central Park in 1934 were part of a 45,000-man army of relief workers financed by the Civil Works Administration and later by the Work Projects Administration (WPA). Moses captured this resource with enormous zeal and energy and diverted it from make-work projects to building new parks, playgrounds, beach facilities and swimming pools. He added 6,000 acres to the parks system in the first six years of his administration.

World War II put an end to the first park-building era of the Moses administration. Throughout the war years, however, Moses kept his staff of architects and engineers busy planning and designing over $100 million worth of new postwar construction: 273 projects including everything from refurbishing small playgrounds to constructing new beaches and parkways. In 1945, when the war ended, finished plans were already in hand for the Wollman Rink, the Loeb Boathouse and the 110th Street Boathouse—all in Central Park.

Moses believed that there was popular demand for this program and that it would provide jobs in the transition economy. He assumed that somehow the city would come up with money to maintain the increasingly complex parks system. His acclaim and that of the mayors he served rested on groundbreaking ceremonies, not on routine maintenance. But with the

A tree is planted in 1880 . . .

. . . and in 1980.

A swimming meet in the Lake, 1927.

A foot race, 1985.

withdrawal of the federal relief programs in the late 1930s, the work force leveled off at around 4,500 full-time maintenance personnel and 2,800 seasonal workers, and it was never increased.

Even though the Parks Department budget represented 2 percent of the overall city budget throughout the Moses years (a healthy figure by today's standard, which is less than 1 percent), it was never adequate to maintain a system that had grown to 35,760 acres by 1964. In the late 1960s and early 1970s, as the city's expenses began to exceed its revenues, cuts in the form of work-force attrition were imposed on the Parks Department.

Ironically, these cuts came at a time when Central Park's popularity was growing exponentially and as many as 1,000 special-event permits were being issued each year. It was during this period that emphasis in the use of manpower shifted from day-to-day maintenance to the setting up and taking down of equipment and the removal of tons of garbage generated at an ever-increasing round of festivals, concerts and political rallies. The allocation of its scarce manpower resources is still a problem that plagues the Parks Department. Nowhere in the system is this problem more difficult to resolve than in Central Park, the traditional gathering spot for large celebrations and the sideline host for dozens of parades along Fifth Avenue.

The abuse of the Park by large crowds and the abandonment of consistent-use policies were demoralizing

to longtime Park workers. Motivation was further sapped by lack of tools and equipment. There was another problem as well. Productivity was hampered by narrowly defined job titles and elaborate work rules of the civil service system. For example, motor-vehicle operators who drove crews to work locations were not permitted to assist the crews in their work. A 1974 Bureau of the Budget report assessed labor crew productivity at 30–35 percent and took the Parks Department to task for the inadequacy of its long-range planning, management-information systems, standard operating procedures and manuals, work-force supervision and management of capital projects.

Some of the same criticisms were leveled in a 1975 report prepared by E. S. Savas, a professor of public-systems management and director of the Center for Government Studies at Columbia University. Savas observed declining personnel numbers and man-hours worked by Park employees. He saw insufficient reliance on part-time employees, inadequate mechanization of work and, most significant, the complete absence of a parkwide administrative structure to make long-range plans, policies, budgets or even routine day-to-day work assignments. The actual manpower level, though declining in the early 1970s, was, Savas felt, "sufficient to provide a much higher standard of performance than is currently achieved" but did not do so because of management failure.

There were, in fact, considerably

more people working in Central Park in the early 1970s than there are today, and funding was actually rising during those years. Savas calculated Central Park expenditures during 1972-73 as follows.

Expenditures in 1972-73

Source

Department of Parks*	
Personnel	$5,913,451
Materials	179,651
Capital expenditures	289,987
Department of Cultural Affairs	171,750
Department of Recreation	265,641
Police Department	2,977,158
Private contributions	27,094
Total	$9,834,732

*Includes fringe benefits

Included among the recommendations of the Savas report were the appointment of a chief executive officer for Central Park and the creation of a Board of Guardians to bring continuity of policy and planning to the Park and oversee its budget and operations. Both of these recommendations were implemented some five years later with the creation of the office of the Central Park Administrator and the establishment of the Central Park Conservancy by Mayor Koch.

In some ways, the fiscal crisis proved a spur to reform. With the layoff of 800 workers in June 1975, it became necessary to "broadband," or generalize, the proliferation of civil service job titles. After two years of negotiation with District Council 37 of the Municipal Workers Union, which represents the Parks Department's civil service work force, 23 titles were collapsed into 6. There have been other significant changes since the beginning of the Koch administration in 1978, as a comparison of Central Park staffing in 1977 and 1984 shows.

Central Park Staffing
April 1977

Functional Assignment	Central Park Totals
1. *Management and Field Support*	1
2. *Maintenance*	
79th Street Yard	24
Sector maintenance (excluding Lower Park and north end of Park)	87
Subtotal	111
3. *Park Operations & Recreation*	
Wollman Rink and Lower Park (including Central Park Zoo)	26
Lasker Rink and north end of Park	17
Children's Zoo	15
Puppets, marionettes, other recreation	26
Subtotal	84
4. *Horticulture*	
Conservatory Garden	3
Total	199

Central Park Staffing
April 1984

Functional Assignment	Department of Parks	Central Park Conservancy	Total
1. *Management and Field Support*	2	2	4
2. *Maintenance*			
79th Street Yard	33	—	33
Sector maintenance	49	—	49
Subtotal	82	0	82
3. *Horticulture*	7	14	21
4. *Preservation*	8	8	16
5. *Park Operations & Visitor Services*			
Rink and pool operations	25	—	25
Puppets, marionettes, preschool	16	—	16
Belvedere/Dairy visitor services	4	5	9
Volunteer coordination	1	1	2
Subtotal	46	6	52
6. *Central Park-Based Security*★			
Communications Center	11	—	11
Night security	17	—	17
Park Enforcement Patrol (PEP)	17	—	17
Urban Park Rangers	14	—	14
Subtotal	59	0	59
Totals	204	30	234

★Security forces based in Central Park serve the entire borough of Manhattan, including Central Park. The Communications Center provides radio communications for all five boroughs.

A mounted Park policeman in the 1860s.

Mounted Park Rangers, 1984.

Between 1977 and 1984 a borough-wide security program started operating out of Central Park, and a work force of Urban Park Rangers was organized to provide public assistance and education. Park education and other visitor services are now provided at the Dairy and the Belvedere by the Central Park Conservancy, and 37 new workers, recent graduates of horticulture and preservation programs, are doing a variety of specialized tasks such as graffiti removal, rustic-shelter reconstruction, masonry repair, shrubbed replanting, tree pruning and turf care throughout the Park. These employees act as an in-house landscape construction crew part of the time and as general groundskeepers and repair crews the rest of the time.

In summing up these two tables, taking into account that only 15 to 20 security workers are active in Central Park at any given time, it becomes apparent that the overall work force has actually decreased between 1977 and 1984. What emerges, in fact, is a fairly sharp diminution of city funding for the traditional Park maintenance worker. As new programs in security, horticulture and preservation have started up, scarce budget dollars have been shifted away from the basic work force and into these areas.

Central Park's Management Today

The Parks Commissioner is involved in many decisions regarding Central Park's day-to-day management because of the Park's prominence in the system and the presence of the Parks Department's headquarters in the Arsenal building in Central Park. The Commissioner's role is essentially a policy role. He has final authority over rules and regulations governing Park use and enters into legal contracts with concessionaires, contractors, entertainers and service organizations such as the Conservancy and others performing operations in the Park. He has final approval over the budget, acts as its chief advocate before the City Council and Board of Estimate, and makes final deisions regarding staffing. Finally, he is the chief protector and defender of the Park from encroachment and misuse.

The Central Park Administrator, the chief executive officer of the Park, reports to the Parks Commissioner and the trustees of the Central Park Conservancy for all policy, planning and budgetary matters and to the Deputy Commissioner for Operations of the Parks Department for all matters involving Park operations. The Administrator supervises and makes decisions regarding restoration planning and construction; the allocation of maintenance resources; and the style, content and level of visitor services, including Park security, sports, events programming and food concessions.

Supporting these operations are two budgets, that of the City of New York and that of the Central Park Conservancy. It is the Administrator's job to see that the private funds raised by the Conservancy are spent wisely and are not applied to items that should be funded by the city and to ensure that city funding in Central Park is maintained at an amount proportional to its present share of the Parks Department budget. Finally, it is the Administrator's task to use these two budgets in a complementary fashion to run the Park.

The Deputy Central Park Administrator is the chief of operations in the Park and reports to the Central Park Administrator. He is responsible for the cleaning and repairing of the Park's structures and furniture, the care of the Park's lawns, trees and other vegetation, and the removal of tons of daily litter. With the Administrator, he oversees the hiring and allocation of the work force necessary to perform these tasks as well as the purchase and delivery of vehicles, equipment and supplies. He is responsible for the administrative record-keeping and management analysis that tracks Park operations and provides data for budget-making, work planning and other decisions. With the Administrator, he coordinates the delivery of services to Central Park provided by other city agencies.

The Assistant Administrator for Construction and Preservation oversees the day-to-day progress of both public and private, in-house and outside-contracted construction projects in Central Park. He reports directly to the Central Park Administrator but coordinates his operations closely with the Deputy Central Park Administrator. He is responsible for reviewing project budgets, handling the bidding process if work is to be done by outside contractors, monitoring construction schedules and handling problems that might cause delays and cost overruns. He also supervises the day-to-day operations of

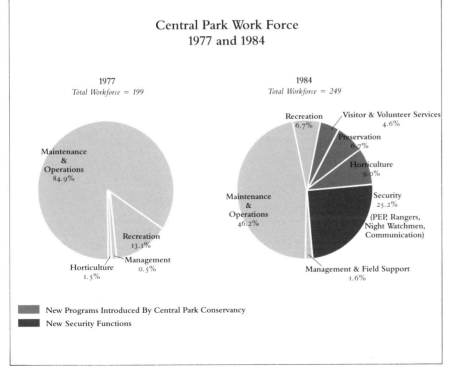

**Central Park Work Force
1977 and 1984**

1977
Total Workforce = 199

Maintenance & Operations
84.9%

Recreation
13.1%

Management
0.5%

Horticulture
1.5%

1984
Total Workforce = 249

Recreation
6.7%

Visitor & Volunteer Services
4.6%

Preservation
6.7%

Horticulture
9.0%

Security
25.2%
(PEP, Rangers, Night Watchmen, Communication)

Maintenance & Operations
46.2%

Management & Field Support
1.6%

■ New Programs Introduced By Central Park Conservancy
■ New Security Functions

Keeping the Park clean is the primary maintenance function, and one that must be performed every day of the year.

the crews engaged in graffiti removal, stone and bronze conservation, and specialized carpentry.

The Assistant Central Park Administrator for Visitor Services supervises educational, cultural and volunteer programs offered to the public in Central Park. She assists in the development of policy guidelines governing the use of the Bandshell and other Park venues for entertainment and recreation; supervises the operation of the Park's Visitor Center—the Dairy, and the Children's Learning Center—Belvedere Castle; administers the Central Park L.I.V.E. (Learning and Involvement for Volunteers in the Environment) program; and produces informational signage, exhibits and publications on Central Park.

The Director of Central Park Horticulture establishes policies, programs and procedures for all horticultural operations in Central Park. He participates in the landscape design process, sets priorities, supervises the preparation of work schedules for the horticultural crews, monitors performance in the field and tracks productivity. He also plans all horticultural work performed by outside contractors, formulates de-

tailed specifications for such work and supervises its execution. He prepares the horticultural program budget for Central Park, organizes staff training and communicates with other professionals in his field and with the general public.

Central Park Operations

Maintenance

The maintenance of Central Park falls into three basic categories: (1) *Cleaning and repair.* This includes the monitoring of general Park conditions, the removal of the approximately 330,000 cubic feet of compacted trash each year, and the cleaning, painting and minor repairs to buildings, ball fields, playgrounds, benches, comfort stations, fences, fountains, pipes, paths and so forth. (2) *Preservation and conservation.* The range of work in this category includes small-scale restoration and preventive maintenance of such artistic and historic components of the Park landscape as statues, bridges, arches, stairways, walls, boat landings, arbors and rustic shelters. (3) *Groundskeeping.* This category includes planting, pruning, mowing, mulching, fertilizing and watering

the Park's lawns, flowers, shrubs, ground cover and trees.

Keeping the Park Clean

As mentioned, since the late 1920s Central Park's 843 acres have been divided into maintenance districts, or sections. Each section has a foreman and crew who operate out of small buildings that usually also serve some public function as well. In addition, there is an operations headquarters— the 79th Street Maintenance Yard— from which parkwide crews are deployed by the principal Park Supervisor and where Park vehicles are stored and serviced.

Central Park is divided into seven maintenance sections. The job of the section crews is to make routine sweeps beginning on the Park's perimeter sidewalks, then moving to the Park Drives and finally to the main pedestrian walkways. Afterward, they clean up the Park's 25 playgrounds, 26 playing fields, 24 bathrooms and various sitting areas and lawns.

Section workers report such things as new graffiti and broken tree limbs, benches, lights and playground equipment to section foremen, who then write up work orders for handling by

Groundskeeping involves an unusual root-pruning operation as well as . . .

planting . . .

pruning . . .

irrigation . . .

sodding . . .

dethatching and many other routine tasks.

the Manhattan Borough Shop or the department shop located on Randall's Island.

Supporting and supplementing the work in each section of the Park is the 79th Street Maintenance Yard. Specialized Yard crews paint benches, clean catch basins and perform various minor repairs; however, the principal function of the Yard is collecting garbage and transporting it to one of three Sanitation Department dumps, ferrying workers and equipment to various job sites in the Park, and trucking barricades and men to set up for events.

Preserving and Conserving the Park

It was clear in 1980, when the Parks Department and the Central Park Conservancy embarked upon the program to rebuild the Park and restore many of its historic landscape features, that specialized crews of craftsmen would be

First aid.

Dispatchers at the 97th Street Security Center respond to calls.

needed to rebuild rustic arbors, shelters and bridges; repair boat landings, pergolas, walls and fences; dredge streams; reconstruct stream and lake embankments; remove graffiti and conserve bronze statuary and plaques.

Since 1980, three crews of mostly young craftspersons have been fielded under Conservancy sponsorship and subsequently funded by the Parks Department. One crew is engaged primarily in carpentry; a second performs masonry jobs, including the implanting of boulders in the landscape for erosion and embankment control; and a third has removed 50,000 square feet of graffiti to date and is also engaged in learning various techniques of bronze conservation. Thus, Central Park has become a laboratory and training ground for a new kind of versatile multidisciplinary worker: the Park Craftsperson.

Groundskeeping

As groundskeeping forces have been reintroduced since 1980, the long-neglected trees and turf of Central Park have undergone a remarkable transformation. Some of the accomplishments in this area include: a comprehensive inventory of the Park's 24,000 trees over six inches in caliper; pruning 6,000 trees and fertilizing 350; planting 275 major new trees and 25,000 new shrubs and understory trees; resodding 21 acres of lawn and intensive turf

management of 38 acres; the establishment of a soil laboratory that can handle 500 samples a year; and the hiring of specialists with various types of horticultural expertise to consult on Park problems.

Four programs are now in operation within the field of horticultural maintenance: an arboriculture program, an

understory vegetation program, a turf-care program and a soil-management program. The Central Park Horticulturalist coordinates and supervises the work in these four interdisciplinary programs and, in addition, cooperates with the Director of Preservation and Conservation on a variety of in-house restoration projects.

Nature study.

Visitor Services

Several promising developments relating to Visitor Services have occurred over the past four years.

Security

The Park was originally patrolled by its own security force of "Park keepers," who reported to Olmsted. Replaced by city policemen after 1897, the approximately 75 full-time officers and 40 seasonal officers assigned to Central Park today operate out of the Central Park precinct located on the 86th Street transverse road in a converted stable that is a landmark building in extremely dilapidated condition.

Currently, Central Park is patrolled in much the same fashion as the surrounding precincts. Patrolmen with two-way radio cars tour the Drives and major paths and respond to emergency calls relayed through a central dispatching system. While this computerized emergency dispatching method is effective in getting officers to the scene of a crime after it has been reported, it does not deter crime or assist in the enforcement of Park rules. Elsewhere, it loses some of its efficacy in the Park because many of the Park's 49 emergency telephone call boxes do not function at any given period of time due to constant problems with overhead phone lines that are looped through the trees. In addition, it is difficult for victims and police who succeed in achieving phone contact to give and confirm directions to a crime site in the Park. Cellular emergency telephone call boxes that are answered by the Central Park police precinct and that automatically pinpoint the caller's location are currently being installed by the Parks Department and the Central Park Conservancy. Other strategies have also been initiated to establish a greater security presence within Central Park. In 1980, a special services unit was organized by the Parks Department to work with the police in combating the problem of illegal vendors. Today, this and other Park rule-enforcement work is being carried out by the Park Enforcement Patrol, a ranger unit with peace-officer status. A radio-command post has been installed at the North Meadow Center in Central Park to communicate with, and receive messages from, these PEP officers. In addition, alarms from Park buildings that have had emergency protection devices installed are being relayed to this center. The building also serves as headquarters for a mobile night-security unit composed of maintenance workers who patrol the Park in pickup trucks.

Events

Although diminished in number today from a decade ago, there are still hundreds of events each year in Central Park. Mass events—drawing 500 people or more—are systematically managed. At weekly operations meetings, representatives from the Parks and Police departments plan the details of each event. While this promotes security and cuts down on abuse of the Park, the fact still remains that the volume of Central Park events is such that, while Parks Department workers set up and clean up after them, regular maintenance must be left undone.

Entertainment and Education

Central Park offers regular programmed entertainment—visitor information centers, a marionette theater, Shakespearean plays, storytelling and a carousel. New education and entertainment programs in the Park are the result of fund-raising efforts by the Central Park Conservancy.

The Dairy offers photography and art exhibits on Park-related subjects, lectures, and an information and sales desk where books, maps and a variety of other items can be found. Programs at the Belvedere are aimed at families on the weekend and at schoolchildren during the week, and they consist of treasure hunts, games, crafts projects, music and magic shows.

The Conservancy is responsible for the large framed maps at all major Park entrances and for posting on the reverse side of these Park maps a seasonal calendar of events. It also publishes a quarterly newsletter, the Central Park *Good Times*. Within the Park, new signs tell about restoration projects under way and encourage respect for new plantings.

The Urban Park Rangers are also helping to promote good behavior and obedience to Park rules, and they administer first aid and teach lessons in environmental science. Some serve as auxiliary members of the Belvedere and Dairy staffs.

Sports and Recreation

One of the greatest challenges Central Park's managers face is how to satisfy the demand for sports while preserving

Fun and . . .

games.

After jogging, softball is the most popular Park sport.

Food

Eating is an activity that engages approximately 30 percent of the Park's visitors. Food and food service have been associated with Central Park since its inception. Milk was dispensed from the Dairy, mineral water from the Mineral Springs refreshment building; and the Casino played the role of today's Tavern on the Green, serving elegant meals in a festive atmosphere. Then as now, outdoor vendors sold snacks from carts, some illegally without a permit.

Licensing of vendors and the setting of standards for their attire and products was yet one more way in which Robert Moses set his stamp on Central Park. Today, there are approximately 40 licensed mobile-cart locations in Central Park, mostly clustered around major entrances and prominent crosswalks. In 1984, following the expiration of a single-vendor contract, all of these locations were advertised for bid on an individual basis; as a result, the Park offered more varied food than it has had in several years. Graphic standards and a dress code for these new vendors was developed by the Central Park Conservancy working in close cooperation with the Concessions Division of the Parks Department.

There has been much heated debate concerning the optimum size for Park food facilities. Olmsted warned against restaurants and other attractions that were in and of themselves *destinations* rather than simply *conveniences*.

the Park's lawns. Management of the Heckscher Ballfields proves that this challenge can be met. Resodded three years ago, the 4.5-acre site has been the subject of a turf-management pilot program in which football and soccer have been prohibited, baseball and softball permits are canceled on rainy days when the ground is muddy and subject to compaction, and playing is not allowed before noon on weekdays or after September 15 in order for a fall overseeding to establish itself while the weather is still warm enough for the grass to grow. A telephone message tape advises permit holders whether or not Heckscher is in play, and rangers monitor for infractions if the fields are closed. To apply this management system to the Great Lawn and the North Meadow ball fields when these are also restored will require the commitment of additional rangers to Central Park.

Thirty percent of all visitors consume food in the Park.

Licensed concessionaires sell food from carts.

Restoration crew rebuilding balustrades above the John Purroy Mitchel Monument near 90th Street and Fifth Avenue.

Restoring Central Park

The complete restoration of Central Park is a complicated, long-term process requiring as many as 200 capital projects. In the past, publicly funded projects have been administered by the Design and Construction Division, and Conservancy-funded projects have been handled by the Central Park Administrator. All projects are submitted for a series of reviews by the Parks Department, Landmarks Commission, Art Commission and the Manhattan Borough Board. Projects of unusual community interest may also be presented to individual community planning boards for review and comment. This review process takes from one to three months, or longer in the case of certain projects of an extraordinary nature. It is the legitimate means whereby the democratic process is brought to bear on the city's most democratic public space.

The Design Division of the Parks Department is in charge of supervising projects worth approximately $80 million a year. With such a broad focus, it is difficult for the division to provide, on a continuing basis, resources solely for the restoration of Central Park. Moreover, the public bidding process mandated by the city precludes other than low-bidder contract awards, and this allows contractors who are sometimes incompetent or incapable

of especially sensitive kinds of reconstruction and landscape restoration work to get jobs in Central Park.

Outside construction contracts are not necessarily the most efficient and economical means of accomplishing the restoration program outlined in

this plan. Many areas requiring restoration remain neglected because they are neither large enough to warrant becoming independent capital projects nor small enough to be part of routine maintenance repairs. As we have discussed above, the reconstruction of the Park's features is being accomplished by the new in-house preservation crew. Their work is integrated with landscape restoration work performed by the horticulture crew. These crews form an interdisciplinary and multi-skilled work force. Individuals working on these crews have been trained to do more than one job. Supervisors thus have more flexibility and ease of scheduling than do contractors who must organize the work of various independent building trades. Most important, unlike a contractor, the preservation crew does not go away once a particular project is completed.

In addition, as a by-product of this management and restoration plan, Central Park now has a group of landscape designers thoroughly knowledgeable about the whole Park and capable of developing design contracts for individual projects within it. Registered landscape architects funded by the Conservancy and currently on the Administrator's staff can both prepare design documents and review the plans of consultants.

Bronze conservation crew cleaning Hans Christian Andersen.

Rebuilding the Park

The first part of this book deals with Central Park as a whole. Its various natural and manmade parkwide systems are studied in detail as are the ways in which each one limits and regulates the others. The recommendations offered in these preceding chapters are intended to improve overall design and management of the park while keeping these systems in balance.

A closer, area-by-area examination is also essential in order to deal with the problems that arise at specific sites within the Park. Each site has its own physical characteristics and constituent uses. As a first step in bringing these special situations into focus, Central Park's 843 acres were divided into logical units of study. In some cases the determining factor was historical, in others it was ecological. Sometimes the delineating factor was a "viewshed"; at other times it was a manmade dividing line such as a Park Drive or a Transverse road.

The planning team thus divided Central Park into 21 sectors as shown in the map below. For each one, details of the sector's history, existing conditions, planners' goals and priorities were compiled. Then recommendations were drawn up and a budget was estimated. Sector reports appear on the following pages. The recommendations at the end of each report indicate the basic thrust of the proposed work but of necessity do not include specific design details. These will come later and may alter the plan to some degree as work goes forward. In addition, further environmental and user analyses are contemplated and these will also effect the process. So too will continuing review by Community Boards, the New York City Landmarks Commission, Art Commission and civic groups.

The maps in each of the following sections show the existing Park in 1982. Photographs are used wherever possible to document both change and continuity.

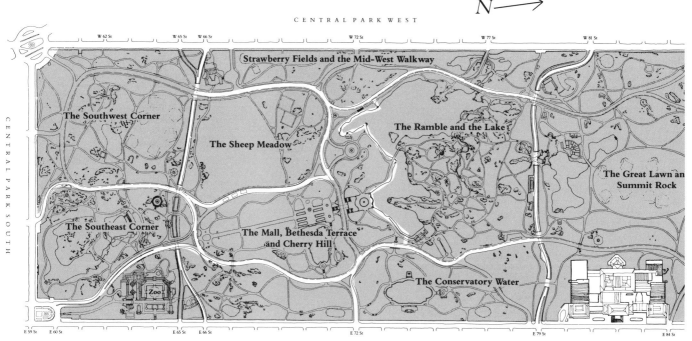

Workers removing carved stone panel at Bethesda Terrace prior to restoration, 1983.

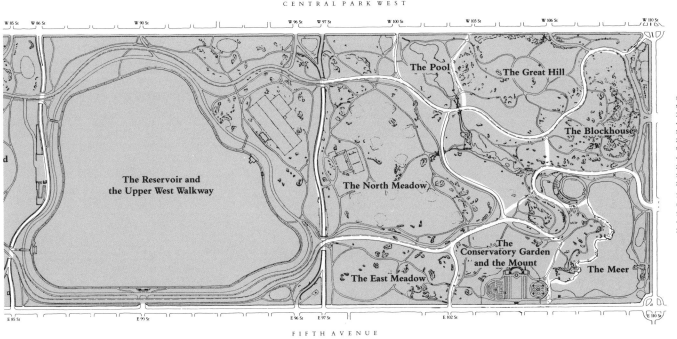

The Meer

The old, natural shoreline of the Meer.

The Harlem Meer is the second-largest water body in Central Park, and it is also the Park's lowest point of elevation. Before the Park was built, the Meer was the westernmost edge of a large tidal marsh reaching in from the East River. Montayne's Rivulet and

Harlem Creek emptied into it from the west.

The northern boundary of Central Park was originally 106th Street. The decision to extend the Park to 110th Street was made in 1858, and the additional 65 acres were acquired by the city—including what is now the Meer—five years later. An 1860 design for this Northeast Corner called for a formal canal and a promenade in the French tradition. The next year, the design was changed to a large, free-form lake with an informal edge, and that is what was constructed. This water body was called the Meer, the Dutch word for "lake." The Meer's shoreline consisted of several coves and peninsulas, and two sandy beaches. There was a small island in the southwest corner.

As with all the other water bodies in the Park, the bottom of the Meer was concreted several times in response to

citywide malaria scares, but the most brutal alteration came in 1941, when the Meer's naturalistic shoreline was bulldozed and smoothed out, its coves and grassy peninsulas obliterated, and the entire edge rimmed in concrete.

At the same time a boathouse, a smaller brick concession and two standard oval-shaped perimeter playgrounds were also built. Though heavy-handed, in the tradition of this era, the placement of facilities at this end of the Park was an acknowledgment that the neglected north end, surrounded by a densely populated urban setting, required services that users of the south end had enjoyed for years.

In 1966, the Meer was altered yet again when the Lasker Pool and Ice Skating Rink was built in the southwest corner directly over the mouth of the stream leading from the Loch to the Meer. A five-foot culvert was installed under the structure so that water from the Loch could continue to the Meer. Lasker Rink, along with the previous alterations mentioned above, reduced the size of the Meer to 11 acres from its original 14. Unfortunately, since the rink was built in a major drainage corridor, it immediately began to have structural problems.

Existing Conditions

Dog walking and bench sitting are currently the main activities in this section of the Park, along with skating and swimming at Lasker.

Most of the project area is in an extremely dilapidated condition, with the exception of the recently renovated 110th Street Playground. The 110th Street Boathouse is a disgraceful eyesore: vandalized, weed choked, burned out and virtually stripped to its shell.

The stones edging the Meer are slowly being dislodged by the erosive force of storm water and lack of maintenance. Approximately 186,000 cubic feet of sediment have accumulated at the bottom.

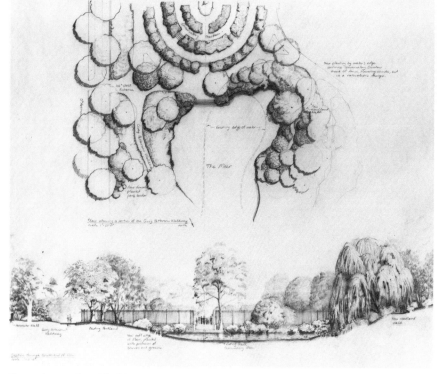

Proposed restoration of the Meer.

The edge of the Meer, with Lasker Rink in background.

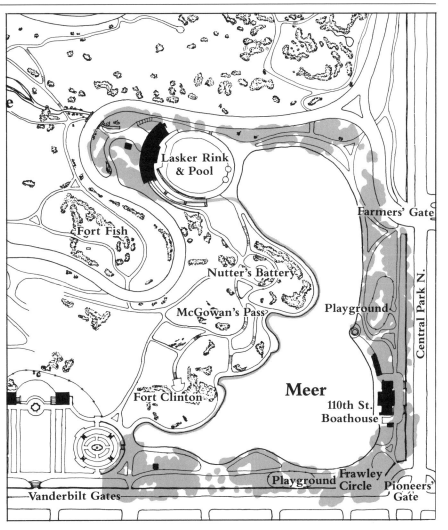

Water quality studies indicate that the Meer is in a hypereutrophic state, but it still supports a diversified fish population. Large-mouth bass, pumpkin seed, blue gill and banded killifish have been collected, but most are quite small. Fishing does occur from the banks, but not nearly as much as when the Meer was stocked regularly (1959-1963 and 1978-1979).

The Meer's drainage watershed is the largest in the Park—192.9 acres—and even though the outlet structures are in fairly good condition, this water body has been rated by engineers as able only to pass a 10-year storm frequency test, meaning that it would be likely to flood at least once every 10 years. This is largely due to its reduced size and hard stone-and-concrete edge.

The surrounding landscape has lost much of its ground cover, and there are virtually no shrubs or understory trees along the perimeter wall. On the other hand, some of the most spectacular large trees in the Park are located on the Meer's eastern edge. A mature stand of turkey oaks, a 44-inch-caliper black willow, a 59-inch-caliper European beech and two outstanding dawn redwoods grace the site. Other trees include elms, lindens, hawthorns, crab apples, black locusts, ginkgoes and several species of oak.

Goals, Priorities and Recommendations

It is of paramount importance that this underused corner of Central Park be transformed into a lively and inviting gateway to and from Harlem. This will require extensive restoration of the landscape, buildings, vegetation, water edge and paths.

Rebuilding the 110th Street Boathouse as a waterside café and boat-rental facility will provide a much needed visitor amenity at this end of the Park.

The Meer needs to be dredged and its natural edge restored. But this cannot be done until erosion control has been completed on the upland parts of the watershed draining into it (the Great Hill, the Forts, the North Meadow, Pool and Ravine). However, the narrow landscape strip bordering the Meer on the north and east forms its own watershed, and work here can begin immediately. In general, the path system around the Meer should be improved so that once visitors have entered the area, they will be encouraged to walk farther into the Park.

A recommendation for the improvement of Frawley Circle, the northeast entrance to the Park, appears in the treatment of the Perimeter (page 151).

In the long term, if it becomes feasible, the Lasker Pool and Rink should be relocated, and the beautiful stream connecting the Loch and the Meer restored.

The Forts

The steep bluffs of Harlem Heights at the north end are possibly the least visited features of Central Park, but they are the richest in historic lore. During the Revolutionary War and the War of 1812, these hills served as strategic military outposts for American troops and for the British enemy as well.

The Revolutionary War: A British Stronghold

In the days before landfills and bulkheads added acres to the edges of Manhattan, the island was not as wide as it is today. Harlem Heights, which stood between the Hudson River and the Harlem Creek marsh, was a natural battlement not easily traversed except through McGowan's Pass, a narrow gap that got its name from a popular roadside tavern. The site of McGowan's Pass is some yards west of what is now Fifth Avenue, just inside the present Park at about 106th Street. It was, as the British noted, a place where "a few troops might stop an army."

This is precisely what the British attempted to do in September of 1776. After defeating the Americans at the Battle of Long Island, the British headed for McGowan's Pass, hoping to trap General George Washington and his troops at the southern end of Manhattan. Washington realized his predicament just in time and hastily left Manhattan, moving his men and arms through McGowan's Pass and retreating to the north.

A rear guard, led by a regiment of Marylanders, delayed the Redcoats long enough for Washington to make good his escape and then just barely made it through the pass themselves. The next day the British occupied the pass. After the Battle of Fort Washington two months later, the victorious British led 2,800 American prisoners back through McGowan's Pass into prisons in British-held New York City. It was not until the end of the war

A pre-Park view of McGowan's Pass.

seven years later that American troops, under the command of General Henry Knox, once again marched through the pass on their way to liberate the city.

The War of 1812: An American Fortress

Thirty years later, McGowan's Pass was a lookout point for the Americans during the War of 1812. Throughout most of the war, the Americans expected a British invasion from the south by sea. Guns and lookouts were trained in that direction from the Battery at the southern tip of Manhattan. However, when the British bombarded Stonington, Connecticut, in August of 1814, the American command began to fear the British might instead be planning an assault by land from the north.

Immediately, the citizenry of New York mobilized to build a chain of fortifications on the high bluffs of what is now Central Park. Butchers, lawyers, Freemasons, students from Columbia College, tallow chandlers and others, working day and night, built several fortifications: Blockhouse 1, a second blockhouse straddling McGowan's Pass, Fort Fish (an open earthwork with a mounting for five guns), Fort Clinton (a three-gun earthwork named after Dewitt Clinton,

Mayor of New York) and the single-gun Nutter's Battery. Three months later the Treaty of Ghent was signed and the war was over. Not a single shot had been fired at any of the forts.

When the north end was added to the original Park purchase in 1863, remnants of these fortifications remained, mainly the foundations. However, not much was done with them by Olmsted and Vaux, who were busy with the construction of the rest of the Park.

Existing Conditions

There has been little regular maintenance of the forts and their environs since improvements involving paths, benches and plantings were carried out during the Moses administration. The consequences of this neglect have made the place more hospitable to wildlife than to human beings. A dense forest of black cherry and other self-propagating species has taken over most of the hillsides, shading out understory and ground plane shrubs and leaving the exposed slopes to erode into the Meer below. Stairs, walkways, benches and lights have all deteriorated.

The Fort Fish site is now barren, devoid of both military relics and grass. Trees block the northern view that once made this a prime defensive lookout. The Andrew Haswell Green Memorial Bench (named after the man who was Central Park's first comptroller and also a founder of the Museum of Natural History and the Metropolitan Museum of Art) stands here unused and unseen.

The Fort Clinton site consists of an asphalt pad dating from the 1940s and little else besides a portion of a fence that once surrounded it and a pedestal that once supported a commemorative cannon, which has either been stolen or rolled into the Meer. A small meadow flanks the crest of the hill and provides views to the north and east.

The site of Nutter's Battery is encircled by a low stone wall and several benches; both wall and benches are in disrepair.

Goals, Priorities and Recommendations

Historic preservation is the top priority for this area of the Park. As a first step, the sites should be cleaned up: The asphalt should be removed from Fort Clinton and Nutter's Battery and replaced with soft surface material; new benches should be installed, but fewer than there are at present.

To point up the historic importance of the forts, the planners feel it is preferable to adorn the walls of the 110th Street Boathouse, once it is restored, with an exhibition of maps, drawings and photographs of this section of the Park during the Revolutionary War and the War of 1812, rather than erect

historic markers on the site of each fort. Just as exhibitions in the Dairy treat the Park's history and design, and those in the Belvedere explain the Park's natural environment, the Boathouse could house an exhibition that covers the pre-Park history of Central Park.

As to the landscape surrounding the forts, a completely faithful restoration would mean cutting down most of the trees. This plan seeks to retain the heavily forested character of the area and recommends only such judicious tree thinning as will promote the ecological health of the entire tree community and provide a safer, more inviting atmosphere.

Looking across the Meer from Fort Clinton today.

The Conservatory Garden and the Mount

The Conservatory Garden, located at 105th Street and Fifth Avenue, is one of Central Park's unique horticultural ornaments. Its formal hedges and flower beds stand in elegant contrast to the rest of the Park's flowing naturalistic landscape.

Olmsted and Vaux intended this area to be part of a large arboretum dedicated to native American trees and shrubs. The arboretum was never built, but the area has always featured specialized plantings of one sort or another. It was first a nursery, and then in 1899 a glass-enclosed conservatory was built on the site.

The glass conservatory was torn down in 1934, and the present three-part Conservatory Garden was laid out in its place. The north garden is built in a circular French parterre style and contains tulips and chrysanthemums, depending on the season; the south garden is planted with perennials; and the center garden is a rectangular greensward edged with yew hedges and *allées* of crab apples. At the western edge of the center section, the garden rises in semicircular tiered hedges with a terrace and an iron pergola supporting wisteria. Brick buildings on both sides of the terrace

Frances Hodgeson Burnett Fountain in the south garden.

are set into the hillside; they house rest rooms and maintenance facilities. The roofs of the buildings function as terraces. Fountains decorate each of the three gardens, and an ornate French iron gate that originally stood at the front of the Vanderbilt mansion at 58th Street (now the site of Bergdorf-Goodman) graces the Fifth Avenue entrance.

Rising above the Conservatory Garden to the west is the Mount, so-called because it was once the site of the Mount St. Vincent convent. The Sisters of Charity moved out when the Park was built, and the convent buildings became a tavern. The tavern burned to the ground in 1881 and was replaced by a restaurant. It was demolished in 1917, and only the foundation remains. A composting operation is currently conducted in this location.

Existing Conditions

In 1982, major restoration of the Conservatory Garden was undertaken by the Central Park Conservancy. Graffiti was removed, trees and shrubs were pruned, new plants were added and a full-time gardener was hired.

Because of its now-thriving condition, attendance at the Conservatory Garden has increased dramatically. Schoolchildren come to learn about plants, volunteers offer their gardening services, tours are conducted, concerts

The old Conservatory on the site of the present Garden.

Chrysanthemums on display in the north garden.

McGowan's Tavern, demolished in 1917.

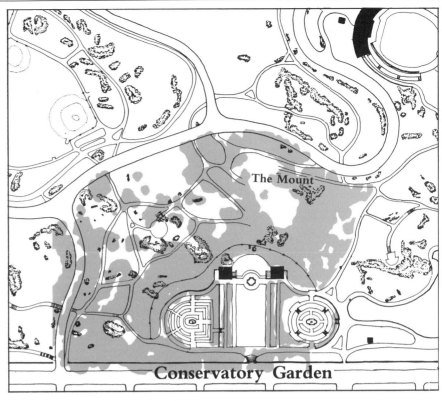

The Mount

Conservatory Garden

are occasionally held and weddings have become a regular warm-weather weekend occurrence.

Goals, Priorities and Recommendations

Restoration of the Conservatory Garden has done more than preserve the Park's horticultural showcase for perennial plants; it has created a major magnet for visitors in the north end of the Park. The Garden could, in fact, become one stop along the pleasant pedestrian route that passes through it if the lawns to the north and south were given general landscape rehabilitation.

Work in the Garden itself is not yet complete. The flagstone pavement needs to be repaired, as do the gates, the fence, the wrought-iron trellis, the benches and the brick walls holding back the slope on the west. The entire circulation system should be repaved. The brick buildings and the terraces require substantial restoration. The men's room is in particularly bad repair.

Reclamation of the Mount St. Vincent convent site, on the high promontory—with its superb views immediately behind the Garden, will constitute a major gain for the Park. The composting operation that occupies it now could be moved to a silo positioned out of sight at the 79th Street Maintenance Yard.

The Terrace above the central garden, today.

The Blockhouse

The hilly and heavily wooded north end of Central Park is more than merely a preserve of trees and wildlife. With its cliffs and bluffs and steep ravines, it is a topographical time warp of Manhattan. The engineers who built the streets of New York City smoothed out and flattened the land that lay outside the walls of Central Park. They used the cut-and-fill technique: Crests of hills were cut off, and low ground was filled in. Although Olmsted and Vaux shaped and highlighted the landscape features of Central Park, they left much of its topography essentially as it was, especially that of the north end. So it remains today as a reminder of how the land around it used to lie.

Just inside the Park at 110th Street, at the top of a steep escarpment, there stands a reminder of something else as well—the War of 1812. The Blockhouse, a square open-roofed fort, was built in 1814, when it seemed that the British might attempt an attack on New York from the north. They did not, and only three months after it was built, the Blockhouse was abandoned.

Nonetheless, to the Blockhouse belongs the distinction of being the oldest building in Central Park and one of only two that predate the Park itself (the other being the Arsenal at 64th Street and Fifth Avenue). The thick walls of the Blockhouse are made of

The lily pool at the turn of the century.

rough-hewn rocks; two horizontal gun ports are cut in each wall.

Olmsted and Vaux envisioned the landscape around the Blockhouse as a woodland with paths leading up to the fort from all sides. The most intricately designed walkway was the beautifully crafted approach from the north. It wound up the cliff in pleasing curves and switchbacks, its broad stone steps cutting through the cliff's rock face on the way.

The Blockhouse at the turn of the century.

The Blockhouse today (interior).

A tree survey made in 1873 shows that Olmsted and Vaux enhanced but did little to alter the character of the existing forest. They encouraged native tree species such as hickory, basswood, American linden and beech. They planted English ivy, honeysuckle, clematis and other vines that tumbled over the rocks. A spring to the east of the Blockhouse created a slender stream that, according to the late-nineteenth-century historian Clarence Cook, ran "with a musical tinkle down the slopes, falling from one rocky or reedy basin to another, until, at length, in a series of pretty miniature cascades, it reaches a circular pool on the level ground at the foot of the hill."

In recent years, the Blockhouse has not received very much attention, either from Park managers or the public. The structure is not maintained at all. The commanding view it used to have is partially obscured by trees. Paths are deteriorating, the lily pond at the bottom of the hill is silted up and overgrown, and water no longer cascades down to it. Because of the steep topography and wooded seclusion, it is infrequently visited.

Goals, Priorities and Recommendations

The Blockhouse presents a special opportunity for historic preservation in Central Park. As a surviving remnant of pre-Park history, it is important for both the city and the nation that it be carefully maintained.

The most pressing need, however, is to make this Northwest Corner of Central Park more attractive to visitors. At present, it is a dense forest that rises in an abrupt precipice at the Park's edge. This kind of terrain is forbidding and daunting to pedestrians. Not surprisingly, it is underused. Visitors need psychological inducements to enter here, and they also need to be reassured in some way that it is safe. Landscape redesign can help achieve these goals.

The immediate perimeter landscape along Central Park West and 110th Street dips far below street grade like a moat and is thus rather uninviting. It should be redesigned. The extent of its redesign will depend on whether the vehicular entrance from Frederick Douglass Circle is transformed into a pedestrian promenade or remains as it is at present (see page 51).

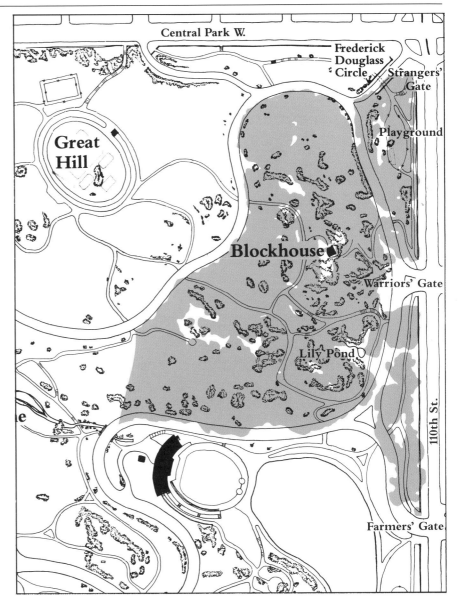

If the vehicular drive is removed here, the arch that links it to the West Drive (and now cuts the perimeter landscape in half) should be removed and the ground raised to street level. This major topographical revision would provide the opportunity to create an entirely new and more agreeable edge landscape.

Whether or not the entrance drive remains for vehicles, some of the open spaces that existed on the steep slopes should be re-created to permit views and let in more light. These glades should be mowed once or twice a year to keep back woody plant growth.

Also, whatever becomes of the drive, the playground at 110th Street should be reconstructed closer to the wall to increase security and make it more appealing.

The deteriorating path system throughout the area should be rebuilt, particularly the winding Victorian fantasy path that approaches the Blockhouse from the north through the rocks.

The lily pond should be dredged and enlarged. The cascades and basins leading to it should be rebuilt. Hemlocks, native shrubs, vines and ground cover should be planted around it.

The Blockhouse itself should be cleaned and its stones repointed. The flagpole in the center, which is neither used nor historically correct, should be removed. A single sign should be installed inside the structure to explain the historic significance of the Blockhouse and this area of the Park as a whole.

The Great Hill

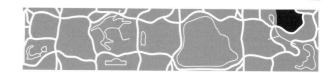

The Great Hill—in the past variously known as Harlem Heights, the Circle, the Concourse and Bogardus Hill—is bounded by Central Park West, the West Drive, the north edge of the Pool and the 106th Street entrance road. It is a 35-acre meadow-and-woodland knoll that rises to a height of 134 feet—the highest elevation in the Upper Park and the third highest overall, after Summit Rock and Vista Rock. Because it once commanded panoramic views of Manhattan, the Palisades and Long Island, the Great Hill was used as a military encampment during the Revolutionary War. Traces of the camp, in fact, were found when the Park was under construction.

Olmsted and Vaux had hoped that a monument of some importance would be placed at the summit, one that could also be used as an observatory. Perhaps, they suggested, there could be a tower to commemorate the completion of the transatlantic cable. None was ever built, although the site was considered briefly as a possible location for Grant's Tomb.

The 1862 plan of the Park shows a carriage road leading up the Great Hill and ending in an oval loop or concourse. The loop served as a carriage overlook. In the middle of it there was a 1.1-acre lawn, and in the course of time, various playing surfaces for racquetball, croquet and shuffleboard were all built there.

A set of wooden steps originally led up from 106th Street, but this was replaced in 1909 by a new walk and a dramatic stone stairway that made its way through clefts in boulders. During the first half-century of the Park's existence, the crest of the Great Hill and its south-facing slope were open meadow. Irregular swaths of turf ran down the other sides. American elms were planted in groups around the concourse on top of the hill, and elsewhere there were clumps of American beech, a few sugar maples and several large clumps of staghorn sumac.

Broken benches were replaced . . .

. . . by new ones in 1986.

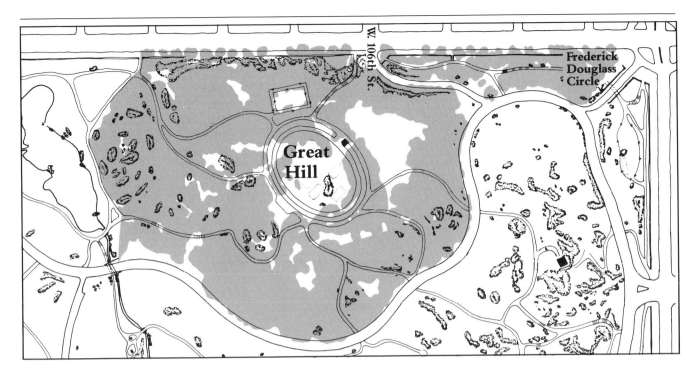

Existing Conditions

Little has been done to maintain or improve the Great Hill since the 1930s. What was once sunny meadow is now largely dense forest. Self-propagated trees have encroached upon lawns and shrouded paths, obscuring the hill crest and obliterating the once sweeping views of the Harlem Plain and, beyond it, Long Island Sound.

These trees consist mainly of ash, black cherry, sycamore and Norway maple, fir, and red oak. As is true elsewhere in the Park, the most numerous species is the black cherry, but here there are other trees of considerable interest, including several American elms surrounding the circular concourse and 22 percent of all the hickory trees to be found in the Park.

Like Summit Rock, the Great Hill's topography and overgrown vegetation tend to isolate it from the surrounding Park, and it is not heavily used. But it does have a growing constituency of families and young professional people from the Upper West Side who populate its remaining open spaces on summer weekends. Dog walkers are the primary users during the week.

Recent steps have been taken to counter the impression of abandonment created by wild vegetation, eroded slopes, unused game courts, broken benches, disintegrating asphalt, dislodged steps and a locked comfort station. The hard-surface playing facilities at the top have been removed and replaced by grass. Plans are now underway to extend the relandscaping to the slopes of the Great Hill, repairing drainage, stabilizing the ground plane and embellishing the area with woodland understory plants.

Goals, Priorities and Recommendations

Thirty years without any form of forest control has permitted an excessively dense woodland to emerge in this sector of the Park. It should be thinned and managed with proper forestry techniques, its few remaining open-lawn spaces enlarged and meadow fingers established in some of the wooded areas.

All of the stone steps should be reset, especially on the 106th Street stairway, and a new walkway constructed to bear the increased pedestrian traffic anticipated in the Northwest Corner of the Park.

Derelict game courts have been returned . . .

. . . to lawn.

The Pool

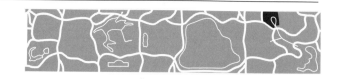

The Pool is a small 2-acre water body located near 102nd Street and Central Park West. Like the other Park water bodies, it is the creation of Olmsted and Vaux. In this case, the designers enlarged a stream, Montayne's Rivulet, to form a picturesque sequence of quiet sheets of standing water linked by five waterfalls that are also artificial, having been created by the massing of boulders in the original streambed. The Pool forms the head of this watercourse, which flows eastward to the Harlem Meer.

Olmsted and Vaux made the Pool a spot of unusual beauty, planting specimen trees on the gently rolling landscape of its south shore. They covered the narrow west edge with dense planting all the way up to the perimeter wall. On the steep slopes up the Great Hill to the north, however, they left an open sunny meadow, and on the southeastern shore they built a small beach that became a favorite haunt of ducks and geese.

Robert Demcker, the horticulturalist who inventoried the Park's plants in 1873, found some interesting vegetation around the Pool. At the water's edge he catalogued, among other things, European wood anemone, skunk cabbage and Dutchman's-breeches. Elsewhere he found dogwood, goldenrod, arrowwood, bog bilberry, ferns, cotoneaster and spring beauty.

A few years later, Central Park Superintendent Samuel Parsons extolled the autumn splendor of the scarlet sumac covering one of the hillsides beside the Pool. In 1903, when Louis Harriman Peet wrote his botanical guide to Central Park, he cited a wide variety of tree species near the Pool. A bald cypress that he found on the west edge is still there today.

In 1961, a water-main break on Central Park West flowed into Central Park, washing away the Pool's tiny rock island and filling in the southwestern cove. This effectively decreased the Pool's surface area from 2 acres to the present 1.5 acres.

Fishing at the mouth of the Pool.

Existing Conditions

Today, the Pool and its surroundings are a composed and peaceful landscape. The grassy topography and majestic trees make it a popular area for family picnics, quiet contemplation, reading, fishing and the investigation of aquatic life. The landscape around the Pool is less distressed than that of other areas of the Park, in part because it is not so intensively used and therefore not subject to trampling.

The area contains a good many mature, well-formed, well-spaced trees, but no single dominant species defines the general character of the space. There are excellent specimens of tulip trees, bald cypress and London plane trees.

In contrast to this general picture of horticultural health, however, the once open meadow on the north slope of the Pool has been filled with volunteer trees and brush, and much of its

ground plane is eroded and bare. The western landscape between the Pool and the wall is now composed of a variety of plants, some of fine quality, but they are now sparser than the original dense shrub layer and therefore do not block out Central Park West as effectively as they should. A semi-swamp now occupies the southwest corner of the Pool, where the cove was filled in during the 1960s. It is constantly wet, generally unused and of only marginal benefit to wildlife.

The Pool itself requires dredging. The depth of sediment in it varies from 7 to 19 inches, and the average depth of the water today is only 2.2 feet, making it likely to flood at least once in a given 10-year cycle. Since foot traffic around the Pool is generally light, there is less erosion along its banks than around any other of the Park's water bodies. Because of its shallow depth, still water and poor flushing movement, the Pool's surface is covered with duckweed and algae in summer.

Goals, Priorities and Recommendations

The Pool is a popular, much-visited feature of the Park. However, lack of maintenance over the years has allowed it to deteriorate somewhat, and the encroaching forest has closed off some of the open spaces in the surrounding landscape.

Straightforward restoration and maintenance is required. This involves dredging the Pool and restoring it to its former area and depth; cleaning its outlet structure so that it can weather storms without flooding; increasing the in-flow pressure to flush the Pool periodically and rid it of duckweed; rebuilding the beach on the south shore to provide easy and nondamaging access to the water's edge; and planting aquatic, emergent and wetland vegetation elsewhere along the shore to stabilize the soil and provide wildlife habitats.

Whereas it would be historically correct to rebuild the island, the Pool is a very small water body and would probably be best off without it.

As with other portions of the Park's north end, the Pool landscape is overgrown in places. The north slope, for instance, should be gradually returned to open space, permitting views to-

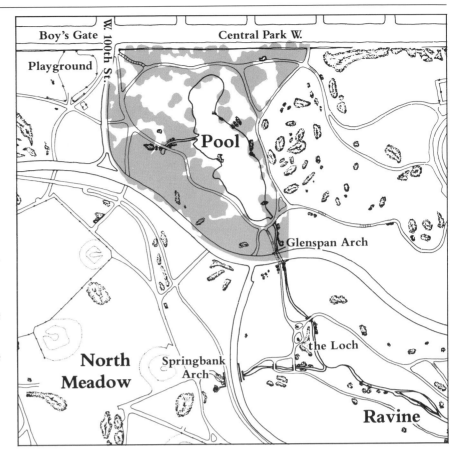

ward and from the Great Hill and providing a sunny south-facing meadow—a rare amenity in this part of the Park. Generally, there should be a selective removal of volunteer trees in order to bring the specimens back into view.

Thick understory trees and shrubs, recommended elsewhere as a screen along the Park's border, should be planted on the western slope beside the perimeter wall. The sumac admired by Samuel Parsons should be reintroduced.

The landscape surrounding the Pool is one of the most romantic and unspoiled in Central Park.

The Ravine

Frederick Law Olmsted had hoped that the whole of Central Park would serve as a place where city people could escape to a country setting, where the sights, sounds, filth and noise of the city would be nowhere in evidence. He even proposed that buildings along the Park's perimeter not be allowed to rise above a certain height so that they could not be seen from within the Park. He achieved only partial success.

Skyscrapers line the edges of the Park today like giant cliffs, an ever-present—albeit stunningly romantic—reminder of the city that surrounds it. The landscapes in the Park are indeed reminiscent of the country, and there are even a few locations from which the tall buildings cannot be seen and the sounds of the city cannot be heard. Of all such places, however, only one truly achieves a transformation from urban to rural ambience. It is a deep, heavily wooded gorge at the north end of the Park with a tumbling brook coursing along the bottom of it. Visitors to the Ravine are totally shut off from the city, magically transported to a woodland environment that resembles the Adirondacks.

The brook at the bottom of the Ravine is called the Loch. Loch, of course, is Scottish for "lake," which is a misnomer and has been for many years. Olmsted and Vaux created the Loch out of Montayne's Rivulet, an ambling stream that flowed west to east at about 102nd Street and emptied into the salt marshes of Harlem Creek at Fifth Avenue and 107th Street, now the Harlem Meer. Montayne's Rivulet was dredged and widened into a varied water sequence that started with the Pool and then flowed over a series of small waterfalls into the 525-foot-long Loch, which in turn emptied into the Harlem Meer. The waterfalls were constructed from exposed bedrock; schist boulders were placed as if by nature to form dams and spillways. In order to obtain a sufficient volume of water to supply this enlarged watercourse, natural drainage into the Ravine had to be supplemented with storm

The original watercourse through the Ravine designed by Olmsted and Vaux consisted of five man-made cascades . . .

. . . and several rustic pedestrian bridges. . . .

The stream flowed under Glen Span Arch . . .

water carried by underground pipes from nearby Drives and walkways as well as by another pipe carrying the overflow from the Reservoir.

To allow the Carriage Drive to pass overhead without intruding, three rustic stone arches were built—Glen Span, Springbanks and Huddlestone. Glen Span and Huddlestone arches crossed over both the stream and a pathway beside it. Springbanks Arch, off to the south, carried pedestrians under a now unused portion of the Carriage Drive to the North Meadow. Fed by a creek from the North Meadow, two pools were constructed at Springbanks, one on either side of the arch. In addition, rustic wood bridges, benches and handrails were placed here and there in the Ravine landscape.

The southeast slope of the Ravine was designed to be a steep meadow dotted with copses of trees. The north-west slope was to be heavily canopied except for a few open glades close to Glen Span. In the early days, stream-side vegetation included bullrushes, rose mallow, skunk cabbage, winterberry, sweet fern, sweet birch and several varieties of iris. Clematis and Virginia creeper were planted around the arches.

Existing Conditions

Compared with other parts of the Park, the Ravine has been the least disturbed by human beings. Nature, however, was quick to reclaim the Loch. Soil from the steep slopes washed into it, turning it into a marshy stream with reeds and stagnant pools. Park managers dug out tons of mud in 1915 and then in 1931 lined the Loch and its banks with large stones in order to prevent further erosion. Today, however, as in 1915, the Loch is filled with a thick bed of silt in which black willow trees have been able to take root and grow. The Loch is now just a sluggish trickle.

The one very clear evidence of human activity in the area is the Lasker

. . . into the Loch . . .

. . . then under Huddlestone Arch . . .

. . . to empty into the Meer.

Same view today, with the stream channeled beneath Lasker Rink and Pool.

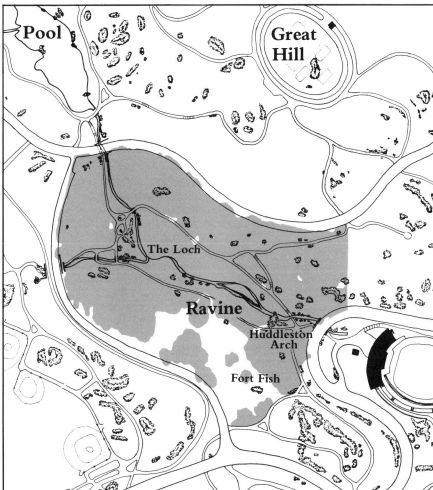

Pool and Rink, built in 1962 at the south end of the Ravine where the Loch flows into the Meer. The rink was positioned below the Loch directly over an island at the mouth of the Meer; architecturally, it has the appearance of a large concrete dam. Not being large enough to carry off all the water from the Ravine during heavy rains, drainage pipes placed under the structure to carry storm water into the Meer periodically clog up with sediment. The result is occasional flooding, particularly around Huddlestone Arch. Farther upstream, the pools at Springbanks Arch have been filled in and no longer serve as a drain-off for storm water.

Even though copious amounts of topsoil from the upper slopes of the Ravine have been lost, a mature woodland canopy has established itself. On the northwest slope, the tree population has not changed much in composition over the past 50 years. Oaks have declined in number, but they are still the third most common species

after the Norway maple and planetree maple. However, self-seeded black cherries have taken over the southeast slope, and in the disturbed soil along the 102nd Street cross drive, where dredge material has been dumped over the years, a 16,800-square-foot plot of Japanese knotweed is rapidly spreading.

The pathway system throughout the Ravine has deteriorated seriously. All of the original rustic wood bridges, benches and handrails are gone.

Goals, Priorities and Recommendations

The beautiful sequence of quiet pools and melodious waterfalls threading through the Ravine—one of Olmsted and Vaux's most sensitive pieces of landscape design—should be at least partially restored.

Some parts of the Ravine slopes should be resoiled. The soil should be kept in

Lasker Pool . . .

. . . becomes Lasker Rink in winter.

place with heavy boulders, dense shrubs and ground cover plantings.

The walkway system should be reconstructed with narrow asphalt paths that catch water from the surrounding slopes and funnel it into a new catch-basin system. Rehabilitation of the drainage system on the Carriage Drive above the Ravine should be done simultaneously, because its runoff directly affects the drainage pattern on the slopes below.

The rustic bridges, benches and railings should be rebuilt. The rock work throughout the Ravine, especially on the bridges, has a good deal of charm and delicacy, and should be restored.

The Ravine is a protected valley, which has its own unique microclimate. In the summer, the sun hits the tops of the trees but does not penetrate, and in winter the wind blows over it, not into it. This spares the Ravine from extremes of temperature and makes it likely that certain plants that are only marginally hardy in this region might survive here.

The East Meadow

The East Meadow is for the most part an open lawn punctuated by rock outcrops and some of the Park's most stately trees. Its terrain is bowl-shaped; the northern portion is steeper and rockier than the pastoral southern section.

The original Greensward Plan envisioned this area—bounded by Fifth Avenue, the East Drive, the 97th Street transverse and 102nd Street—as part of an arboretum that was never built. It became a meadow instead and was planted with beeches, oaks and honey locusts, some of which have grown to magnificent proportions.

The East Meadow has remained essentially unchanged over the years. There is one noticeable difference, however, and that is in the expansion of its tree population. In the 1934 tree count, a total of 278 trees of six-inch caliper or greater were found on the East Meadow. There are now 392. The distribution of species has also changed. In 1934, black cherries accounted for only 3 percent of the total stand; today, they represent 26 percent. Meanwhile, other species have decreased: elms from 33 percent to 15 percent, oaks from 13 percent to 12 percent and beeches from 8 percent to 3 percent. Inasmuch as black cherries are self-seeding and invasive, their vastly increased numbers is not a positive trend.

The meadow's expanse of green lawn receives heavy athletic use by school groups, and as has happened elsewhere in the Park, the soil has become compacted and bare. In combination with the bowl-shaped landscape, this condition results in frequent flooding; after a rain, a pool of water is often left standing here. The steeper sides of the meadow are popular for picnics and sunning. The playground at 100th Street, however, is seldom used. Children and parents seem to prefer the lawn.

An elm in the East Meadow.

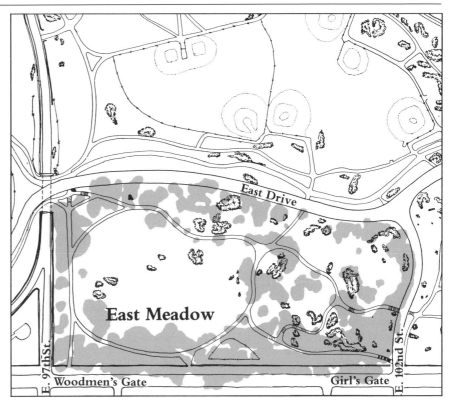

Goals, Priorities and Recommendations

The East Meadow is a prime example of how various neighborhood constituencies compete for use of the same space: in this case, school athletic teams, families and individuals. Permits are presently issued for school athletics, and this policy should continue and be closely monitored so that access by the other users of the East Meadow is not in any way impeded.

Some minor relandscaping is required as well. The lower part of the meadow should be slightly regraded to promote better drainage; paths and steps set into the upper slopes need to be rebuilt; some of the small volunteer trees should be removed; erosion on the slope toward the 102nd Street Drive

should be controlled through new planting; and the infrequently used playground at 100th Street should possibly be reconverted to greensward, thus making this northern section of general-use open space equal in size to the Sheep Meadow farther south.

The East Meadow, 1986.

The North Meadow

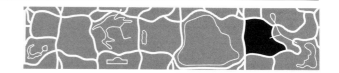

The 19-acre North Meadow is the largest of Central Park's open meadow spaces. Originally, the landscape was a barren plateau that lay between the marshes of Harlem Creek and the plot of land staked out for the new Reservoir. Olmsted and Vaux set to work transforming it into a pastoral meadow.

The clearest indication of how well they succeeded can be seen in the words of the landscape architect and Superintendent of the Park Samuel Parsons. In 1891, Parsons wrote of the North Meadow: "It is a wonderful effect. . . . The sheen of the grass, the varied tints of the foliage sweeping the turf . . . the low-lying hillocks crowned with large forest trees, the great boulders entirely exposed or only half submerged, the meadow beyond running back to seemingly unknown distances. There is dignity, there is breadth, repose. . . . It is genuine park scenery . . . one of the best examples we have of good park work."

In his lengthy and glowing description, Parsons mentions that this former tableland had become not only a rolling meadow but one that was "ridged up in long mounds at places," somewhat like "headlands left unlevelled." There was not, he said, a level spot in the whole meadow.

The meadow Parsons admired no longer exists. Decades of heavy athletic use—including croquet, lawn tennis, cricket, football, baseball and softball—have taken their toll. The rolling turf was flattened long ago to accommodate the ball fields. The unbroken sweeping vista has been cut up with hurricane fences, chain-link backstops and asphalt paths. The effect of an endless meadow with a subtle, undulating border has been destroyed by a dense perimeter wall of trees. The sheen of the grass is but a distant memory. As long ago as 1927, the landscape architect Herman Merkel, in making his report on the condition of the Park, said of the North Meadow: "It cannot longer be called a meadow or lawn by any stretch of the imagination."

Today, the North Meadow has seven baseball fields, five softball fields, six handball courts and concrete bleachers. These facilities get almost constant use. On warm-weather weekdays between 5 and 7 P.M., over 500 people can usually be found playing one game or another in the North Meadow. On Sundays, the number climbs to over 1,000. Baseball leagues use the diamonds during the season; public and private schools are in evidence from early morning until dusk for gym classes and intramural sports. All of these activities require Parks Department permits, but, unlike the Heckscher Playground, play occurs on the North Meadow regardless of ground conditions.

Goals, Priorities and Recommendations

The 1983 user study of Central Park observed that the North Meadow "is Central Park for most of the people who live in lower Spanish Harlem or in the vast housing projects of the Upper West Side." The report concluded that "anything that could be done to upgrade the facilities here and to extend the capacity of the sports fields would be worth serious study."

This plan seeks to enhance the present heavy program of sports and restore some of the aesthetic qualities of the badly damaged landscape. The impression of a limitless greensward "running back to seemingly unknown distances"

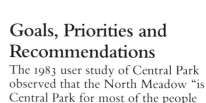

Baseball, North Meadow.

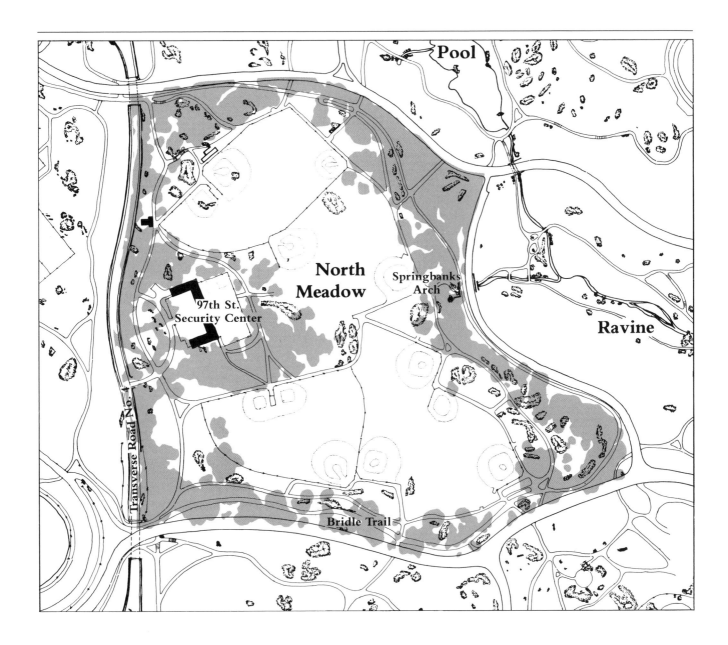

North Meadow

Springbanks Arch

97th St. Security Center

Transverse Road No.

Bridle Trail

Pool

Ravine

Football, softball and soccer are played on the North Meadow.

can be re-created by softening the perimeter tree line.

In addition, Springbanks Arch should be restored—its drainage repaired, plantings renewed and lighting installed—so that it can once again serve as a link between the sunny North Meadow and the shaded woodland of the Ravine to the north.

The portion of the Winter Drive along the western edge of the North Meadow should be restored by the addition of various evergreens, such as pine, azalea, winterberry and cypress. And the section of the Bridle Trail that traverses this area should be repaired.

The Reservoir and The Upper West Walkway

The 106-acre Reservoir is the largest single landscape feature in Central Park. Together with the land around it (from the West Drive to Fifth Avenue, between 86th and 96th streets), it forms a zone of separation between what Olmsted called the Upper and Lower parks.

The Reservoir was built in 1862, when the original Croton Reservoir (now the Great Lawn) became insufficient to serve the water-supply needs of the city. Its curvilinear shape is largely due to the persuasiveness of the man who was then the engineer of the new Park, Anton Viele. Viele argued that the new reservoir should not be rectangular like the old one but should have a more graceful and natural form.

In spite of this aesthetic gesture, the Reservoir posed problems for the designers Olmsted and Vaux. It filled so much of the Park from side to side that it was a virtual barrier to north-south traffic. To the east, between the Reservoir and Fifth Avenue, there remained only a narrow, 200-foot-wide strip. That space was developed to include a pedestrian path, the Bridle Trail and a Carriage Drive, all of which ran in straight lines. The drive was flanked on both sides by double rows of trees, which gave it a formality similar in character to the Mall. The north and west sides were not as constricted as the east side, and so provided opportunity for some open meadow spaces. The South Meadow (actually to the north of the Reservoir) was used for lawn tennis but could be returned to pastoral scenery simply by removing the nets. The west side was horticulturally a part of the Winter Drive and was a composed sequence of evergreens (mostly conifers) and open spaces.

According to the contemporary historian Clarence Cook, the pedestrian walkway around the Reservoir provided an "admirable 'constitutional'" in the early days of the Park. It afforded a fine breeze, dancing waves and a setting for beautiful sunsets. Three cast-iron arches (Bridges 24, 27

Lawn tennis on the South Meadow at the turn of the century.

Permanent tennis courts now occupy the South Meadow.

The Reservoir, 1960s.

and 28) were built to carry pedestrians over the Bridle Trail to the walkway, and two ornamental stone gatehouses were constructed—one at the north shore, where water entered the Reservoir, and one at the south, where it exited to the gravity-fed city water system.

By 1903, the East Drive along the Reservoir embankment was being called "the most popular drive in this country." At the time, however, the entrance at East 90th Street provided only carriage access to the Park. The Upper East Side had become densely populated since the Park was built, and the increasing numbers of pedestrians using this entrance found themselves having to cross both the East Drive and the Bridle Trail to reach the

pedestrian path. To ease this congestion somewhat, the Park managers constructed a new walk along the east side of the drive from 85th to 98th streets and redesigned the entrance at 90th Street to accommodate pedestrians. The 1903 Annual Report described the project as difficult to engineer because of the topography and trees but well worth the effort, "demonstrated by the great numbers of pedestrians who have used this point of vantage on every pleasant day to enjoy the spectacle presented on the East Drive."

In 1908, 10,000 rhododendrons were put into the ground along the East Drive from 85th Street to 97th Street, replacing herbaceous beds and shrubs. Samuel Parsons, then Central Park's

landscape architect, imported most of the plants from England and introduced a wide variety of exotic species intermingled with the native *Rhododendron maximum*. Parsons added new soil and mixed in some rich peat mold to help the plants flourish. He also piped in a special supply of water so that they could be irrigated during the summer months. Nevertheless, because of general site conditions and toxic fumes from automobiles on the East Drive, the rhododendron plantation did not thrive. It has dwindled over the years, and today only a remnant of it is left.

The tree population in the Reservoir area changed considerably over time. A tree inventory compiled in 1873 shows a heavy representation along the West

Drive of evergreens, cedars, junipers, pines—all in great profusion. However, by 1934, when another survey was done, the Winter Drive had only a few scattered pines, while the population of oaks, cherries and maples had surged dramatically. On the south side, along the Bridle Trail, turkey oaks *(Quercus cerris)* are shown on both the 1873 and 1934 surveys; and today many of these survive as venerable specimens, together with the numerous large beeches.

The 1934 survey also indicates the same composition of sycamores, elms and maples along the East Drive with symmetrical plantings of ornamental cherries on either side of the new John Purroy Mitchel Monument. But the meadow area to the north has suffered a substantial loss of tree variety. What used to be an assortment of maples, elms, oaks, ginkgoes and sycamores has now become a forest of spindly wild cherries. Much of the meadow itself has disappeared and has been replaced by tennis courts. The original grass courts were replaced in 1912 with dirt courts, which were improved in 1914 and made permanent in 1929. The Tennis House was completed the next year and was, in the estimation of the authors of the Annual Report of 1930, "probably the finest tennis house in any public park in this country."

One important change throughout the project area has been the development of a more extensive tree canopy, with smaller and fewer open spaces for sunning and picnicking than there used to be. The Reservoir banks, too, are now crowded with weeds and other spontaneous vegetation and have lost much of their open quality—a visual closing-in that has created security problems for joggers using the track.

Existing Conditions

In spite of the fact that the bulk of the project area is taken up by the Reservoir itself, which is fenced and off limits to the public, the site is one of the most heavily visited in the Park. The pedestrian path around the Reservoir was resurfaced in 1982 for use as a running track. For the past 10 years or so, it has been used continuously throughout the day by an estimated 5,000 joggers, quite successfully, with the minor exception that runners frequently take short cuts up the steep slopes of the embankment to the track, wearing away ground cover and causing soil erosion.

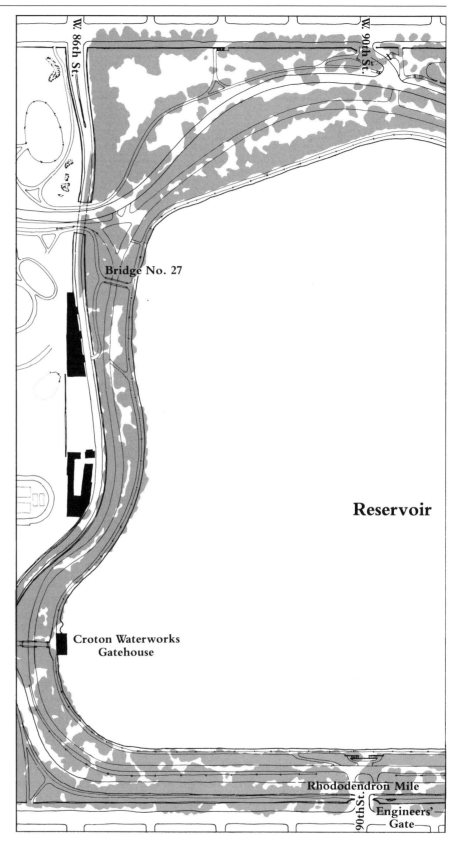

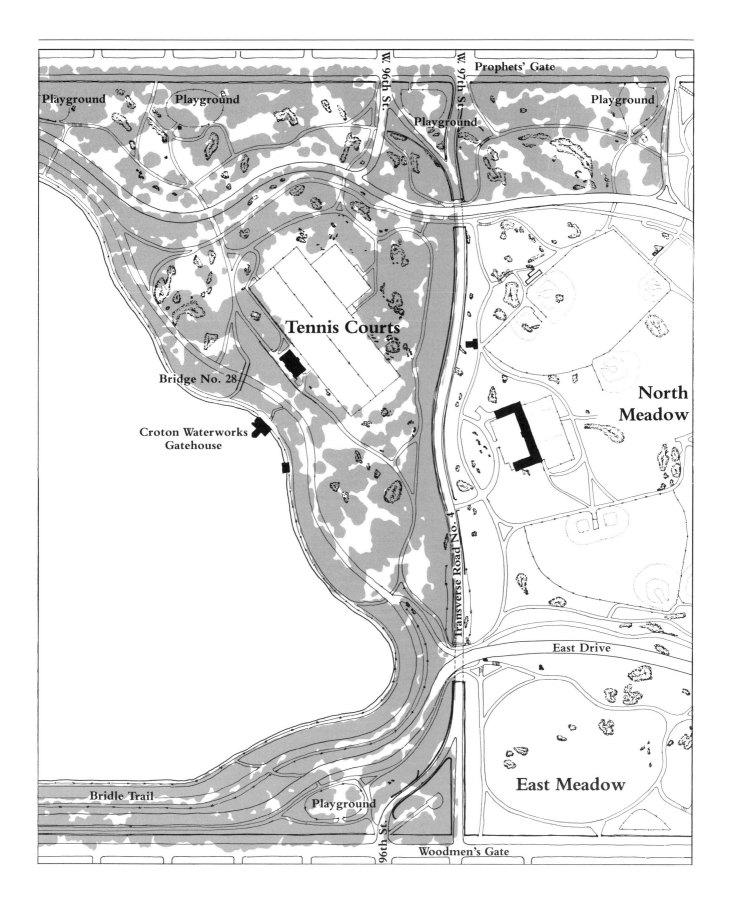

Runners warming up at the East 90th Street entrance.

Erosion is a problem elsewhere in the project area, too. The Bridle Trail is badly worn away where it connects with the North Meadow loop on the east side; its Telford rubble base is now exposed, and little soft surface remains. The most visible and potentially grave erosion in the area, however, is at the Park perimeter between the East Drive and the wall. Dense shade, in addition to the cumulative effects of age and lack of horticultural maintenance, has created a bare ground plane. Surface runoff from the pedestrian path washes soil down against the perimeter wall, where the increased weight heaves stones out of alignment. Water has begun to seep through the wall in places where subsurface drains have broken down. A potentially dangerous situation exists here, because the soil pushing against the wall on the Park side is considerably above the level of the sidewalk on Fifth Avenue.

Each of the features in the Reservoir project area is heavily used, some more efficiently than others, and some by competing constituencies.

The tennis courts are extremely popular, but like most single-use facilities, they lie unused for part of the year. The pedestrian path around the Reservoir is so dominated by joggers that the entrance at East 90th Street has been nicknamed "Runner's Gate" (its historic name is Engineer's Gate). Some pedestrians who want to stroll around the Reservoir for a look at the

view complain that it is a daunting experience, with joggers constantly jostling past them in both directions. The Reservoir loop is the most heavily used portion of the Bridle Trail, because it is broad, flat and in better (albeit deteriorated) condition than

The Bridle Trail south of the Reservoir has drainage problems.

elsewhere. In addition, the commercial riding stable serving the Park is on West 89th Street, which makes this part of the Bridle Trail the most easily accessible. The walk along the East Drive is an important and much-traveled part of the north-south pedestrian circulation spine. Motor vehicles use the drive here with frequency; taxis exit at 90th Street during all hours.

A major conflict involving all of this traffic occurs at Engineer's Gate (East 90th Street), where runners, pedestri-

ans, equestrians and vehicles all criss-cross one another. Runners and pedestrians frequently use the Bridle Trail against Park rules, creating a hazard for themselves and those on horseback. Runners warm up and cool down anywhere they can find the space at East 90th Street, often on the Bridle Trail's straightaway, where horses are likely to be moving quickly (although galloping, too, is against Park rules). With the exception of Bridge 24 (at the South Gatehouse), the cast-iron bridges designed to take pedestrians over the Bridle Trail are so placed that they are seldom used now and have become little more than beautiful artifacts. (Numbers 27 and 28 were recently restored; number 24 is in great need of repair.)

Goals, Priorities and Recommendations

Improving safety, security and circulation are immediate priorities in this project area. The planners' intention is to increase the area's usefulness for both active and passive recreation, while enhancing its scenic beauty.

Security along the Reservoir would be improved by removing the high, thick, concealing plants that surround it. These should be replaced with ground covers and low-growing shrubs that would allow runners a more open view and also perform the vital function of holding the soil in place.

The confusion and traffic hazards at the East 90th Street entrance could be resolved with better articulation of the various routes and directional signs.

The entire loop of the Bridle Trail around the Reservoir needs to be completely rebuilt to include a new drainage system and a restored surface.

The firs and conifers should be restored along the historic Winter Drive on the west side. The Fifth Avenue perimeter should be selectively thinned and grubbed, replanted with shrubs and understory trees, and the drainage system behind the wall rebuilt.

The rhododendron beds at the eastern edge of the Reservoir should be replaced with shrubs and ground covers that will endure better in this location. Erosion-causing drainage problems on the Bridle Trail above should be corrected first and the gouged-out gullies resoiled and replanted.

The Long-Term Future of the Reservoir

A rare and exciting design opportunity will present itself for the Reservoir in 10 or 15 years, when New York City's third water tunnel is completed. At that time the Reservoir will become obsolete, and the Department of Parks and Recreation will take over the management of the site from the Department of Environmental Protection.

Present thinking—preliminary at this stage—envisions keeping the Reservoir as a body of water but redesigning it as a beautiful, natural-looking lake. The shoreline could be made softer and more irregular than it is now, and parts of the artificial berm that rims it could be lowered to create a more natural littoral.

The surface area of the Reservoir is 106 acres at present, five times the size of the Lake. If even part of this were opened up to public use, it would offer an abundance of recreational opportunities. There could be swimming from a beach or pier, sailing, windsurfing, rowboating, canoeing and iceskating. The lake could even be stocked with fish.

On the other hand, another possibility would be to go in the opposite direction and fill in the Reservoir, as was done to the old rectangular reservoir in making the Great Lawn. Such a move would more than double the space available in Central Park for team sports. Clearly, a separate and detailed study on the Reservoir options will be necessary before any decision is made.

Whatever course is taken, planners will have an opportunity to redesign this sizable piece of Central Park—12 percent of the Park's total area.

The Upper West Walkway

Rolling terrain, typical of the upper west side perimeter.

The narrow undulating landscape along the western edge of Central Park from 86th Street to 100th Street is particularly interesting because it contains some of the most beautifully sculptured landforms in the Park. Its rolling lawns and meadows are ribboned with curving paths that disappear behind knolls and then reappear.

Because the West Drive in this section was part of the Winter Drive, Olmsted and Vaux banked it with pines and other evergreens set off by a counterpoint of white birches. Today, only 3 percent of the trees are pines; 20 percent are the prolific self-propagating black cherry.

Between 1935 and 1938, no fewer than four playgrounds were built in this area of the Park—at 91st, 93rd, 96th and 100th streets. Today, only those at 93rd and 100th streets are heavily used. Neither the playground at 91st Street, which is badly sited on top of a hill, nor the playground in the triangle created by the entrance and exit of the transverse road is as popular.

Strollers, picnickers and sunbathers are the most typical users of this perimeter strip. The meadow from 86th Street to 88th Street is used for active sports and has a large bare patch of compacted soil to prove it—the one unsightly element in an otherwise green landscape.

There are circulation problems created by poor design at one entrance, competition between horses and pedestrians at another, and the lack of any clear routes leading to the Reservoir running track, a major destination for Park runners.

Goals, Priorities and Recommendations

Only minor work is necessary in this project area.

The Winter Drive should be restored by the planting of additional evergreens.

The meadow at 86th Street should be regraded to improve its drainage. It should then be resoiled, seeded and carefully managed to prevent damage to the turf in wet weather.

The entrance at West 88th Street, added in recent years and poorly designed, should be closed. A new entrance should be opened between 86th Street and 87th Street, where the grades are gentler.

The entrance to the Park Drive at 90th Street, where there is now competition between cars and horses, should be reconstructed as an equestrian path leading to the Bridle Trail. New pedestrian paths should be built to take people from perimeter entrances to the Reservoir running track.

Reconversion of the underutilized playgrounds into parkland should be studied.

The Great Lawn

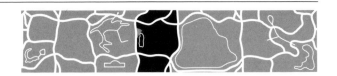

The Great Lawn is an almost flat open space of some 15 acres in the center of Central Park. It is the largest single feature that was not part of Olmsted and Vaux's original design, and there is no way it could have been. It stands on the site of the old Croton Reservoir, a huge, high-walled rectangular structure that had to be incorporated in the original Greensward Plan because it was a functioning part of Manhattan's water supply at the time.

Olmsted made no secret of his unhappiness about the reservoir. "It occupies the whole of the middle of the Park," he wrote, "and is a blank, uninteresting object that can in no way be made particularly attractive." The reservoir, together with a "new" reservoir to the north that was contemporary with the Park's construction and that still exists, interrupted the flow of the landscape and effectively divided the Park into upper and lower sections. Olmsted and Vaux sought to ignore the reservoirs, pretending they didn't exist, by aligning north-south pedestrian paths in such a way as to bypass them and draw the eye away from the high stone walls.

When the old Croton Reservoir was dismantled and filled in to make the Great Lawn in 1934, the sense of a divided Park was somewhat lessened. But the site's isolation from the rest of

A temporary shantytown appeared during the Depression after the old Croton Reservoir was drained and prior to the construction of the Great Lawn in 1934.

the Park's circulation system was never adequately redressed, and pedestrian access to the Great Lawn remains a major problem today. Since continuity between the Great Lawn and the surrounding landscape is still an objective to be achieved, the peripheral borders are included in the Great Lawn project area, which encompasses the entire width of the Park between the 79th Street and 86th Street transverses.

When the old Croton Reservoir was turned over to the Parks Department by the Department of Water Supply in 1929, numerous proposals were submitted for how to use the space. The plan ultimately put into effect by Parks Commissioner Robert Moses in 1934 called for a central Beaux Arts oval lawn with a small lake (Belvedere Lake) at the south end. At the north end, there were to be two large chil-

The Croton Reservoir being filled with rubble in the 1930s (viewed from the north).

The newly completed Oval, 1936, with the shoreline of Belvedere Lake in foreground.

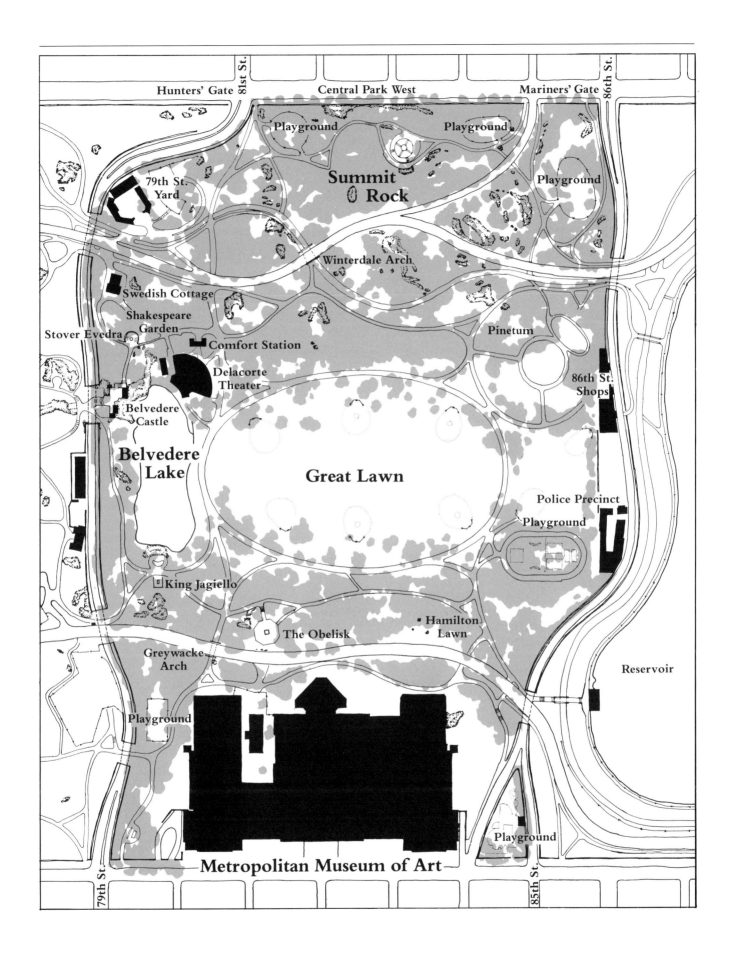

Hunters' Gate 81st St. Central Park West Mariners' Gate 86th St.

Playground Playground

Playground

Summit Rock

79th St. Yard

Winterdale Arch

Swedish Cottage

Shakespeare Garden

Pinetum

Stover Evedra

Comfort Station

86th St. Shops

Delacorte Theater

Belvedere Castle

Belvedere Lake

Great Lawn

Police Precinct

Playground

King Jagiello

The Obelisk

Hamilton Lawn

Greywacke Arch

Reservoir

Playground

Playground

79th St. 85th St.

Metropolitan Museum of Art

The view from the Belvedere, 1890.

The same view today with the Delacorte Theater, the restored Belvedere pavilion and Belvedere Lake in place of the old reservoir.

dren's playgrounds, and the rest of the area was to consist of landscaped walks, shuffleboard, croquet and lawn bowling. The oval lawn was closed to the public to preserve the grass.

Moses's plan represented a victory for those who were determined to prevent conversion of the area into extensive athletic fields, but it was a temporary victory. There are now a half dozen ball fields with backstops on the lawn. And since the restoration of the Sheep Meadow in 1979, the lawn has been used as the site for large outdoor concerts that attract over 100,000 people.

Existing Conditions

The space, despite its problems, is one of the few great, dramatic open plains in New York. In one corner, Belvedere Castle perches romantically on the top of a steep rock outcrop that rises from the water surrounding it. On the east, west and south rise the towers of New York; on the north, the horizon appears limitless because of the unbroken

sky. Some of the Park's best specimen quality trees surround the oval. But the Great Lawn and its environs are in declining condition. Some portions of this large Central Park space are unused, others are overused, and design shortcomings reduce both its recreational utility and aesthetic quality.

After its construction in 1934, the Great Lawn became a popular user destination—something the area had not been designed for originally. The original pedestrian paths, laid out to avoid the new and old reservoirs, have never been properly redesigned to accommodate the flow of foot traffic, particularly the crowds that attend free concerts on the Great Lawn. Pedestrian access to and from the Great Lawn is confusing and inadequate, and lanes of exit are too few and dangerously constricted.

Free concerts by the Philharmonic and Metropolitan Opera as well as popular entertainers on the Great Lawn have become a contemporary tradition that is highly prized by thousands of New Yorkers. But in addition to the

management problems these mass gatherings pose, the large number of people who attend them—300,000 at the Elton John concert in 1980 and nearly 750,000 at the Anti-Nuclear Rally in 1982—compact the soil and hasten erosion. Indeed, 34 percent of the ground plane throughout the Great Lawn project area is bare.

The chief erosion factor, however, is not the concerts but the intensive athletic use of the Great Lawn, which has turned it into a hardpan desert. No fewer than 40 permitted baseball and softball games take place on the Great Lawn every day throughout the season, plus uncounted dozens of pickup soccer and touch football games. The eight ball fields are in deplorable condition, with barely discernible diamonds and large, visually obtrusive backstops.

To the north of the oval, the two Moses-era playgrounds have fallen into disuse and disrepair. One has a broken mud-filled wading pool, and the other is also deserted except for two basketball courts that do receive some use. Between the playgrounds, two barren

Forty softball games can be played by permit holders on the Great Lawn daily.

Impromptu soccer games.

114

makeshift ball fields contribute to the atmosphere of abandonment. To make matters worse, maintenance and security vehicles scar the northern edge with tire ruts in an effort to achieve a parkside access to the 86th Street shops and the Central Park police precinct. Police personnel park their cars and gain entry to their facility, located on the transverse road 13 feet below the grade of the Great Lawn, by climbing down a wooden ladder. Park workers make attic-level deliveries to their building as well as to the attic level of the police precinct, which is currently used as an auxiliary Parks Department shop and storage area.

These conditions would not seem propitious for the siting of the Arthur Ross Pinetum, but this was, in fact, the location chosen by the Parks Department in 1971, when Mr. Ross initiated the installation of the conifer collection that bears his name. There are many choice specimens here that, if sited elsewhere or rearranged somewhat, could make a much more striking landscape composition.

The landscape immediately to the south of the oval is a crowded one. Belvedere Lake, less than three acres in area, is bounded on the west by the Delacorte Theater and on the east by the folk-dancing circle and a statue of a medieval king of Poland, Wlayslaw Jagiello. Vista Rock stands at the southwest edge of the lake; and the Shakespeare Garden and the Swedish Cottage lie at the foot of its western slope.

In the early days, a fire tower stood at the top of Vista Rock, but when the Croton Board transferred title to the Parks Department in 1867, Calvert Vaux designed a fanciful Victorian castle to take its place. The castle was constructed mostly out of parent rock from excavations elsewhere in the Park. The United States Weather Bureau set up a weather station in the castle in 1919, but after the introduction of mechanized instrumentation in the 1960s, the building was left unmanned and fell prey to vandalism. It was restored in 1982, and two pavilions that had been removed 50 years earlier were rebuilt. At that time, the castle became an environmental education center for children.

Belvedere Castle serves as a picturesque focus for visitors looking south from the Great Lawn. It is also the visual terminus of the northward view from the Mall, its tower visible over

Belvedere Castle was designed to crown Vista Rock.

the wooded Ramble, perfectly centered above Bethesda Fountain. Unfortunately, the view of the castle from the Great Lawn is substantially blocked from the west by the Delacorte Theater, a 1960 addition to the landscape, and a row of tall poplar trees planted to hide the theater from view.

The shores of Belvedere Lake are a popular gathering spot for picnickers and theater and concert patrons in the summer months. The lake itself is quite small and has none of the naturalistic coves and inlets typical of the Park's older water bodies. Eroded soil from the surrounding lawns washes directly into it, and the accumulated sedimentation has created a hypereutrophic condition: the lake is marshy and dying. The narrow embankment lawns around it are often filled to capacity with picnickers and sunbathers, hemmed in by sidewalks to the north and south, by the Delacorte Theater to the west and by the folk-dancing area to the east. The folk dancing has outgrown the paved area designated for its use. Dancers must continually widen their circles beyond the pavement and onto the lawn.

Farther to the east of the Great Lawn, the landscape surrounding the Metropolitan Museum of Art was originally designed as a pastoral meadow dotted with trees. The meadow was linked to the Great Lawn by Greywake Arch under the East Drive. As the museum expanded through a succession of additions over the years, the meadow became smaller and smaller until its general character was quite lost. At the same time, north-south pedestrian circulation became increasingly pinched, and the path traversing this landscape eventually became pinned to the East Drive.

Opposite the museum, the Obelisk, or Cleopatra's Needle, which once stood on the seashore at Alexandria, was installed just west of the East Drive in 1881 after a complicated and sometimes comical diplomatic roundabout between the United States and Egypt. It stands on the southern edge of Hamilton Lawn, a small meadow surrounded by trees framing a statue of Alexander Hamilton, which was erected at the same time as the Obelisk. The Levy Memorial Playground just southwest of the museum was constructed in 1957.

To the west of the Great Lawn lie the Shakespeare Garden and the Swedish Cottage. The Shakespeare Garden, a series of pathways, pools and cascades interspersed with examples of plants mentioned in the works of Shakespeare, was built into the western slope of Vista Rock in 1917. The garden thrives with the help of a group of volunteer gardeners, but its visual relationship to Belvedere Castle above is unfortunately obscured through poor design.

The wooden-lodge-style Swedish Cottage at the foot of the garden was a gift of the Swedish government following the 1876 Centennial Exposition in Philadelphia and was used as a comfort station until 1912, when, because of protests by Swedish-American citizens, it was turned into an entomology laboratory. In 1973, the cottage

was renovated a second time and converted into the present marionette theater.

Another feature distinguishes the area to the west of the Great Lawn: Summit Rock, the highest natural point in Central Park, at the westernmost edge of the Park at 83rd Street. Summit Rock once offered a commanding view of the landscape below. Over time, however, the slopes have been so heavily planted with trees that there is no longer any view at all. A children's sand pit and sitting area was constructed on the top of the rock in the 1930s, but because of its excessively secluded character the area is now unfrequented; the sand pit lies vacant, the benches around it broken. As for the evergreens planted along the Winter Drive by Olmsted, they have almost all died out.

There are three perimeter playgrounds on the west side of the Park—at 81st Street, 85th Street and 86th Street—all constructed in 1935 in a standard oval shape, 100 feet by 200 feet. The one at 85th Street is largely unused. The 79th Street Yard, a set of low buildings that was originally used as a stable, now houses maintenance and horticultural operations, and there is a well-maintained comfort station next to the Delacorte Theater.

Goals, Priorities and Recommendations

Two overriding issues affect all sectors of the Great Lawn project area: circulation and programming. The east-west pedestrian routes must be redesigned to provide convenient access to this piece of the Park and to tie it in to the surrounding landscape. Programming should accommodate a variety of activities—team sports, large public gatherings and informal relaxation.

Project Subsector 1:
The Great Lawn oval, Belvedere Lake and the North End

Apart from the two objectives cited above, the chief concerns in redesigning this subsector are to relieve congestion of sunbathers and picnickers beside Belvedere Lake and increase the naturalistic, Olmstedian quality of this flat open space that is so uncharacteristic of Central Park's gently rolling topography.

The congestion would be relieved if the oval were shifted 200 feet north-

ward. Such a move would allow the amount of space allocated for sports to remain the same, while making better use of the "no-man's-land" at the north end of the Great Lawn near the 86th Street transverse.

More important, moving the oval would open up valuable space to the south, making it possible to double the size of Belvedere Lake and the embankments around it. This would create more space for sunbathing and picnicking along the lake edge and provide a more romantic foreground for Belvedere Castle. When it is enlarged, the lake shore should follow a more undulating line, like that of a natural stream-fed pond.

The lawn inside the new oval should be graded with a slight roll to break the monotony of the terrain and make it look more natural. The grade, however, must accommodate eight ball fields with clay infields and slightly overlapping grassy outfields. These should be equipped with black vinyl-clad backstops that blend more readily into the surrounding landscape than do bare, metallic chain-link fences. The outfields and other lawns in the project area should be reconstructed using new "tough turf methods" (see page 72). A number of the trees planted when the oval was built in the 1930s have matured into beautiful specimen trees. These must be spared when the oval is shifted—a consideration that will, in fact, determine the eventual configuration of the oval and whether it retains a perfectly ovoid shape.

The unused portions of the two playgrounds to the north of the oval should be removed and returned to lawn, shrub plantings and new walkways. The basketball courts in this locale do have a constituency and should remain.

The Arthur Ross Pinetum would be enhanced by repositioning the walk that cuts across it, relocating some of the trees and planting new ones to achieve a better landscape composition. Trees should be labeled in order to instruct the public about the many fine species in the collection.

Management policies for this subsector should combine horticultural maintenance with use control. Activities on the ball fields should be regulated as they are at the Heckscher Playground: (a) Play is not allowed during or immediately after a rainstorm; (b) a 24-hour telephone tape message indicates whether the playing fields are in usable

Summit Rock once had commanding views to the east and south. Trees now obscure the view.

condition and (c) permits are required throughout the season.

Regarding concerts and other major events on the Great Lawn: (a) Efforts should be made to limit gatherings to a maximum of 100,000 people; (b) no more than six large concerts should be permitted per year and (c) concert producers should post a bond to cover the costs of cleanup and repairs.

Project Subsector 2:
Belvedere Castle, the Delacorte Theater, the folk-dancing circle and the Swedish Cottage

Enlarging the lake and widening its embankments will make a dramatic difference at the south end of the oval. But overcrowding in this area could be reduced still further if folk dancing were moved to the Cherry Hill concourse. This new site—at the crest of a hill with specimen trees, sweeping lawns and one of the best views in the Park—has a sufficiently large paved area already in place to accommodate the dancers. If this move were made, the present paved area at the eastern edge of Belvedere Lake could be taken up and replaced with a pathway of standard width.

Both the Delacorte Theater and the Swedish Cottage offer examples of unfelicitous siting within the Park landscape, but the functions they serve—outdoor Shakespeare and marionette theater—are delightful and popular additions to the Park's menu of visitor services. These structures

should stay in their present locations for the remainder of their useful lives, but at some future date, when their physical restoration may be warranted, the feasibility of re-siting them elsewhere in the Park should be seriously studied.

Project Subsector 3:
The landscapes west of the Great Lawn oval, Winterdale Arch, Summit Rock and Mariner's Gate

Circulation is the prime concern in this subsector. It offers a particular challenge: how to get large numbers of people from the west side of Manhattan to the Great Lawn without trampling the landscape in between.

Winterdale Arch is an important key to the resolution of this problem. This arch takes east-west pedestrians under the drive to and from the Great Lawn. At present the arch is dark and secluded, so people avoid it and walk across the drive instead, creating a serious traffic hazard. The suggested remedy is to make the path through Winterdale Arch feel like the appropriate and natural path to take. This will require clearing the tangle of volunteer trees and shrubbery and relandscaping the ground beside it.

Some additional tree thinning is required throughout the landscape west of the Great Lawn and along the slope around Summit Rock in order to stabilize the severe erosion there with understory plants. The pavement, sand

pit, flagpole and benches now crowning the top should be removed; new benches should replace the old ones, and walkways to the north and south leading to Summit Rock should be reconstructed.

The portion of the Bridle Trail that runs through this area should be converted to a major pedestrian spine to give strollers an uninterrupted north-south walk on the west side similar to the one that exists along the east side.

The Mariner's Gate landscape at 85th Street was restored in 1982. Lawns here should be overseeded and some additional plants installed.

Project Subsector 4:
The Metropolitan Museum of Art landscapes, Hamilton Lawn, the Obelisk, Greywake Arch and the Levy Memorial Playground

To the west of the Metropolitan Museum, the lawns should be reseeded and some border shrubs planted. (The landscapes to the north and south of the museum have already been reconstructed.)

Hamilton Lawn needs to be overseeded, and the trees on the adjacent border should be thinned and planted with understory shrubs and ground cover. The statue requires surface restoration. The overgrown shrubs around the Obelisk should be cleared and replanted, and the platform and benches should be repaired.

The Ramble and the Lake

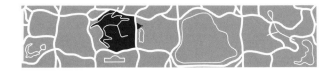

The Ramble is a 38-acre woodland with rocky outcrops, secluded glades and a tumbling stream called the Gill. It is nestled in the center of the Park just below the 79th Street transverse. The Park's designers, Olmsted and Vaux, sculpted the Ramble out of a wooded hillside that lay immediately south of the old Croton Reservoir. It was, in their estimation, the richest and most interesting part of the pre-Park landscape, both topographically and horticulturally.

The native growth in the area included sweet gum, spicebush, tulip tree, sassafras, red maple, black oak, azalea and andromeda—all of which Olmsted termed "exceedingly intricate and interesting."

The Ramble quickly became a haven for nature-lovers and others seeking quiet solitude. It had no carriage drives or equestrian paths. Winding footpaths led visitors on a tour of constantly changing terrain, highlighted by a carefully planned succession of scenic views.

Detailed notes of Olmsted's design for the Ramble survive, and they reveal a passionate dedication to landscape composition. One of Olmsted's painterly effects, for instance, was the illusion of depth in the view of the Ramble from Bethesda Terrace. He achieved it by putting dark shrubs in the foreground and lighter foliage farther back near Belvedere Castle.

The 20-acre Lake, which wraps around the Ramble on the south and west, was built out of a swamp. In the original design, there were five coves (one leading to a cave, which was bricked up in the 1930s), an island (now eroded away) and a butterfly-shaped arm of water called the Ladies' Pond, which was filled in 50 years ago.

A wooden Victorian boathouse stood on the easternmost shore. It provided docking space for rowboats and a tour boat that took passengers around the Lake, stopping at five boat landings and Bethesda Terrace. In winter, when there was ice-skating, the

The Ramble, nineteenth century.

Rustic bridge across the Gill, nineteenth century.

Rustic umbrella structure overlooking the Lake, nineteenth century.

secluded Ladies' Pond offered novice skaters a place to practice their skills.

Today, the Ramble is prized by a varied constituency that includes strollers, picnickers, nature-lovers, sunbathers and bird watchers, who come especially during the spring and fall when 200 species of migrating birds are attracted to the green canopy and the water surrounding it. Since its restoration in 1982, Belvedere Castle has been used as an environmental learning center, and the Ramble now serves as an "outdoor classroom" where 4,300 schoolchildren receive instruction every year in natural science and other Park-related subjects.

Changes in the Ramble

In the 125 years since this elaborate piece of landscape was built, a number of changes have taken place. All five original boat landings have disappeared; three facsimiles were constructed in the 1960s. All but one of the 12 rustic shelters that crowned the rocky outcrops are gone.

The Victorian boathouse was replaced in 1954 by the Loeb Boathouse, along with a 2-acre parking lot directly north of it that destroyed a lovely, small south-facing meadow and the original entrance into the Ramble from the east.

The pedestrian path system generally follows the historic layout, although a few new paths have been added. The paths are now paved with asphalt instead of pebble and gravel. There is also a multitude of desire lines crisscrossing the landscape; some are harmless and simply add to the country feeling of this part of the Park, but many are on extremely steep slopes and promote erosion.

The beehives, birdhouses and pergolas that contributed to the Ramble's early charm have all disappeared, as have the original rustic benches, which have been replaced by the concrete-and-wooden benches typical of the rest of the Park. The Ladies' Pavilion, a cast-iron structure on the western

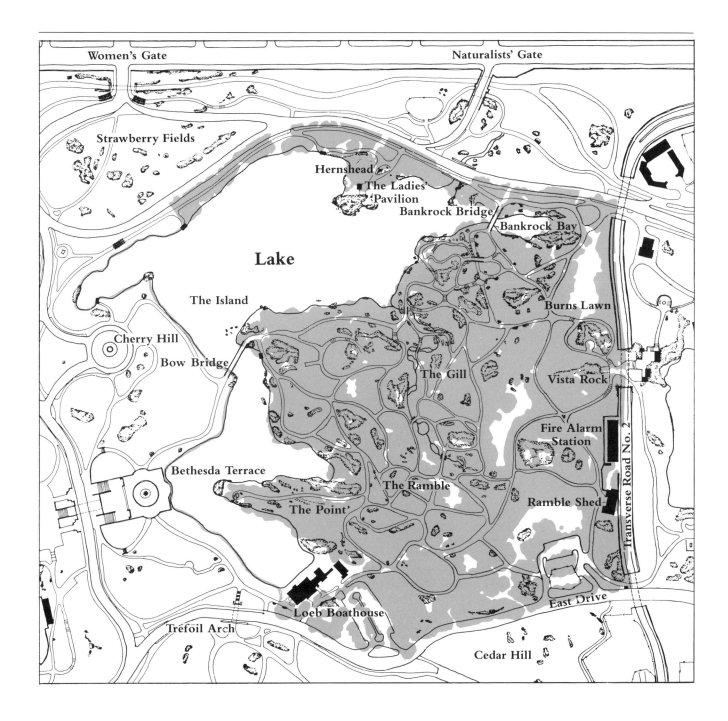

shore of the Lake, has recently been refurbished.

The original topography is largely unchanged, because there has never been any major regrading or recontouring of the Ramble since it was built. However, the soil is badly eroded. Crests of slopes are denuded of topsoil, which has washed down into the valleys and coves of the Lake.

The vegetation of the Ramble is still quite varied and interesting, though no plants date back to its construction,

and the landscape is not as crammed as it once was with subtle and delicate horticultural effects. An in-depth study of the Ramble was conducted in 1979 (by Bruce Kelly, Philip Winslow and James Marston Fitch), and in the course of it 6,000 trees were identified and catalogued, and each was graded according to its scenic and horticultural value. The survey found 60 specimen trees, including various oaks, Kentucky coffee trees, cork trees, cucumber magnolias and Japanese

pagoda trees. Red maple, tupelo and sweet gum have prospered in the flatter, wetter areas, and recent dense plantings of seed- and berry-producing shrubs on the Point and along the Gill have proved very attractive to birds and other wildlife and are helping to hold the topsoil in place.

Elsewhere, however, vegetation is generally in poor health. Black cherry and Japanese knotweed are spreading rapidly; 80 percent of the open lawns have surrendered to these species. In

A nineteenth-century rustic bench.

Contemporary rustic bench.

contrast to the rich inventory of tree species, there is very little botanical variety in the understory or ground plane.

Much of the Ramble's original drainage system has ceased to function; catch basins are filled with silt and debris, and walkways are often flooded with water and mud. In some areas, especially on the steep slopes, broken drainage tiles can be seen on the surface.

The bed of the Gill, the charming artificial stream traversing the Ramble, lost its original wide "V" shape when it was reconstructed in the early 1900s, and its further rechanneling with the installation of a concrete bridge in 1935 reduced its original cascading waterfall to a trickle. Even though recently dredged, the Gill is a repository for silt and debris from the upland watershed. It will continue to fill up with sediment until the slopes above it are stabilized and the underground drainage system is restored to working order.

Changes on the Lake

In 1903, the natural edge and clay bottom of the Lake were replaced with gravel and cement in response to an order by the Health Department. In 1929, the edge was again reconstructed and rimmed with natural boulders, a less artificial-looking way of controlling shoreline erosion. At the same time, the Ladies' Pond was filled in.

The Lake has always been a popular Park attraction. In the 1920s, special

Off-path foot traffic on the Ramble's steep slopes causes severe erosion.

events were held on it, including canoe regattas and swimming meets. Rowboating continues, but the tour boats no longer operate, and swimming is prohibited for safety reasons. Skating was discontinued when the artificial rinks (Lasker and Wollman) were installed elsewhere in the Park. At various times during the past 25 years, the Lake has been stocked with fish by the Department of Environmental Conservation, and fishing is still a popular pastime for some.

The health of the Lake has suffered. More than a half-million cubic feet of sediment have washed into it from the surrounding watershed. With the current restorations of the Bethesda Terrace and Cherry Hill landscapes, much of the ground plane on the southern part of the watershed will be re-greened, which should help control erosion. But elsewhere, particularly on the steep western bluffs of the Ramble, erosion is taking a heavy toll, and because of the high organic content of the sediment, the Lake has become hypereutrophic.

Overall, the history of the Ramble has largely been one of management neglect. Not since Samuel Parsons was Superintendent of Central Park (1880-1910) has there been a consistent, systematic effort to maintain it. It is because of the richness of the soil and the abundance of moisture that the Ramble has survived as well as it has. Unfortunately, its decline is increasing at a progressive rate, so landscape restoration has now become essential.

The Azalea Pool, a favorite haunt for bird watchers.

Birders standing on newly restored rustic bridge, 1986.

Goals, Priorities and Recommendations

There are four major areas of concern in the Ramble: (1) erosion control, (2) wildlife ecology, (3) safety and security, (4) landscape architecture.

Erosion Control

The combination of a steep terrain, underground springs, a dense forest canopy and errant pedestrian circulation make erosion control the most urgent priority in the Ramble today. A number of remedies are required, one of which should be the revegetation of the severely eroded ground plane. Planting should include shade-loving ground covers in the woodland and native grasses in the meadows and on the sunnier slopes.

Maintenance of the Ramble's horticulture must take into account that the Ramble is one of the few places in the Park that supports a native plant community rather than a wholly imported one. In fact, several types of trees and shrubs now growing in the Ramble were growing on the original pre-Park site: tupelo, red maple, sweet gum, spicebush, sweet pepper bush and witch hazel. It makes sense here to preserve, strengthen and enhance these native species in every way possible.

Wildlife Ecology

The Ramble's value as a wildlife refuge should be protected. Hemlocks, American hollies and other shade-loving native evergreens should be reintroduced. Berry- and seed-producing

Depleted understory, typical of most of the Ramble, contrasts with . . .

. . . healthy understory on the Point, which was restored in 1982.

plants should be planted at the edges of herbaceous openings to attract birds, and a certain amount of deadwood should be left in place to provide thick brush cover for small animals and insects. All landscape restoration work should be developed in consultation with a wildlife advisory committee and a professional urban ecologist. It must

be understood, however, that while the Ramble can be maintained as a thriving wildlife environment, the wildlife habitat cannot be maximized without impinging on human use of the area. Certain compromises will have to be made on both sides.

Safety and Security

Because so much of the Ramble has become overgrown, many visitors find it a disturbing and mildly threatening place to be. In the ubiquitous woody tangle, the visitor becomes disoriented; the paths are complicated, and one easily gets lost in innumerable dead ends. Visual cues are needed: Rock outcrops should be accentuated and small woodland glades opened up to admit more sunlight and sighting of recognizable landmarks.

The underground drainage system throughout the Ramble and along the Lake edge needs to be rebuilt. Also, paths should be regraded and new stone gutters placed beside them to channel storm water in the proper direction.

The Point, 1906.

Woodchucks are one of the Park's resident mammals.

The Point, 1979.

Landscape Architecture

There is little question that the Ramble represents a man-made landscape of historic importance. One of the first parts of the Park to be built, it is a monumental achievement of natu-ralistic design—an early and unique example of this style in America. For this reason alone it deserves to be carefully preserved. Olmsted lavished attention upon the Ramble. In his writing, he devoted more words to it than to any other part of the Park, and he made it the focal point of the Park's chief visual axis northward from the Mall across Bethesda Terrace and the Lake to the Belvedere.

Clearing of the rampant Japanese knot-weed, an invasive plant that chokes out other vegetation, is necessary if a more varied woodland plant community, similar to the one lovingly created by

The Point, 1985.

Ladies' Pavilion on the Hernshead.

Olmsted, is to be reintroduced into the Ramble. Off-path foot traffic should be discouraged in order for these plants to thrive.

Because of the delicacy of the Ramble both as a landscape and as an ecosystem, most of the recommendations made here should be accomplished by a series of small projects using, wherever possible, trained in-house crews rather than outside contractors. Some contract work (for paths, benches, drainage, etc.) will be necessary, but this work should be limited in scope and carefully supervised. Since restoration of this woodland cannot be done all at once without disturbing its function as a wildlife haven, it should be done as a series of mini-projects over time.

The Lake

The Lake should be dredged once soil stabilization is complete throughout the entire watershed. Since this action will not occur for several years, short-term emergency dredging should be done in the two westernmost coves in order to keep them from reverting to dry land. Eventually, the entire Lake edge should be reconstructed, with boulders implanted in the shoreline to control erosion.

The island, most of which has eroded away, should be reconstructed.

The boathouse parking lot and the parking lot next to the Ramble maintenance building should be reduced in size and the reclaimed portions returned to lawn.

A Venetian gondola delighted crowds at the turn of the century.

Another Venetian gondola, 1986.

The Conservatory Water

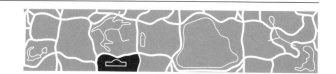

The Conservatory Water project area, which extends from 72nd Street to 79th Street on the east side, is a particularly pleasant and popular part of the Park. It was originally part of the same low-lying swamp as the area now occupied by the Lake. In order to accommodate the East Drive, an earth dam was created, effectively bisecting what was once a single drainage system.

At the bottom of a bowl of land near Fifth Avenue and 74th Street lies the Model Boat Basin. It has roughly the same shape as a formal flower garden originally planned to occupy the same spot. A preliminary design by Olmsted and Vaux called for a two-story glass structure to be built with an entrance on Fifth Avenue and stairways leading down to a formal landscape below. As soon as the foundation work began, however, it became apparent that costs were going to be too high, and work stopped. A conservatory was eventually built at Fifth Avenue and 105th Street, and the intended formal garden at 74th Street became instead the Conservatory Water, a pond that has been enjoyed by generations of model-boat yachtsmen, ice-skaters and their spectators.

Model-boat contests became an annual event in the 1920s, and in 1929 the basin was rimmed with a low concrete wall at a height so that children could kneel on it and push their boats into the water. Skating championships were held there in the winter during the Twenties, drawing crowds of up to 20,000 people. In 1954, the Kerbs Memorial Boathouse was built to store model boats and house a small food concession and rest rooms. At the same time, a small brick concession stand was built at the southern end of the Conservatory Water.

Existing Conditions

Today, the gently sloping landscape around the Conservatory Water attracts strollers, sunbathers, picnickers, the elderly and parents with children.

The slope south of the Conservatory Water, c. 1910.

The same slope, 1976 . . .

. . . and today.

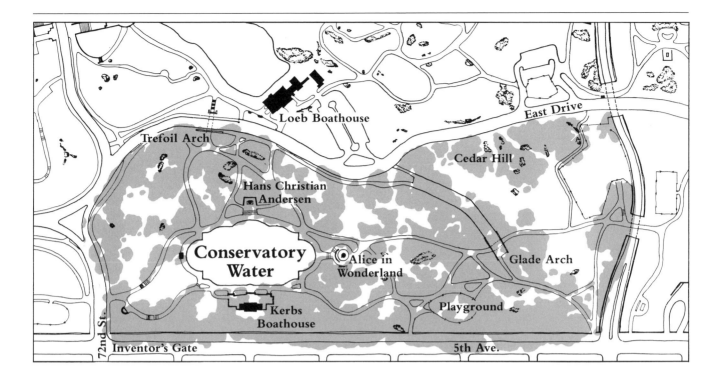

Skating on the Conservatory Water in the 1940s.

Model boating is still popular. The two storybook statues—George Lober's 1956 Hans Christian Andersen and José de Creeft's 1960 Alice in Wonderland—have gleaming bronze patinas from the buffing thousands of clambering children have given them. In winter, ice-skaters and hockey players enjoy the frozen boat basin, and sledders glide down Pilgrim and Cedar hills.

The landscape surrounding the Conservatory Water has always been horticulturally diverse. Because it is a valley with an orientation perpen-dicular to the prevailing winter winds, microclimatic conditions exist here that are hospitable to more southerly species that would perish elsewhere in the Park. In 1873, such exotics as beach plum, Persian walnut, marsh stone fruit and Carolina allspice grew here. Today, there are nine species of oak on the south lawn. The lawn northwest of the boat basin now contains an exceptionally beautiful oriental cherry grove and a stand of Australian pines, as well as several fine specimens of beech, larch, hemlock, birch, tupelo, papaw, and crape myrtle. But the landscape beneath the tree canopy presents a less desirable picture.

Intensive use by gym classes of the relatively flat parts of lawns has worn away turf and compacted the soil. This, coupled with the tendency for the low-lying areas to flood during storms, has exacerbated the problems of the ground plane. A wide, well-worn desire line traverses Pilgrim Hill, the slope to the south of the boat basin. All the blue stone steps in the area are in disrepair. The concrete holding basin of the water body is itself succumbing to the effects of age. There are indications that the founda-tion is developing cracks, and once a thorough investigation is completed, restoration should immediately follow.

The playground at 76th Street and Fifth Avenue is a typical Moses-era playground, with an asphalt play sur-face and a few pieces of standard pipe-rail equipment. It is currently being renovated as a playground for very young children.

Goals, Priorities and Recommendations

Drainage and circulation are the most serious problems in this sector. The Conservatory Water basin and adjacent landscape is a natural low point, and the area is dependent upon catch basins

Slopes around the Conservatory Water are popular for sledding . . .

. . . and for school groups at play.

to take storm water away. Today, much of the drainage system is clogged and in danger of collapsing. The water body itself, the only one in the Park with a formal edge, overflows its basin during severe storms. Since the same storms pour water into the area from the steep slopes of Cedar Hill to the north, this area has become notorious as one of the most susceptible in the Park to bad flooding. A rebuilt landscape with a new walkway-related drainage system and a new water outtake system for the basin is necessary to correct this problem.

Errant circulation is also a major concern. The desire line between Bethesda Terrace and the Kerbs Boathouse is one of the biggest in the Park. Although fences would probably help guide circulation, this desire line is so heavily used that it should probably be confirmed with a newly designed path set appropriately into the landscape.

In the interest of these and other priorities, the following additional recommendations are made:

Walkways in the area should be repaved; benches and drinking fountains, replaced.

Understory plants should be installed on the steep slopes adjacent to Glade Arch in an effort to control erosion.

Management policies regulating activities of school groups in the area should be instituted in order to protect the restored lawns.

The Kerbs Boathouse and terrace should be rehabilitated. The rest rooms, particularly, should be redesigned for efficient maintenance and to allow accessibility for the disabled. The model-boat storage room is currently being converted to winter use as an indoor space for Park volunteers.

The Ice Cream Café at Kerbs Boathouse.

A young yachtsman.

The Mall, Bethesda Terrace and Cherry Hill

The Mall and Bethesda Terrace form a north-south axis designed to draw visitors into the heart of Central Park. From the south entrance to the Mall, the eye travels northward along a broad promenade flanked by double rows of American elms that form a vast open-air cathedral of green. At the north end, the Mall terminates at Bethesda Terrace in an elegant cascade of Victorian stonework and one of the Park's most dazzling views: Bethesda Fountain, the Lake and the wild Ramble beyond.

The combination of the Mall and Bethesda Terrace is the only original formal element in Central Park, and it was designed to be the centerpiece of the Lower Park. "In giving it this prominent position," Olmsted wrote, "we look at it in the light of an artificial structure on a scale of magnitude commensurate with the size of the park, and intend that it should occupy the same position of importance that a mansion should occupy in a park prepared for private occupation."

The Mall was one of the first Park features to be built. From the beginning, it was as much an axis of motion and activity as it was of vistas. Strollers, bicyclists, goat carts and roller skaters have all paraded along it. Concerts were performed in an octagonal, Moorish cast-iron bandstand. These concerts grew so popular that eventually they became a daily event, and in 1873 the paved area had to be enlarged to accommodate the crowds. Atop a slight rise to the east, visitors could pull off the East Drive, alight from their carriages, stop off for refreshment at the Casino ("a pretty domestic-looking cottage") and walk over to the Wisteria Pergola to enjoy the concert and the sight of the spectators in the Concert Ground below.

Boats that were tied up at the western edge of Bethesda Terrace took passengers around the Lake, stopping at various landings along the way. A Venetian gondola, presented to the Park in 1862, floated nearby, "looking

Promenading along the Mall, 1894.

sufficiently romantic, lying in all its low, black length upon this water hardly more ruffled than that of its native canals."

Cherry Hill, to the west, afforded another magnificent view of Bethesda Terrace, the Lake and the Ramble.

Carriage-borne visitors could water their horses in the circular granite fountain pool at the top, overlook the grassy lawns sweeping down from the summit and admire Bow Bridge and, on the other side of the Lake, the rocky and lush Ramble.

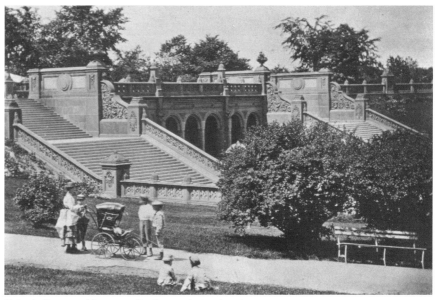

Bethesda Terrace and its surrounding lawns, nineteenth century.

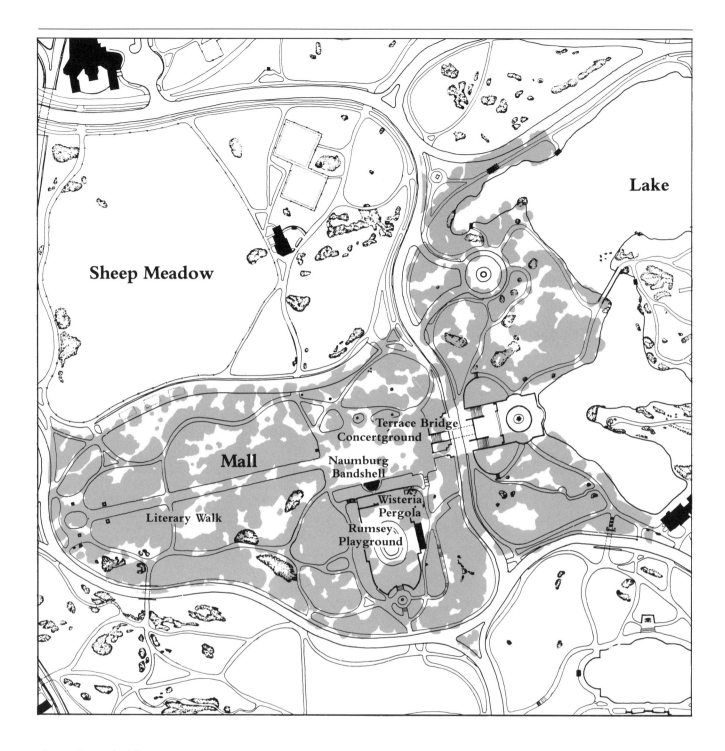

Continual Change

Over the years, the Mall's features have been repeatedly altered and redesigned. In fact, the Mall is one of the most redesigned features of the Park. Some of the changes have been for the better, many for the worse.

In 1873, 11 years after Bethesda Fountain was built, its single jet of water was replaced by Emma Stebbins's sculpture Angel of the Waters, commemorating the biblical passage in which an angel bestowed healing powers on the pool of Bethesda in Jerusalem. By association it also commemorates a great public-health victory for New York City, the construction in 1842 of the Croton aqueduct and reservoir system that brought the population pure, uncontaminated water. The statue of Sir Walter Scott was placed at the southern end of the Mall in 1871, the first of several sculptures that would give the name "Literary Walk" to the promenade. The Belvedere, built at the north perimeter of the Ramble in 1869, brilliantly punctuated the view from the terrace. In 1912, the paving of the terrace was considerably enhanced by a herringbone pattern of red brick, which replaced the crumbling asphalt.

Eventually, the public decided that the bandstand was acoustically inade-

Bethesda Fountain, original appearance.

Bethesda Fountain, late 1970s.

quate. So in 1923, it was demolished, and the Naumburg Bandshell was built on the eastern edge of the Concert Ground. The Concert Ground was again enlarged, and its planted islands, gilded bird cages, pools and fountains were sacrificed for pavement. The bandshell was positioned immediately to the west of the Wisteria Pergola so that the audience could face away from the setting sun during early evening concerts. But this blocked the pergola from view and abruptly shut off any view from the pergola itself. However, few people minded. This was the big band era, and large audiences enjoyed the concerts and dances that were held at the bandshell.

The vacillating fortunes of the Casino came to an end when, after having been enlarged and remodeled a number of times and converted from a simple refreshment stand to a posh nightclub, it was razed by Robert Moses and replaced by the Rumsey Playground in 1937.

Over the years, Bethesda Terrace succumbed to gradual deterioration. Vandals chipped away at the delicate stone tracery. The open spaces framing the terrace were obliterated with the planting of 24 pin oaks after World War II, a horticultural mistake that caused shading out of grass and severe erosion on the slopes leading down to the lower terrace. In 1967, the Parks Department installed the Fountain Café. Although it damaged both the paving and the architecture, the café was an enormously popular summertime attraction until the early 1970s, when a burgeoning open-air drug traffic and the lack of security to deal with it discouraged patronage and caused it to close. By this time, the lawns on the terrace slopes were gone and roots of the pin oaks, planted too close to the terrace structure, were interfering with the drainage system and beginning to dislodge the stone walls. Pavement was cracking and heaving, and the fountain was broken.

Meanwhile, the Mall had become the locale-of-choice for a variety of

Recarving a stone owl, Bethesda Terrace, 1985.

Use Guidelines for the Bandshell in Central Park

The New York City Department of Parks and Recreation has adopted the following guidelines for the Bandshell to assist outside sponsors of events in understanding their responsibilities; to prevent overuse, crowding, security problems and excessive noise; and to avoid conflicts with other users of Central Park.

The Bandshell guidelines may, in some instances, amend and supersede the Department of Parks and Recreation's Special Events guidelines.

If your proposed event does not meet these guidelines, consider using an alternate site. Throughout New York City there are underutilized parks and bandshells. Many communities would welcome a performance or special event.

Sponsors planning to use the Naumburg Bandshell must obtain the following permits:
1. Special Event Permit
2. Central Park Bandshell Permit
3. Sound Permit
4. Vehicle Permit(s)
5. Concessions Permit

Permits are non-transferable and non-assignable.

Permits (originals only) must be in the possession of the person designated on the Bandshell Permit. This person and persons named as responsible for cleanup must be present for the entire event.

Hours/Dates of Use: Hours of use may vary depending on the type and anticipated size of the event. Most performing arts events can be permitted for 2 hours, with a maximum of 2 hours pre-performance setup and a maximum of 2 hours post-performance break down.

Festivals and multiple performance events can be permitted for a maximum of 6 hours, with a maximum of 2 hours pre-performance set up and a maximum of 2 hours break down. Festivals may be permitted between 12:00 P.M. and 6 P.M. In deference to nearby residential neighbors and Park users who enjoy quiet mornings, sound amplification is permitted only after 12:00 P.M.

Evening performances are permitted only under certain circumstances. Evening events must be finished by 9:30 P.M.

Sound Amplification: To ensure high quality sound for all events, while respecting the peace of nearby residents, the Department of Parks & Recreation provides a sound amplification system designed for the specific demands of the Central Park Bandshell. All event sponsors must use only the Department of Parks & Recreation sound system. The Department of Parks & Recreation is to be the sole and only provider of sound amplification, including though not limited to amplifiers, speakers, monitors, microphones and processors.

Clarity of sound results from a combination of amplification equipment and a sound technician's familiarity and proficiency with that system. The Department of Parks & Recreation employs a professional sound technician familiar with the Bandshell. The technician is fully versed in sound bounce patterns, daily air currents, and sound skipping within the Park. The sound technician also takes into consideration the Bandshell's proximity to the Sheep Meadow, an official Park "quiet zone," activities at Bethesda Terrace, and the recommendations of New York City Department of Environmental Protection.

Insurance: Many events are required to have insurance in effect at all times in the amount stated on the Special Event Permit.

Display and Distribution of Literature: Sponsors may not distribute, post, display or affix handbills, flyers, posters, flags or banners. Sponsors may distribute a program for the event.

Vehicles: All vehicles must have permits. Permitted vehicles may arrive a maximum of two hours pre-performance and depart a maximum of two hours post-performance. Upon arrival at the Bandshell, vehicles are given one hour to unload. The vehicles may then be parked at a designated parking area. No vehicles of any kind may be parked at the Bandshell, Concert Ground or adjacent areas during an event or performance. After the event, vehicles may load for a maximum of one hour.

Concession of Goods: Any event staged strictly for advertising and promotion purposes is not allowed. Sponsors wishing to sell items related to the event must have a Concessions Permit.

Revenue: Sponsors and individuals may not solicit funds or derive revenue within Central Park. The Department of Parks is the sole and only party allowed to collect contributions.

Safety: Concern for public safety prohibits the following:
- Use of fire of any sort.
- Use of weapons and dangerous implements.
- Cooking grills, stoves, hibachis, and other portable ovens.
- Portable showmobiles, stages and trailers.

Portable Toilets: At times when the anticipated general park use is high, and therefore the nearby restrooms will already be heavily used, the sponsor may be required to provide one portable toilet for every 250 anticipated attendees. Vendor information can be obtained from the Bandshell Program Director. All delivery vehicles must have vehicle permits.

Cleanup: All sponsors must provide ample industrial weight (3 ply) plastic garbage bags and personnel to clean the Bandshell site. Sponsors must list on the permit application the name, phone number, and address of the person responsible for directing cleanup operations. This person must be identified to the Bandshell Program Director or his representative at the beginning of the event, and show proof of garbage bags. The sponsor's personnel must bag and tie all garbage. The stage and backstage areas must be swept clean.

Evaluation: All events will be attended by a representative from the Parks Department. Each event will be evaluated according to these Bandshell Guidelines and the Department of Parks & Recreation Special Events Guidelines. Specific attention will be paid to sound level, attendance, cleanup, and respect for Central Park and its users. Sponsors will also be provided with an evaluation form for compliance with these guidelines.

Failure to follow these guidelines as proven by evaluation and documentation can result in forfeiture of bond, and provide reason to deny the sponsor or major responsible parties any and all future Bandshell permit applications.

Guidelines for the use of the Bandshell Concert Ground were published in 1986. They are representative of the management policies that are being promulgated for other areas in the Park.

The Mall: Literary Walk, 1986.

gigantic festivals. One food fair attracted 250,000 people, creating a miasma of dust and garbage. It became clear that things had gotten out of hand when one Sunday in May 1977, a bike-athon and a foot race were scheduled for the same time and both had to cross repeatedly over the line of a parade march as well as the path of vehicles transporting performers, supplies and floats to a cultural festival.

Of the changes that have taken place in the Mall, among the most damaging have been those that compromised the Mall's original north-south axis. Early on, crosswalks were sliced across the promenade to make approaches from the east and west. At the north end, the ever-larger Concert Ground became a shapeless, directionless open space of creeping asphalt, further confused by the placement of aluminum highway-light standards at the very center of the axis. The realignment of the Park Drive for high-speed traffic in the 1930s cut off pedestrian access to the Mall from the south, severely weakening the Mall as a magnet to draw people from the city streets into the heart of the Park.

Goals, Priorities and Recommendations

Despite the many alterations over the years, the Mall still functions as Olmsted originally intended—as a busy promenade and meeting place

where people go to enjoy the sight of other visitors in the Park and to be seen themselves. The Mall and the adjacent Bethesda Terrace receive mostly transient use. The 1983 demographic study found that "only 20 percent of people who arrive [at Bethesda Fountain] actually stop for any length of time. . . . After strolling the Mall, people generally decide to settle on a nearby green or to continue on a Park ramble."

Referring to the "happenings," the drug market and the political rallies of the 1960s and 1970s, the study pointed out that "this period of loosening public decorum has largely passed." A legacy of this era is perhaps discernible in the fact that today there is a greater concentration of street performers on the Mall than in any other part of the Park, and when programmed events are not occurring at the bandshell, various spots along the Mall serve as the informal venue of impromptu mimes, musicians and acrobats.

The Mall and its environs—Bethesda Terrace, Cherry Hill, the Wisteria Pergola and the area where the Rumsey Playground is located—were conceived by Olmsted as a single design element. An objective of the present plan is to restore the coherence of that unit.

The Mall and the Concert Ground

The Mall has been literally cut off at both ends. Realignment of the Park

Drive in the 1930s detached it from the Marble Arch underpass and pedestrian circulation from the Fifth Avenue entrance at the south, and the gradual paving over and rearrangement of the Concert Ground seriously weakened the once-strong axis linking it to Bethesda Terrace at the north.

It would be very costly today to restore the original Park Drive and the Marble Arch that led visitors from the Fifth Avenue entrance to the south end of the Mall. However, a central entrance at the Mall's south end would both visually and physically help to restore this important connection.

At the north end, the rows of American elms that used to be a feature of the Concert Ground should be restored in order to reemphasize the Mall's axial quality and its relationship to Bethesda Terrace. The elms should be surrounded by specially designed cast-iron and wood benches, which would protect the lawns at the base of the trees and provide seating for 550 people. Additional portable benches would enable the space to accommodate audiences of up to 3,000.

The two circular fountains that originally stood at the north end of the Mall should be rebuilt. The pool edges should be set at bench height to serve as informal seating.

The bandshell, which has blocked the view of the Wisteria Pergola for over 60 years, has outlived its usefulness as a

Cherry Hill concourse and fountain after restoration, 1981.

performance stage. Performers today use electronic sound systems, and the bandshell's acoustics are therefore redundant. If the bandshell were removed, events requiring a stage could take place in a newly designed music pavilion at the location of the original octagonal Victorian structure. Modern sound systems and an expandable stage area could be built into this concert structure. In addition, if the Wisteria Pergola were no longer hidden behind the bandshell, it would not be able to serve, as it now does (in spite of police surveillance), as a market for furtive drug dealing.

The Elms

The double rows of elms along the Mall survive, although they have been imperiled since the 1930s by Dutch elm disease. This grove of elms, together with others nearby, contains over 300 trees—one of the largest contiguous stands of American elms in the world.

They are being closely watched and well tended. Each year, the trees are vigilantly monitored, and if an infested tree is discovered it is quickly treated or removed and a new elm planted in its place. However, if Dutch elm disease prevails, a decision must be made whether to continue planting elms or to replant from end to end with another species. Some prospective candidates include cucumber magnolia *(Magnolia acuminata),* silver linden *(Tilia tomentosa),* common bald cypress *(Taxodium distichum),* katsura tree *(Cerci*

diphyllum japonicum), European hackberry *(Celtis laevigata)* and dawn redwood *(Metasequoia glytostroboides).* Whereas all of these are impressive and beautiful, none adequately replicates the structure of the elm, and, hence, the beautiful "cathedral nave" effect of the present Mall would not be achieved with any currently known substitute planting.

Bethesda Terrace

The reconstruction and restoration of Bethesda Terrace and the Terrace Arcade beneath the 72nd Street Drive have been completed, thereby returning the Park's most elegant space to public use.

Cherry Hill

The Cherry Hill concourse, which had become a parking lot by 1934, was restored in 1981.

The Rumsey Playground

In 1985, the Rumsey Playground, which had been abandoned by parents and children in favor of the newer playground near the Park's perimeter, was converted into an athletic field to serve the many schools that use this part of the Park for their sports programs.

New and Proposed Management Strategies

Planners must ask what sort of activities and how many people the Mall

area can accommodate without losing its spontaneous character or suffering physical damage. With the Parks Department's reestablishment of management policies for all of Central Park, the policies for events on the Mall and at Bethesda Terrace now discourage or rule out: commercial or promotional events; events likely to draw more than 2,500 people; hard rock and disco concerts; food fairs; political rallies; and events that include animals, private parties or boxing matches. Events that are considered least likely to result in damage are those that require no special benches or lights and attract small audiences of regular Park visitors rather than crowds that come specifically to be entertained or to exploit the Park for political purposes.

Application for an event permit now requires a nonrefundable processing fee of $100, an additional application fee of $50-$100, depending on the type of application, proof of an insurance policy protecting the Department of Parks and Recreation from liability for injury during an event, and a bond covering the cost of cleanup after the event. Food carts on the Mall and Bethesda Terrace are licensed according to strict health standards.

Cherry Hill should continue to be managed and operated as it is now—as general parkland for passive use. The specimen trees now thriving on the upper meadow should continue to receive special care, as they rank among the finest trees in the Park.

The Sheep Meadow

Guidelines for the original Central Park design competition in 1857 stipulated that plans had to include a parade ground of some 20 to 40 acres for military exercises. Olmsted and Vaux selected a fairly flat tableland for this purpose and called it the Green. It was the 22-acre site of the present Sheep Meadow in the center of the Park between the 65th Street transverse road and 72nd Street. "Such a broad open plain of well-kept grass would be a refreshing and agreeable feature," Olmsted wrote.

The design of the meadow emphasized openness. Trees along the edges were scattered singly and in small clusters so that light mingled with shadows, giving the impression that the meadow extended beyond its true borders. In 1868, the fanciful cast-iron Mineral Springs Pavilion was erected in the northwest portion of the meadow. It was a concession that sold healthful spring waters, and it was positioned to be visible as one entered the Park at West 72nd Street. Demolished in 1960, it was replaced with a large brick structure nearby, one that was not visible, however, from the West 72nd Street entrance.

The meadow was never used for military exercises, as it turned out. A flock of 150 sheep was put there in the 1860s, along with a keeper who carried a crook. Baseball was introduced in the 1880s. In 1911, 10,000 girls from the Public School Athletic League danced around maypoles, accompanied by a 60-piece band. A few years later, 38 temporary lawn tennis courts were laid out.

Activity exceeded the limit of the lawn's endurance during the 1960s and 1970s, when mass rallies and concerts drew crowds of over 200,000 people. These events, together with unregulated baseball, football and soccer games, compacted the soil and destroyed the turf. All that was left was a bare dustbowl.

The historic Sheep Meadow with grazing sheep.

The contemporary Sheep Meadow, Manhattan's "front yard."

Unregulated sports and mass gatherings destroyed the Sheep Meadow.

Restored in 1979, the meadow is protected by a low fence, and regulations are enforced by rangers.

Existing Conditions

In 1980, the Sheep Meadow was re-graded, a drainage system was constructed, an automatic irrigation system was installed, and a thick carpet of bluegrass sod was laid down over a layer of new topsoil. It quickly became one of the most popular parts of the Park. Five years later, at the time this report was written, the restored lawn remains a lush and healthy sweep of green, a favorite spot for sunbathing, picnicking, kite flying, strolling barefoot and relaxation in general.

Goals, Priorities and Recommendations

The 1980 Sheep Meadow restoration unfortunately did not extend to the whole of Olmsted's meadow, which originally included the area that is now a lilac grove just beyond the gravel path that carries pedestrian traffic past the Mineral Springs Pavilion to the Mall. Further diminishing this important Park space is the 1961 Mineral Springs Pavilion replacing the graceful Victorian, Moorish-style structure that stood several feet to the northwest. The two bowling greens next to it also create a visual barrier to Olmsted's "broad open plan," effectively bisecting the meadow.

In order to restore the original dimensions of Olmsted's lawn, consideration should be given to removing the gravel path (installed in 1981 to legitimize a major desire line, it guides pedestrians directly to another wide desire line that invades the Mall lawn) and incorporating the pleasant lilac grove area into the Sheep Meadow.

At some future date, when the current Mineral Springs building is deemed obsolete, consideration should be given to building a replacement structure on the original site.

The careful management policies that protect the restored Sheep Meadow should be extended to the areas surrounding it, and when such comprehensive use-enforcement policies are achieved, the chain-link fence that now sets the Sheep Meadow apart as a selectively managed zone should be removed.

Old cast-iron Mineral Springs Pavilion.

Contemporary Mineral Springs structure with tromp l'oeil mural by Richard Haas.

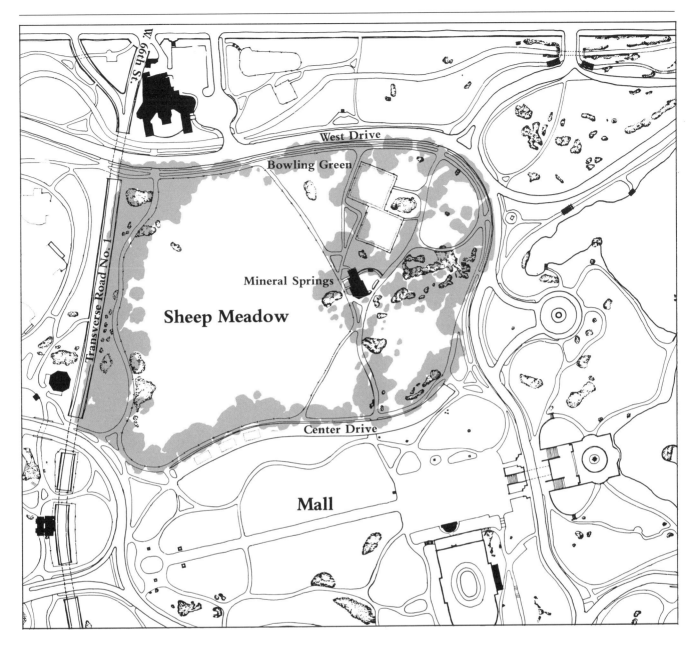

West Drive

Bowling Green

Transverse Road No. 1

W. 66th St.

Mineral Springs

Sheep Meadow

Center Drive

Mall

Maintenance of high-quality greens for lawn bowling . . .

. . . and croquet.

135

The Dene

The landscape along the east perimeter of the Park from 66th Street to 72nd Street is known as the Dene. It is a combination of gently rolling lawns and shaded walks punctuated with rock outcrops. Notable features include a rustic Summer House, two playgrounds and Balto (the statue of an Alaskan husky). The Dene's easternmost walkway is a heavily used north-south pedestrian commuter route as well as a leisurely promenade between the Conservatory Water and the Central Park Zoo.

Before the Park was developed, the Dene was a relatively flat site, part of a plateau from which the Mall and the Sheep Meadow were formed. Though it lies at a higher elevation than the swampy valley to the north (which became the Conservatory Water), parts of the Dene were originally a bog, particularly in the southern end, where the elevation drops off substantially.

Olmsted and Vaux made several changes in the topography of the Dene in order to increase its visual interest and rectify its drainage. Lawns were graded and seeded, trees and shrubs were planted, and by 1891, Central Park Superintendent Samuel Parsons wrote of it: "This place reminds one of an English lawn. It is five or six acres of fine turf, unbroken except by a few scattered shade trees of large size. Each tree is a fine specimen. There are horse-chestnuts and some excellent American beeches, oaks, tulip trees, maples, elms, purple beeches, liquidambers, etc."

Willowdell Arch, built in 1860, passes under the East Drive and provides pedestrian access to the Mall. This red-brick arch was named for a group of large willow trees that stood nearby. They were among the few specimen trees on the mostly barren pre-Park tract of land.

The rustic Summer House, which sits atop one of the Park's largest rock outcrops, affords a view of the Dene landscape and the Mall beyond. Historian Clarence Cook wrote in 1869 that the structure was positioned to max-

A restored rustic shelter.

imize the Park experience. "Shut off from the view of passers in the street," he wrote, "one can find here almost as complete a seclusion, for an hour's reading or meditation, as he could obtain in the centre of the Park itself, so judicious has been the planting. . . ."

The Cricket Players' House was constructed in 1870 beside the lawn south of the 72nd Street entrance. Known first as the Cricket Ground, the lawn was later called the Croquet Ground and finally the East Green. The Cricket Players' House was eventually torn down, but the green continued to exist and has recently been resodded and serviced with a new drainage system and irrigation pipes.

Plantations of trees and shrubs were regularly added to the Dene during the first 50 years of its existence. Fifty winter honeysuckles and 70 spicebushes were planted near the Summer House and along the perimeter wall in 1908 and 1909.

The two playgrounds in the Dene area were constructed in the 1930s as a part of Robert Moses's plan for a series of perimeter playgrounds, each placed near the edge of the Park for the sake of convenience and safety. The 71st Street playground was redesigned in the 1960s, and the 67th Street playground is currently in the process of being rebuilt.

Existing Conditions

Over the years, nearby private schools have used the East Green for active team sports, repeatedly trampling the lawn into hardpan. As with the restoration of the Sheep Meadow, the recent rebuilding of the East Green has been followed by strict regulation allowing only passive uses. Active sports have been diverted to the nearby site of the former Rumsey Playground on the other side of the East Drive, where a clay sports surface has recently been installed.

As in other parts of the Park, heavy pedestrian use of the Dene has resulted in a web of desire lines, leading, as it inevitably does, to erosion. The rock

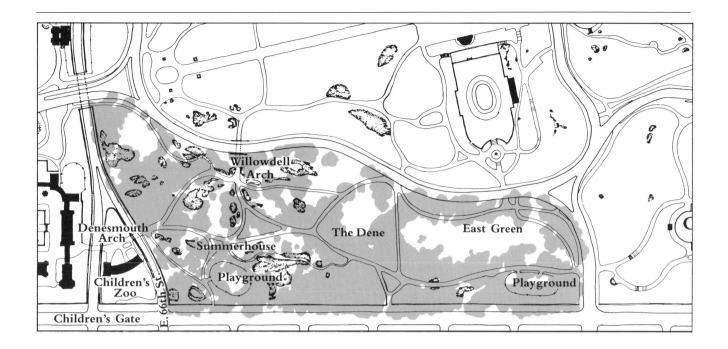

outcrops are popular for climbing and sunning, but they also encourage additional off-path foot traffic. Broken subsurface water pipes, which send water gushing to the surface, complicate matters and make some of the lawns soggy and unusable.

An exact replica of the original Dene rustic shelter was rebuilt by the Central Park preservation crew in 1983. At the same time, the horticultural crew made soil improvements and planted evergreens and shrubs around the rock outcrop upon which the shelter sits.

Goals, Priorities and Recommendations

Restoration of the Dene project area has already commenced with the reconstruction of the rustic shelter (completed in 1983), the redesign and reconstruction of the 69th Street entrance (1983), the restoration of the East Green (1984) and the rebuilding of the 67th Street playground (1985).

The Dene will be receiving increasingly heavy use as a corridor zone when the new Zoo opens, and efforts to stabilize the landscape and prevent future erosion are a top priority now. Repairs to the drainage system are most urgent. Some pathways need to be realigned and others repaved. The slopes along the perimeter wall and the East Drive should be resoiled and replanted.

Rock outcrop in the Dene.

Strawberry Fields and The Midwest Walkway

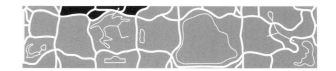

The western perimeter of Central Park from 66th to 81st streets contains Tavern on the Green, three playgrounds, a portion of the Bridle Trail and a teardrop-shaped parcel of land known as Strawberry Fields.

In 1868, when this part of the Park was completed, fewer than 3 percent of the Park's visitors entered through the Women's Gate at 72nd Street. Today, 35 percent come in that way. These two figures tell the story of the western perimeter and, for that matter, the development of Manhattan's Upper West Side.

This section of the Park was originally far more simple in design and content than it is today. There were no entrances between 59th and 72nd streets (there are now two, at 67th and 69th streets); Tavern on the Green did not exist; and a stream flowed under Balcony Bridge at 77th Street, leading to the tranquil, butterfly-shaped Ladies' Pond (since filled in).

The Sheepfold, built in 1870 as a Victorian brick and stone barn, housed the sheep that grazed on the Sheep Meadow. Olmsted had left the Park administration by the time the Sheepfold was built, and when he returned in 1872 he was critical of what he found. He wrote that he had intended the view from the Mall across the meadow "to become dim under large

trees." Olmsted thought the Sheepfold was not only poorly sited but hazardous to reach: Pedestrians had to cross the Bridle Trail to get to it.

This circulation problem became even more acute when in 1934 Robert Moses decided to convert the Sheepfold to a restaurant, Tavern on the Green. The change was protested by the Central Park West and Columbus Avenue associations on the grounds that it would create traffic congestion and represent yet another encroachment on the Park. Plans proceeded, however, and the sheep were sent off to Prospect Park. An entrance was cut into the Park wall at 67th Street to serve the restaurant, and the adjacent landscape was paved to make a parking lot.

Existing Conditions

The main problem in this area today is that there is no strong north-south pedestrian spine, as there is on the east side. Access from the new entrances at 67th and 69th streets leads directly across the Bridle Trail at grade level. Pedestrians and dog walkers often use the Bridle Trail instead of the pedestrian paths. At the 72nd Street entrance, many pedestrians prefer to walk on the Park Drive rather than take the path under the wisteria arbor.

The Ladies' Pond, 1906.

The Ladies' Pond filled in, today.

Overgrown shrubbery, the lack of visual cuing and the fact that the arbor is a bit dark and intimidating may explain why.

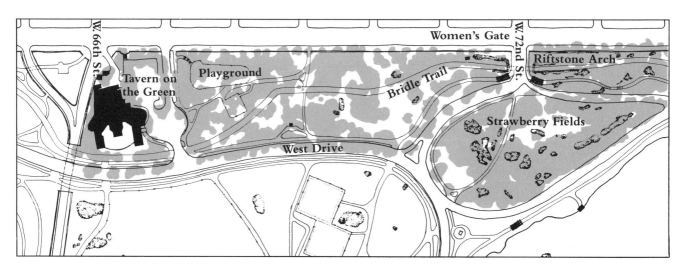

Eroded ground in Strawberry Fields before restoration.   *Strawberry Fields restored, 1986.*

The landscape of Strawberry Fields has been restored as a memorial to John Lennon, the costs of construction and future maintenance having been underwritten by Yoko Ono Lennon. Among the 161 species of trees being planted here are a number of evergreens that will reestablish the start of Olmsted's Winter Drive. The meadow and the playground in the area once occupied by the Ladies' Pond are not frequented very much, and the landscape of the northern half of the project area is generally overgrown, derelict and a bit intimidating.

Goals, Priorities and Recommendations

The three major problems to be addressed in this area are circulation, erosion control and rejuvenation of plant material.

The southern loop of the Bridle Trail, below 86th Street, should be reconstructed as a badly needed walkway. This would accommodate strollers and pedestrian commuters and, in addition, make Tavern on the Green more accessible from the Park side. A swath of turf beside the new walkway would help visually unite the restaurant and the Sheep Meadow across the Park Drive.

Open spaces—small meadows for sunning and sitting—should be reestablished between 67th and 72nd streets.

Riftstone Arch, at 72nd Street, should be relandscaped. The high shrubbery on top should be replaced with a low-growing tumbling variety to allow views into the Park. This, plus the reconstruction of the historic rustic arbors on either side of the Park Drive at the lower intersection, would encourage pedestrians to use the path

rather than the drive as the main route to the Sheep Meadow and the Mall.

The rocky outcrops and slopes along the perimeter north of 72nd Street should receive major regrading, resoiling and replanting.

The Ladies' Pond should be restored as a small secluded backwater for aquatic birds and other animals. The area surrounding the pond should be landscaped as open sunny lawns for picnics and small gatherings. The banks of the pond should be planted with lush vegetation to provide color and textural interest as well as animal habitats.

A major new entrance should be built at 79th Street across from the American Museum of Natural History. This would open up an unused strip of perimeter landscape from 77th to 81st streets, improve east-west pedestrian circulation, and provide a link between the museum, the Belvedere and the Metropolitan Museum of Art.

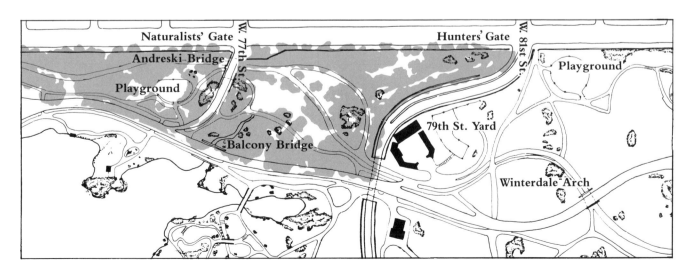

The Southwest Corner

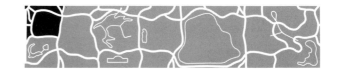

The Southwest Corner of Central Park—that area bounded on the north by the 65th Street transverse and on the east by the Sixth Avenue Park Drive entrance—is today the site of six permanent softball diamonds, the Heckscher Playground, the Carousel and sections of the Park Drive and the Bridle Trail. Before the Park was constructed, this piece of land was essentially a swamp. Its topography was that of a shallow valley with several large rock outcroppings and De Voor's Mill Stream flowing out of it.

Following the original design, the stream and the swamp were filled in and graded in order to construct an open meadow surrounded by irregularly spaced groves of trees. The Carriage Drive and the Bridle Trail ran parallel to each other as they passed around the meadow's perimeter. A substantial amount of landfill was added to bring the Park up to street level at the Southwest Corner so that a major entrance—Merchant's Gate—could be built at Columbus Circle. Four major bedrock outcroppings were left exposed: Umpire Rock, Drip Rock, Spur Rock and the bedrock that formed the support for Pine Bank Arch. Visible from Merchant's Gate and from the Sheep Meadow to the north, Umpire Rock was the dominant landscape feature.

When the Park opened, Merchant's Gate was the second most heavily used entrance for horses, carriages and pedestrians. Those walking through the gate could pass over the Bridle Trail or under the drive to get to the central meadow (then called the Ball Ground).

They did so by means of arches—three masonry arches under the drive and two of cast-iron over the Bridle Trail. The Bridle Trail itself passed under the drive at two points in this area.

The 10.5-acre meadow was originally reserved for children and school groups and was used variously for softball, cricket, croquet, football, coasting and picnics, depending on the season.

The original architecture of the site was highlighted by seven arches of various design and composition. Four other structures served different functions and represented varied architectural styles: the wooden Carousel, a rustic cedar shelter on a knoll overlooking the meadow, the Ballplayers' House and the Gate Keeper's House just inside Merchant's Gate.

Aerial view of the Southwest Meadow in the late 1920s.

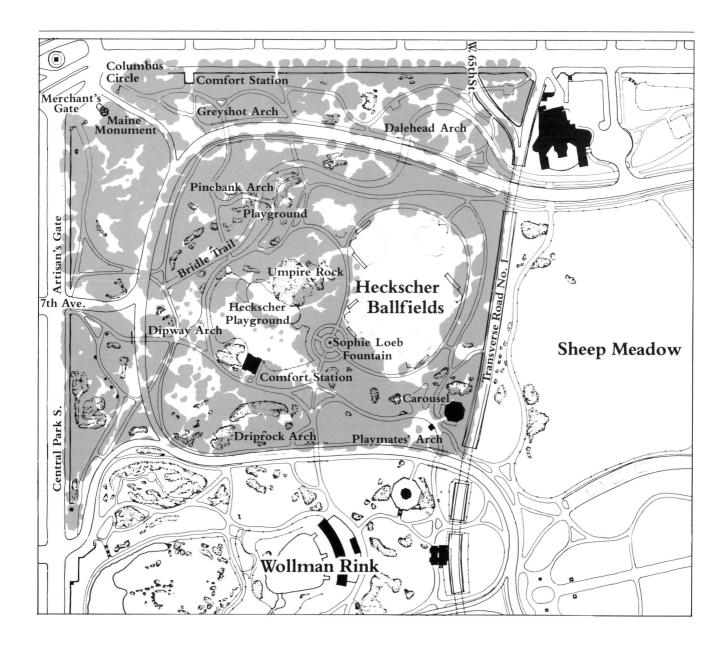

While the area did not have any main landscape theme such as those that distinguish the Ramble and the Mall, it was unified and very simple, and it offered immediate pastoral scenic relief from the city. Over the years, however, it has undergone substantial change.

Early in the 1900s, in response to increased street traffic, a drive and Bridle Trail entrance was constructed at Seventh Avenue, effectively cutting the landscape along the Park's southern perimeter into two sections. A vehicular entrance that was subsequently added at Sixth Avenue sliced across this southern perimeter landscape once again. New walkways had to be added to accommodate the altered pedestrian flow caused by the changes to the drive circulation, and as a result this part of the Park is now little more than a series of islands surrounded by automobile and foot traffic.

Incursions into the meadow began in 1927 with the building of the Heckscher Playground. The playground had two pavilions, a boy's and girl's rest room, the most advanced play equipment of the day and a wading pool—all of which took up about four acres. The playground's surface, originally dirt-fill, was soon paved with asphalt.

Most of what was left of the meadow became, in 1934, five softball fields with backstops, four handball courts, a horseshoe-pitching area and

Water feature at Heckscher Playground.

Heckscher Playground: the first of 27 permanent man-made hard-surface playgrounds in Central Park, as it was in 1927 . . .

. . . and as it is today.

more paths. Two years later the Sophie Loeb Fountain was constructed between the playground and the ball fields, with a paved plaza, paths, a gate and a closely planted circle of plane trees. These combined changes thus turned the meadow from being a flexible unprogrammed space like the Sheep Meadow into an area of defined uses for specific recreational interests.

The Gate Keeper's House was the first original building to be removed; it disappeared at about the time the gatekeeper's job was eliminated. The rustic shelter was demolished sometime after 1934; the wooden Carousel, having burned, was replaced by a brick structure in 1951; and the Ballplayers' House was demolished in 1969. Meanwhile, the Maine Monument was added to Merchant's Gate in 1913, and in 1928, another comfort station with a plaza for a roof was built into the exterior Park wall at 60th Street.

Over the years the vegetation in the Southwest Corner has become more and more dense. The grassy area behind the Maine Monument was closely planted with a grove of oaks. Small clearings elsewhere were filled in with new trees, and the pathways around the meadow were planted so heavily that the area became a circular wall of trees instead of a loosely defined pastoral edge.

Because of overplanting, brutal circulation alterations and architectural additions, all of which were done without any respect for the landscape integrity of the Park, from a design point of view the Southwest Corner is today the Park's most incoherent part. Closer inspection reveals just how unfortunate the situation is.

Existing Conditions

We have seen how over the years a unified landscape has been parceled up into increasingly smaller sections. The landscape has been divided into areas of specialized use, and so many paths have been etched across the grass to new destinations that the linear footage of asphalt has doubled since 1873. The original meadow has all but disappeared, and the original circulation patterns have been lost in a plethora of new paths laid out in a spirit contrary to that of the original design.

Columbus Circle and the adjacent West Side of Manhattan are currently in a period of tremendous growth and development. Within the past 10 years,

Umpire Rock: the most important landscape feature in the area.

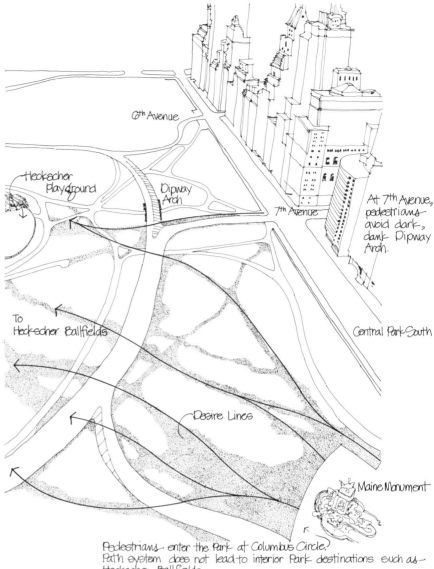

Heckscher Playground

Dipway Arch

6th Avenue

7th Avenue

At 7th Avenue, pedestrians avoid dark, dank Dipway Arch.

Central Park South

To Heckscher Ballfields

Desire Lines

Maine Monument

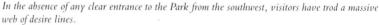

Pedestrians enter the Park at Columbus Circle. Path system does not lead to interior Park destinations such as Heckscher Ballfields.

In the absence of any clear entrance to the Park from the southwest, visitors have trod a massive web of desire lines.

new residential high rises have sprouted up in the Lincoln Center area, and a developer has been selected to replace the Coliseum with a sky-scraper. The West Side boom has al-ready created a new pattern of everyday use in the Southwest Corner. Future development will bring even more visitors to this part of the Park.

Fifty-ninth Street along the Park's southern boundary has long been a densely populated hotel and luxury residential district. With Midtown and the theater district directly to the south, the entrances on Central Park South (59th Street) and the landscape beyond draw a constant flow of office workers, tourists and residents of nearby neighborhoods.

Columbus Circle is a major trans-portation node for both buses and subways. Six subway lines converge

Pine Bank Arch following restoration in 1985

under it: IND lines A, D, AA and CC; BMT line B; and IRT line 1 (with an indirect connection to IRT express lines 2 and 3 and the rest of the system). Four bus lines stop at the Park's edge, and four more have stops a few blocks away on Broadway. Thus the South-west Corner is one of the Park's most accessible areas, and, even if nearby transportation facilities are able to ac-commodate the increase in traffic, the question remains: Can the Park bear the traffic as well?

Unfortunately, as a functioning land-scape, the Southwest Corner has, as we have seen, already become some-thing of a muddle. To begin with, conditions at Merchant's Gate seem to

Heckscher Ballfields before and . . .   *. . . after restoration.*

defy most users' comprehension. There are several reasons for this. The Maine Monument blocks the view into the Park. A 150-foot-wide area behind and to both sides of the monument has been left without the low perimeter wall so that pedestrians flow somewhat aimlessly into the Park across the entire width. The two major pathways, instead of heading to the northeast, where most people want to go, veer either north or east through dark and dank below-grade arches. Not surprisingly, the public has abandoned these paths and trod a massive web of desire lines across the Park toward such popular destinations as the Wollman Rink, the Zoo and the Heckscher Playground.

Despite a complex drainage system, vestiges of the original bog in the Southwest Corner remain. All of the below-grade arches have drainage problems, and most have been damaged by soil erosion. Topsoil has flowed under Dalehead Arch, and the condition of the Bridle Trail that runs under it is so deteriorated that it has to be periodically closed at the western side.

The Heckscher Ballfields were rehabilitated in 1980. Their condition has remained excellent due to rigorous management. The fields are closed after a rain, when the ground is spongy and liable to damage, and a telephone message tape so advises permit-holders. They are taken out of play each year after September 15, when they are

aerated and overseeded. With the addition of lime and fertilizer, they are made ready for play in the spring.

The 20,000-square-foot plaza in front of the Maine Monument presents a more troublesome picture. A high concentration of pedestrians passing through makes it a prime market of illegal drug sales. All the benches inside the south perimeter were removed in the 1970s in an effort to force dealers out of the Park. The move was partly successful. However, "stashes" are still kept inside the Park.

The ball fields, the Heckscher Playground and the Carousel are popular excursion sites and are well used. But the barren expanse of asphalt in the center of the playground gets almost no use at all and is extremely hot in summer. The Sophie Loeb Fountain (not presently in working order) has drainage problems that cause the plaza around it to flood. The London plane trees around the fountain have filled out so that light barely penetrates, which means that the area remains dark, dank and infrequently used or enjoyed.

Lunchtime use is concentrated around rock outcroppings and what turf remains. The picnic area south of the Carousel is popular with school groups, even though summer winds swirl dust from the clay infields through the area.

The original composition of the landforms in the Southwest Corner still exists. However, as has been

noted, much of the spatial design has been compromised over the years. Only 4.5 of the original 10.5 acres of open meadow remain, along with a few open glades. Trees planted closely together in the past have not been thinned or transplanted, and because of excessive competition, the turf has died out in many places, particularly behind the Maine Monument.

There are few specimen quality trees in the area, and most of the understory and shrub material that remains is old, scraggly and cannot hold the topsoil in place. Much of the edge is not planted thickly enough to filter out the sights and sounds of the city.

Goals, Priorities and Recommendations

The Southwest Corner is ailing in so many ways it would be difficult to select a top priority were it not for the certainty that massive crowds will be flowing through Merchant's Gate with the completion of Wollman Rink, the Zoo and the proposed skyscraper on Columbus Circle. For this reason, the first order of business clearly must be redesigning circulation.

In order to control and direct entrance traffic at Merchant's Gate, a 150-foot-long wall should be constructed behind the Maine Monument in the style of the existing adjacent walls. The granite block pavement now behind the monument should be removed and

Proposed Ballplayers' Refreshment Pavilion.

the Park. Through appropriate planting and tree removal, the edge surrounding the Heckscher Ballfields and the handsome protruding bedrock outcrops should be redefined along their original naturalistic lines.

The six masonry arches in this section need to be rebuilt and their watersheds restored. (Pine Bank, the only remaining cast-iron bridge in this area, has already been restored.) Spindly shrub and understory material around the arches should be removed and replaced with species whose root structures are better able to grasp the topsoil, thereby reducing erosion, and whose forms allow for a better visual connection from the walkways to the arches.

The Heckscher Playground, one of the most important and popular playgrounds in Central Park, is in reasonably good condition, but it can be made more attractive by the reduction of some of its extensive asphalt surface and the introduction of some plant material within it.

The meadow adjacent to the western edge of the Park near 65th Street should be permitted for school use during the academic school year but should be kept unprogrammed at all other times.

The existing management of the ball fields should be continued. At some time in the future, the entire meadow should be irrigated with an automatic watering system so that maintenance time can be reduced and the fields kept in play for more hours.

replaced with hexagonal blocks so that the entire plaza is visually united.

Pedestrian circulation throughout the whole area must be redefined. Though the historic circulation plan can be kept in much of its original form, new or redesigned walkways should be laid out to allow direct connections with important destinations in the Park. Redundant and confusing paths must be removed. The segment of the Bridle Trail from 60th to 67th streets should be turned into a walkway connected with other new and improved paths

that carry pedestrian traffic north and northeast.

The restructuring of the circulation system will mean that new underground drainage, electrical and potable-water systems associated with the walkways (for path lights and drinking fountains) will have to be constructed, too. New benches should be placed along the new paths and concentrated in areas that offer good views of people at play.

Another major priority is to restore some sunlight to the ground plane in this now dark and overgrown corner of

The Carousel.

Heckscher Playground today.

The Southeast Corner

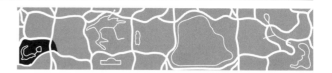

The Pond near 59th Street.

Historically, the Southeast Corner has always been the most important entrance into Central Park. In the early years, when the city still lay some distance to the south, it was fashionable to ride by carriage into the Park at 59th Street and Fifth Avenue and parade up the drive to the Mall. Today, with the towers of Midtown looming above, almost half of all Park visitors—about 6 million people a year—still enter at this point.

The Southeast Corner project area as a whole is bounded by Central Park South and the East and Center drives. Before it was developed, the site was a varied landscape: low-lying swampland and steep slopes crowned by craggy rock outcrops. This inhospitable terrain was occupied by squatters, farmers and foul-smelling industries. At Olmsted and Vaux's direction, the swamp was excavated and turned into a pond with an irregular shoreline that included a sandy beach at the southern shore. "The picturesque effect of the

bold bluffs that run down to [the Pond's] edge and overhang it must be increased," Olmsted wrote. "In the rugged portion, stiffer forms of evergreen trees [hemlock, black spruce, Norway spruce, European larch, Scotch fir, etc.] will best accord with and set off the picturesque rocks. . . . In the more sheltered low ground, the Deciduous Cypress, the White Cedar. . . ." Olmsted accented the rock outcrops along the Drives, increasing their height with soil and plantings in order to give variety to the horizon line and to draw attention inward toward the Mall.

Olmsted and Vaux designated the south end of the Park as the Children's District, because it could be reached most conveniently. In those days, New Yorkers were frightened by the increase of infant mortality in midsummer, and the Park was used as a substitute for a fresh-air ride in the country. To this end, several attractions were built. The Kinderberg and the

Cop Cot were rustic open-air structures on top of rock outcrops. The Dairy, a gray stone Victorian building nearby, dispensed fresh milk at a moderate charge, and on hot days mothers and children enjoyed the shade of its broad loggia and the breezes wafting up from the Pond. These features, together with the nearby ball ground and Carousel, made this part of the Park indeed a delight for children.

The Pond has served as a setting over the years for boating and skating. In its early days, rowboats could be rented, and a swanboat took passengers for rides. Calcium lights made nighttime skating possible in 1912, and in the 1920s the Pond was the scene of a winter carnival.

The Pond's bottom was lined with cement in 1903, when, in fact, all the Park's water bodies became suspect as malaria breeding grounds. The shoreline was given a new "natural" rock edge in 1928. In 1934, both the Pond and the four-acre Promontory at the western end were set aside as a bird sanctuary. Then in 1951, the northern arm of the Pond was filled in to become the site of Wollman Rink. This structure, while immediately popular, represented an encroachment upon the pastoral setting surrounding the Pond, and it caused the Bridle Trail to terminate abruptly in a *cul-de-sac*, rather than, as before, at Scholar's Gate. Fortunately, further encroachment was avoided in the early 1960s, when a citizens' protest prevented the building of the Huntington Hartford Café just inside the Park at Fifth Avenue and 59th Street.

In the 1970s, Wollman Rink was the site of popular music concerts. With their overflow crowds of up to 30,000 people, the concerts damaged the slab supporting the rink and spilled out onto the adjacent slope, destroying the grass and creating severe erosion.

Large-scale reconstruction of the Southeast Corner began in 1979. The Pond was dredged, and a rubble-rock edge set with mortar was installed. Both the rock edge and the landscaping

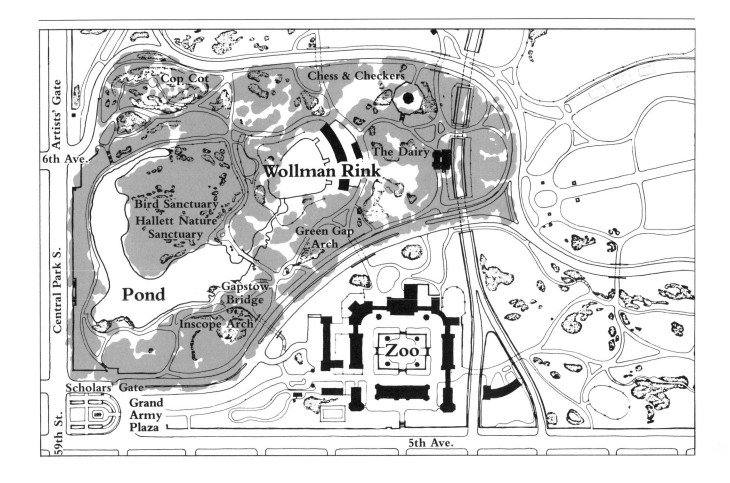

around the Pond were given an artificial look, contrary to their original appearance.

The reconstruction of Wollman Rink and its surrounding landscape is currently under way. The slab of the new rink is nestled gracefully into its site this time, and it can be flooded in summer to make it seem as though it is, once again, part of the Pond.

Both the rustic Cop Cot and the Kinderberg were razed many years ago, after having fallen into disrepair. The octagonal Chess and Checkers Building was built on the site of the Kinderberg in 1952. The Dairy, which had also become dilapidated and was being used as a Park maintenance storage facility, was completely restored in 1979. It is now a visitor information center, an exhibition space, and the setting for meetings and social events.

There is a daily rhythm to the ebb and flow of visitors to the Southeast Corner. In the early morning and again in the evening, a wave of pedestrian commuters moves though the area on its way to and from Midtown. At lunchtime in warm weather, the

benches, rocks and lawns around the Pond are filled with Midtown office workers.

Goals, Priorities and Recommendations

Errors made in early restoration work in the Southeast Corner provide examples of how a purported naturalistic

The restored Cop Cot.

treatment can end up looking "engineered." Remedial work is needed in this section to soften the landscape and harmonize its design with that of the rest of the Park.

The restored embankment of the Pond is a rigid curb of large flat rocks cemented together. Some of the rocks should be removed and shrubs, vines, grasses and emergent vegetation should be planted in their place. In the same way, vines should be planted on and near the walls on the south and west sides of the drive. Some of the redundant paths should be removed. So should the heavy concrete curbs. Large, natural-looking boulders should replace the unattractive rubble walls set into the hillsides for erosion control.

The Promontory's value as a bird sanctuary should be further enhanced by the addition of food-producing plants and more ground cover. Its tree canopy should be opened up in places to permit growth of the understory. The prohibition against general public access to the Promontory should continue, but the program of guided nature tours and study groups should be expanded.

The Arsenal and
The Zoo

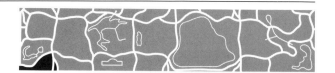

The Arsenal is one of two buildings in Central Park that are older than the Park itself (the other being the Blockhouse at 110th Street). Built in 1848 as a munitions supply depot, the Arsenal originally stood alone in vacant, rubble-strewn terrain just west of Fifth Avenue at 64th Street.

Though the Arsenal was a picturesque brick structure with castellated Norman towers, Central Park's designers, Olmsted and Vaux, considered it fairly unattractive. For this reason, they planted trees around it that would grow into large, handsome specimens and reduce its impact on the landscape. In 1871, Boss Tweed had the Arsenal's facade covered with stucco and its turrets topped with pointed wooden towers. Sixty-three years later, Robert Moses ordered the stucco sandblasted off and the wooden towers replaced with concrete battlements. At the same time, he commissioned murals for the entrance hall.

Aside from its military function, the Arsenal has at one time or another housed a livery stable, the Museum of Natural History and the U.S. Weather Service Station for New York. It now serves as the administrative headquarters for the Parks Department.

The Zoo behind the Arsenal was not built until 1934. Olmsted and Vaux had long resisted pressure to include any zoo in the Park. Reluctantly, they drew up plans for four different sites, and work was started and abandoned at all of them. In the meantime, animals were kept in a menagerie in the Arsenal's basement or in a succession of makeshift wooden sheds outside. Robert Moses finally got the Zoo built in his first year as Parks Commissioner, and it quickly became the most frequently visited feature in the Park.

Currently, the Zoo is closed and being rebuilt according to a design that will allow the animals greater freedom of movement. Four buildings of the old Zoo will be kept for new uses: the Monkey House as a zoo school and education center; the Birdhouse as a gift shop and exhibition space; and the

The Arsenal as viewed from the East Drive in the 1860s.

The Seal Pond, one of the Zoo's most popular attractions, 1960s.

148

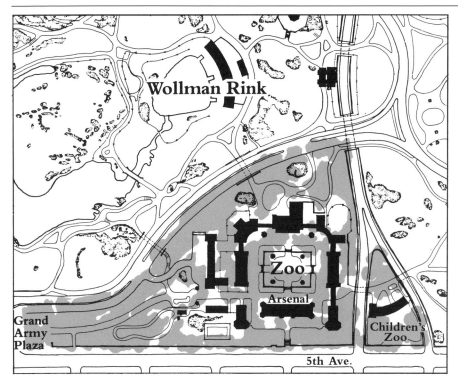

A detail of the gate by Paul Manship at the Children's Zoo.

Deer House and the garage as administrative offices. The Parks Department will relinquish jurisdiction over the redesigned Zoo to the New York Zoological Society.

The Children's Zoo is located in the triangle of land formed by the entrances to the 65th Street transverse. It was built in 1960, a gift of Governor and Mrs. Herbert H. Lehman. Its buildings are designed as Disneyland-style nursery rhyme settings. The gates, installed in 1961, were created by sculptor Paul Manship.

The Arsenal-Zoo project area as a whole extends along the eastern perimeter of the Park from Grand Army Plaza to the 65th Street transverse. It is a popular corner of the Park, particularly in the summer. Some work has already been done to restore its landscape. In 1982-83, the lawn between the East Drive and the walkway was resodded and fenced, and new perimeter plantings were installed.

Goals, Priorities and Recommendations

Demographic studies of Central Park in 1973 and 1982 revealed that the Zoo is the Park's number-one attraction. The newly restored Zoo is, if anything, likely to draw even larger crowds than the old one, putting more stress than ever on the nearby lawns and landscape.

The four stone arches in the project area—Denesmouth, Inscope, Greengap and a vehicular overpass next to the Children's Zoo—require masonry and landscape restoration. Walkway reconstruction and bench replacement are needed below 64th Street.

The Zoo under reconstruction.

The Perimeter

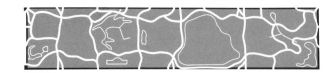

Central Park's rusticated stone wall—plain, understated and less than four feet high—may appear to the casual observer to have been a mere afterthought. It was anything but.

Olmsted and Vaux insisted that the Park's perimeter be of a scale and design compatible with the naturalistic theme of the Park itself. A formal wrought-iron fence would not have been appropriate, nor a monumental work of sculptured stone. So strongly did the two men feel about this, in fact, that they resigned in 1863 when it appeared that a wall with grandiose, ceremonial gates by the sculptor Richard Morris Hunt might be built instead. The Park Committee came around to Olmsted and Vaux's point of view two years later and reappointed them to work on the Park.

Olmsted's concept for the border included a broad, tree-shaded walk, a simple low wall and just inside the wall a planted slope, which in combination with the street trees would provide a substantial visual barrier between the Park and the city. Stately American elms were planted in *allées* along the streets on all four sides of the Park.

Traffic circles at each of the Park's four corners signified major entrances. The two at the south end—Grand Army Plaza (59th Street and Fifth Avenue) and Columbus Circle (59th Street and Central Park West)—were designed to serve both vehicles and pedestrians. The two at the north—Frawley Circle (at 110th Street and Fifth Avenue) and Frederick Douglass Circle (110th Street and Central Park West)—were originally for pedestrian use only.

Existing Conditions

The present state of the wall ranges from good to poor. In some locations, erosion inside the Park has exposed the wall's foundations. In other places, the opposite has happened: Soil has washed down slopes and piled up against the wall, heaving it out of alignment. Often, where drainage has

Typical view of the Park perimeter, showing street trees, sidewalk, benches and Park wall.

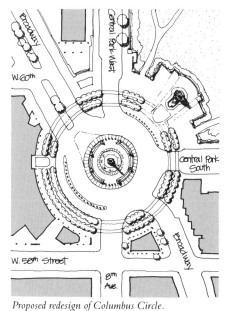

Proposed redesign of Columbus Circle.

broken down, water seeps through the wall, as it does rather copiously at 85th and 96th streets on Fifth Avenue.

Graffiti is now being removed routinely, but excessive moisture, which causes the growth of algae, fungi, moss and climbing plants, is causing mortar to crumble and stone to disintegrate. New entrances have been cut into the wall over the years, so that instead of the original 17 there are now 60. The vehicular entrances added on Central Park South at Sixth and Seventh avenues and the one at Frederick Douglass Circle have changed the character of the Park considerably.

The border of elms has not survived intact. It is still in evidence on Fifth Avenue. However, ginkgo trees run across both Central Park South and 110th Street, their spare columnar form providing neither the shade nor the covered *allée* effect that was intended. Central Park West has a variety of oaks with high, round heads.

As for the circles, neither of those at the northern end is particularly distinguished; in fact, they could be described as bleak.

At the Park's southern end, Columbus Circle has become a major traffic rotary, jarring physically as well as aesthetically. Continuations of Broadway and Eighth Avenue have been sliced though the center of the circle, and parking islands have been installed. The space is cluttered, its symmetry ruined. Traffic is confused and hazardous. The statue of Christopher Columbus in the center, surrounded by its pool and fountains, has been challenged by a grandiose embellishment on the Park side: the Beaux Arts Maine Monument, erected in 1913. A second vehicular entrance to the Park has been sealed off, further confusing the pattern of circulation.

From a design point of view, Grand Army Plaza is the only really successful Park corner. It is a major focus of Midtown Manhattan and an elegant urban space. The statue of William Tecumseh Sherman by Augustus Saint-Gaudens in the north plaza is considered one of the great American equestrian monuments. The Pulitzer Fountain, topped by a statue of Pomona, the goddess of abundance, is a graceful ornament in the south plaza. The fountain, however, has ceased to function; its stonework is broken, and the surrounding space is in need of repaving and relandscaping.

Goals, Priorities and Recommendations

The perimeter trees and the wall are the first elements of the Park one sees from the surrounding streets. Their appearance reflects the health and well-being of the whole Park, and their maintenance is therefore an important priority. Three of the four corner traffic circles are urgently in need of redesign to improve circulation and make them more inviting and accessible as entrances to the Park.

Major reconstruction of the wall is required at several locations: on Central Park West between 61st and 62nd streets, 82nd and 84th streets, and 103rd and 106th streets; and on Fifth Avenue between 100th and 102nd streets. The entire wall should be repointed.

Large tree roots that are causing the wall to buckle should be cut back. In cases where this would harm the tree, a masonry bridge should be constructed to pass over the root.

The ailing ginkgoes on 110th and 59th streets should be replaced with a more graceful street tree that will provide shade and a visual screen between the Park and the street.

Artist's rendering of Grand Army Plaza as it may look when restored.

Grand Army Plaza
The restoration of this major civic space is recommended. Though not within the actual boundaries of Central Park, Grand Army Plaza has traditionally served as its "gateway." Beaux Arts in style, it is—like the Mall—a formal counterpoint to the picturesque Park.

Columbus Circle
Along with the current redevelopment of the Columbus Circle area, the chaotic traffic situation must be studied and a remedy devised so that the circle can once again become a smoothly functioning "Place d'Etoile" of New York City.

Frawley Circle
As part of a major effort to draw Harlem residents into the Park,

Frawley Circle should be redesigned so that it appears more welcoming and the Park more accessible. A proposed statue of Duke Ellington might give the circle a sense of place it now lacks.

Frederick Douglass Circle
Because it is a vehicular entrance, Douglass Circle is hostile to pedestrians entering the Park. It should be converted into a pedestrian entrance if a feasibility study indicates that such a move is advisable. If it is, the edge landscape should be raised to street level and the entrance turned into a major, and very inviting, pedestrian walkway into the Park. A statue of Frederick Douglass would be an appropriate feature here, since the circle already bears his name.

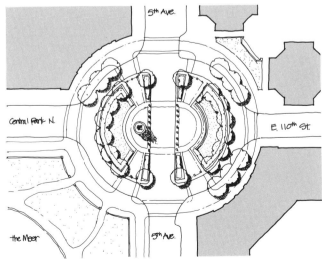

Proposed redesign of Frawley Circle.

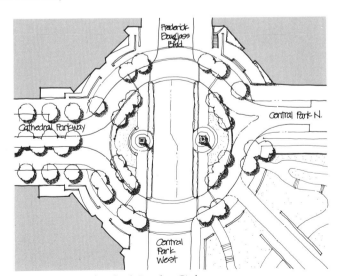

Proposed redesign of Frederick Douglass Circle.

Bankers Trust helped the Central Park Conservancy field a graffiti-removal crew in 1981. Subsequent funding for this crew was provided by the city, and graffiti-removal operations were extended to other parks—a good example of private investment initiating significant public action.

The Central Park Conservancy:
An Experiment in Private Sector and Governmental Cooperation

Public parks, unlike profit-making theme parks and amusement parks, are normally the province of the municipal, state or federal government. Their day-to-day operations are generally supported by tax revenues or special tax assessments, and their capital improvements are paid for through bond issues. Better perhaps than almost any other country, the United States has built a rich mix of local, state and national parks that provide its citizens with wonderful scenery and a multitude of easily accessible recreational opportunities.

Overall, the administration of these parks is effective and their funding generally adequate. This is less apt to be true in our older cities, however. Municipal parks created in the last century or in the early years of this century as emblems of civic beauty and experiments in social reform have deteriorated as their surrounding neighborhoods have declined. Where there is little political will to reverse the general urban deterioration, such parks inevitably become ill-tended, unkempt and insecure. Shunned, they are abandoned to socially undesirable uses like drug sales or opportunistic robbery, and their increasing notoriety gives them an ever bleaker reputation until they become fearful places indeed. Invariably, the socially hostile environment of these parks is reflected in their lack of maintenance. Park workers become demoralized and administration becomes indifferent.

Such was the case in New York City during the 1970s. The city's once incomparable park system was on the skids, and this was nowhere more evident than in Central Park. If the nation's first and most famous municipal park could slip into irreversible decline, what hope might there be for other aging and deteriorating parks elsewhere? Opportunity, however, is often born of adversity. And, although hard to discern at the time, a happy confluence of circumstances was occurring during some of the darkest days in

New York's history, as the city teetered on the verge of bankruptcy. In retrospect, the lesson learned from what happened is that necessity and the will to address it, or a dream and a vision to achieve it, is an important underlying factor in the creation of new institutional arrangements.

Formation of the Political Will to Meet a Manifest Need

By the mid-1970s, Central Park was viewed as too popular and too precious an urban resource to write off. While there was general agreement about this, there was little agreement on how to rescue the Park. Some suggested making it a state park; others, notably Senator Daniel Moynihan, proposed turning it over to the National Park Service. But Central Park was to be saved not by a higher governmental authority but rather by a grass-roots initiative supported by a sympathetic mayor.

The birth of the partnership between city government and the private sector represented by the Central Park Conservancy was a matter of luck and timing. Since 1974, a modest amount of private sector support for the Park had come from two citizens' groups formed to respond in provisional ways to the crisis. The Central Park Community Fund was providing money for some badly needed maintenance equipment, and the Central Park Task Force sponsored youth employment and school volunteer programs. Because there was considerable duplication of effort, the two organizations soon considered becoming one.

By 1979, the basic conditions for the formation of a working partnership between city government and the private sector were favorable. With the election of Mayor Edward I. Koch and the appointment as Parks Commissioner of first Gordon J. Davis (from 1978 to 1983) and then Henry J. Stern (the current commissioner), the necessary political conditions of mutual

need and mutual respect existed to foster the public-private sector alliance that resulted in the formation of the Conservancy.

Role Definition and the Concept of the Park as a Cultural Institution

As long as the operation of parks was considered just another municipal service, there could be no public-private partnership. But a park can be viewed as being as rich as a library in opportunities for instruction, as well endowed as a museum with visual beauty, as emotionally uplifting as a symphony orchestra and as entertaining as theater. Such, after all, are the "cultural" qualities of Central Park and many other parks as well. Parks are continually vulnerable to encroachment by well-intentioned citizens and public officials seeking readily available open space for transportation improvements, new schools and medical facilities, and other cultural interests such as museums and zoos. A self-perpetuating board that holds Park interests as high as those of traditional civic, educational, cultural and social-service institutions is necessary to guard and maintain this interest *over time*.

In the case of Central Park, a necessary first step in creating the Conservancy was the acceptance of the Park as its original creators saw it—a scenic retreat, a peaceful space that would act as an antidote to urban stress. The next step was a commitment on the part of the Mayor that the city would not withdraw its support of Central Park in the face of private funding. Since Central Park did not have a separate budget at the time, it was necessary to review departmental records—payroll, work orders, purchasing and so forth—in order to find out what the city's actual manpower and dollar commitment to Central Park had been. This was done in 1980, and the exercise provided a benchmark by which to set the government's future commitment.

A further declaration was obtained from the Mayor that the Park would continue to enjoy the *same proportionate* amount of the city's annual budget regardless of how much money was forthcoming from the private sector. Private philanthropy was construed as providing "the critical difference" between simply maintaining the Park and managing it as a first-class institution. Specifically, private philanthropy was assigned the task of accomplishing what could not be done with city funds.

Leadership and Board Formation

The choice of board chairman and a board of directors was critical. The chairman's personal prestige and commitment to the cause would influence the character and strength of the rest of the board and its ability to work alongside government. In the case of the Central Park Conservancy, the first chairman, William S. Beinecke, was appointed by the Mayor as one of three mayoral appointees to the board. Because of his standing in the New York corporate and philanthropic communities, Beinecke was able to recruit a board of distinguished individuals to serve as Conservancy trustees. Recently retired as chairman of the Sperry and Hutchinson Company, he had the time and energy to devote to this task.

The two prior Park assistance groups, the Central Park Community Fund and the Central Park Task Force, dissolved their boards, and three members of each organization were asked to join the new board. Respected corporate executives were also sought, as well as community leaders whose backgrounds reflected the Park's democratic nature and pluralistic usership. The Parks Commissioner and the Central Park Administrator were directly involved in soliciting and approving board appointments. In this fashion, the new organization was exceptional in that it was forged both from within and without city government. Still, it was legally no different from any other not-for-profit corporation within the meaning of sections 170(c)2 and 501(c)3 of the Internal Revenue Code of 1954. It had six "inside" board trustees—the three mayoral appointees plus the Manhattan Borough President, the Parks Commissioner and the Central Park Administrator serving *ex officio*—

and 30 self-elected trustees divided into three annual classes of three-year terms of service, all of whom had been selected with the concurrence of the officials with whom they would be working. The next step, therefore, was to set the organization in motion and begin practical operations.

Staff Building and the Importance of Working from the Inside

From an operational point of view, the Conservancy's partnership with the city was focused through the office of the Central Park Administrator. The Administrator is appointed by the Mayor and reports to the Parks Commissioner but is paid by the Conservancy. The Administrator thus serves at the pleasure of both the Conservancy board and the city. A member of the Parks Department administration with line authority over Central Park personnel, the Administrator is also the chief executive officer of the Conservancy. This unification of responsibility means that Conservancy staff and Parks Department staff function in concert. No matter how amicable the relationship between an outside group of Park supporters and Park officials may be, it can never be as truly effective as this integrated arrangement.

Staff building for Central Park's management and operations has been strategic, and its growth has been by stages. Programs conceived and launched on a large scale, particularly those developed by outside planners rather than by the people who will actually run them, are more failure-prone than those that start on a provisional, pilot basis and then grow. Accountability for funds spent and demonstration of results are important before subsequent funds are allocated.

The Conservancy's success has been predicated on proving itself step by step as Park management was re-established in Central Park. Many of the innovative steps to reinstitute good groundskeeping and maintenance have been started with private funding only to be subsequently taken over by the city as items in its parks budget. For instance, a grant from Bankers Trust in 1981 funded a graffiti-removal team and equipment; subsequently, anti-graffiti personnel and supplies were absorbed by the city. Because of its demonstrated success in Central Park,

the program was subsequently expanded to Riverside and other New York City parks.

Much of the planning and design that have resulted in a commitment of both city and private funding for capital projects—including this management and restoration plan—have been initiated by the Conservancy. The Conservancy's budget and planning are carefully overseen by the Parks Commissioner as well as by the board. Its expenses are scrutinized by the audit and executive committees, and city budget officials and private donors provide further accountability.

The final forum for review is, of course, public opinion. Approval or disapproval of the Park's vast array of constituents reinforces or curbs managers in direct and indirect ways. Successful operation in such an intensely public, heavily and diversely used space depends to a considerable degree on politics and public relations.

Image Building and the Importance of Working on the Outside

The articulation and marketing of the cause of Park preservation and improved management are essential both for successful fund-raising and political support. Without a clearly defined shopping list of gift opportunities, well-intentioned philanthropists will frequently suggest gifts that do not really fit the organization's goals. And the support of political leaders will be lacking unless the organization's message is explicit, popular and reasonably well developed. "Development," a current euphemism for "fund-raising," really means the development of the cause and its support and growth through public relations.

Favorable media representation can be enormously beneficial to the organization. Newspaper stories and television coverage usually do not just happen where simple good deeds are concerned. Opportunities for publicity must be arranged and the press contacted. Controversies, when they occur, can be turned to public-relations assets if they are sensitively, forthrightly and courageously handled.

Fund-raising must be pursued systematically and professionally. Grant proposals and letters must be written, and personal calls on prospective donors made. A direct-mail campaign is a useful way to increase name recognition and build a family of regular contributors. Board involvement is important in building a network of private-sector support. An articulate, energetic and knowledgeable spokesperson for the cause is also a must. Political leaders and interested community groups need to be contacted frequently. Their friendship and support are very valuable. In the case of the Central Park Conservancy, its administrative staff, like the staff of its various programs, began on a small scale, worked experimentally and flexibly as it took on new organizational tasks, then grew slowly in response to clearly demonstrated need. Outside consultants were used in the beginning for a direct-mail campaign and for foundation solicitation; later these functions were moved in-house. A corporate campaign was organized through a committee of executives representing various sectors of New York City's economy—banking, finance, retail, consumer products and so forth. "Cross-over" contacts based on personal and business friendships were, of course, welcomed. Because of its good leadership, systematic organization and conscientious tracking, the Conservancy's annual corporate drive now brings the organization nearly $1 million for general support.

Staged events are a necessary means of creating organizational recognition and increasing the donor base. The Conservancy organizes two major annual events as well as several smaller ones to raise both money and Park-consciousness. The Frederick Law Olmsted Awards Luncheon, held in May, honors one or more notable Park benefactors. Besides this festive benefit, there are other, smaller benefits held upon suitable occasions such as the reopening of a restored facility like the Loeb Boathouse. "You Gotta Have Park" weekend in mid-May solicits the general public; brightly colored booths at Park entrances are manned by volunteers who request a $1 donation from each Park visitor, who in turn receives a large button bearing a YOU GOTTA HAVE PARK emblem. The emblem, new each year, is the product of

Mime entertaining guests at Frederick Law Olmsted Awards Luncheon, May 1985.

a design contest involving local graphics students.

Personal calls on potential large donors, tours, special presentations and various other kinds of education and entertainment relating to the organizational mission all help to extend and reinforce a network of friends and supporters.

Planning—A Process, Not a Product

The restoration and management plan in this book represents the best collective thinking of Central Park's current managers. It is not sacrosanct, however. It represents a vision rooted in a particular time and culture. Good plans will necessarily be amended, altered and updated. While outside consultants have and will continue to contribute to the plan, its principal authors are the people who are charged with its implementation. This staff is continuing, at a finer level of detail, the analyses, recommendations and design development outlined in these pages. As they do so, their thinking will be shaped by new observations as well as by public opinion. In the process, some elements of the plan will change, and new management will undoubtedly bring in new ideas. It is hoped that this plan for Central Park's management and restoration will grow and change but not be abandoned, that it will be a continually evolving springboard for action long into the future rather than a onetime prescription that provides only a limited and temporary cure.

Index

Photo credits